WRITING SUCCESSFUL COLLEGE APPLICATIONS: IT'S MORE THAN JUST THE ESSAY

Cynthia Clumeck Muchnick

PETERSON'S

About Peterson's

Peterson's provides the accurate, dependable, high-quality education content and guidance you need to succeed. No matter where you are on your academic or professional path, you can rely on Peterson's print and digital publications for the most up-to-date education exploration data, expert test-prep tools, and top-notch career success resources—everything you need to achieve your goals.

For more information, contact Peterson's, 3 Columbia Circle, Suite 205, Albany, NY 12203; 800-338-3282 Ext. 54229; or find us online at www.petersonsbooks.com.

ISBN: 978-0-7689-3889-0

Printed in the United States of America

10 9 8 7 6 5 4 3 2 1   16 15 14

First Edition

Dedication

To my children: Justin, Jacob, Ross, and Alexa. I wish you each
your own unforgettable college experience someday!
To Adam, the greatest guy I met in college.
And to my incredible parents who always support and
believe in me.

Table of Contents

Chapter Four

The Activity Paragraph **155**

Chapter Five

The Academic and "Thinking" Paragraph **173**

Chapter Six

The "Why This School?" Question **191**

Acknowledgments

Thanks to the college counselors who reached out to their students to share their essays with me, especially: Vicky de Felice of de Felice & Geller, Jenn Curtis from FutureWise Consulting, and my former colleague, Linda Winrow. Also thank you to my intern, Karli Dugan, and former Stanford classmate and colleague Alexandra Dumas Rhodes for always being on deck to consult on questions that arose.

And thank you to the incredible, professional, and fastest-responding group of people I have ever worked with, the staff at Peterson's, who believed in and helped shepherd this project: Robyn Thurman, Bernadette Webster, Julie Ammermuller, Stephanie Benyo, and my amazing editor Jill Schwartz.

I am grateful to the Deans of Admission from such diverse colleges and universities for sharing their honest insights, advice, and wisdom to this project.

Justin, Jacob, Ross, and Alexa, thank you for your patience while I was busy writing and researching this book. At times I know it took me away from you all in some form or another. And, Adam, thanks for holding down the fort and supporting me so that I could meet my deadlines.

Finally, thanks to the hundreds of student contributors who shared their writing with me. And special thanks to the specific students selected (see page 293), as well as the ones who allowed me to publish their work but preferred to remain anonymous. (You know who you are.) No book is ever written alone!

Introduction

I am guessing that you picked up this book because you wanted to learn the tricks and secrets to great college application writing. You're looking for advice and a direction for your all-important personal statement and other supplemental essays, right? Maybe you feel that nothing worth writing about has happened in your life up until now. Perhaps you think your GPA or test scores are not going to boost your chances of getting into a school, so your writing sure as heck better be strong! Or, maybe you think you aren't a great writer. Now, let go of your worries (however legitimate and anxiety-inducing they seem), and look no further: help has arrived!

Writing Successful College Applications will assist you with all of your writing concerns. But, in truth, you must know that you cannot really write your way into a college. The writing you produce for your application provides your readers (the admission officers) with just a glimpse of who you are. It allows them to "hear" your voice and gain insight into how you think and articulate your ideas. But, really, your writing alone will not make or break your chances at any particular college.

Remember those other key parts of your application. First and foremost, your high school transcript is the most important piece of any college application. How you perform as a student is a college's best indicator of how you will fare at their campus. Colleges evaluate your transcript by looking at the classes you select, the intensity of the high school track you are on, and how you do in these courses within the context of your school. Did you take all college-prep courses? Did you push yourself with some AP® and Honors-level courses (if your school offers those)? How did your grades progress as the school year progressed, semester to semester? How did you grow as a student as the schoolwork intensified and you got older, year to year? These are just some of the ways your transcript is reviewed by admission offices.

Also important to many schools are your standardized test scores, namely the ACT® or SAT® and often your SAT Subject Tests™ and AP scores. (If test scores are of high concern to you, check out fairtest.org, where you will find a list of over 850 colleges and universities that do not require you to submit test scores, "deemphasize" standardized testing in their evaluation of applicants, or are test-score optional.) In addition, your activities and how you spend your time outside of class—whether in athletics, community service, clubs, employment, or extracurriculars, as well as any awards or honors you have received—make up your "brag sheet" or student résumé. In addition, teacher and supplemental recommendations are important and serve as another piece of the puzzle to help admission officers better understand who you are in your classroom, school, and community. Some schools also offer admission or alumni interviews to further get to know their applicants.

But, overall, the writing you compose for your applications brings your voice and human experience to the admission office, and you want that writing to be an honest reflection of who you are. *Writing Successful College Applications* will help you navigate and execute all of the writing required for your various college applications. By perusing a wide array of real essays from the most competitive students to the most mainstream on a vast range of topics; learning helpful tips from students, teachers, and your author; considering practical advice from leaders in the admission profession; and trying to find your authentic voice in this overwhelming process, you can use *Writing Successful College*

Applications to de-stress and de-mystify this rite of passage (and *write* of passage) that you are about to embark upon.

College applications—in their content and as a process—are always evolving. At the time of this book's publication, the Common Application was going through its annual changes as it has more significantly in recent years. As you read the instructions throughout this book, be sure to double-check The Common Application website closely, as well as your selected college websites, for any new changes that may have occurred, such as the number of writing pieces required, supplements to the Common Application, wording of essay questions, word count limits, upload or other space restrictions, and so on.

So, to review, just so you understand that your writing is only one piece—albeit an important piece—of the application process, here is a list of all of the components that make up your college application:

1) **Biographical Information:** name, address, important numbers, parental info, and so on.

2) **Transcript:** the grades you have earned from ninth grade on, including summer school, community college courses you may have taken, etc. (If you took any high school classes before high school, such as an advanced math or language in eighth grade, you will also get credit for those classes most likely on your high school transcript, but not always—so check with your school counselor.)

3) **Standardized Test Scores** (SAT®, ACT® and, in some cases, SAT Subject Tests™, TOEFL®, AP® scores, etc.).

4) **Brag Sheet/Student Résumé:** a list of everything you have done after school, outside of school, on the weekends, and in the summer: clubs, community service, jobs, internships, other activities, sports, summer experiences, honors and awards earned, and hobbies and interests. Time commitment should also be included.

5) **Teacher Recommendations** (usually two, one from math/science and the other from history/foreign language/English): Get good ones!

6) **Personal Interview** (not always offered; by alumni or admission officer): be prepared and do your homework before the interview. Know why you want to attend that school. Bring questions, and be sure to write a thank-you note to your interviewer afterwards.

7) **Personal Statement** (and additional writings for many schools that can include short answers, paragraph answers, etc.): That's what *this* book is all about!

And sometimes you will be asked for:

8) **Supplemental Recommendation** (sometimes requested from a friend, employer, religious leader, or someone else who knows you well)

9) **Graded school paper** or project: You may be asked to submit a copy of a piece of schoolwork with your application. Don't throw away any strong high school writing assignments or projects with good grades and teacher comments that you have earned!

10) **Prepare a music or art portfolio** if your college requests one. Also, be prepared to audition for dance, drama, or music if your college offers or requires auditions. If you cannot attend in person, some schools will allow video or website submissions. Check with your institution for requirements, dates, and locations for auditions and portfolio submissions.

After fifteen years of working as a private college counselor and prior to that as a college admission professional, high school teacher, and test-prep tutor, I have gathered information and insights to assist my students with the task of college application writing. The big secret (or bad news) is that there is no magic formula for writing your essay. The best advice I can offer: *write an essay that only you could write*. It should be personal (hence the name personal statement) and not generic (i.e., it could not be written by anyone else). The topic can be simple and mundane, but it has to genuinely reflect *your* voice, *your* passion, *your* insights, and *your* perceptions. So, you could actually put this book down now and read no further, or continue on and let the essays that follow enlighten, inspire, and encourage you to be yourself and write an essay that genuinely reflects *you*.

All of the essays in this book "worked," meaning all of the students who wrote them did ultimately get into and attend college, and these writing samples are what they crafted and used to get into college. Was it just these essays that got them admitted to college? No. Obviously, based on the criteria that are reviewed in every file, the essay is just one piece of the application puzzle that is evaluated. As Elizabeth Harlow, a Duke University admission officer, describes beautifully in her blog[1]:

"Evaluating a file is an art akin to assembling a jigsaw puzzle without a box. We aren't starting with any preconceived pictures, and we don't possess every piece of information that might be interesting or valuable. We do not presume we know everything about all our applicants, but the application provides enough interlocking pieces, many of them very big, for us to identify a picture of each student as a person."

If anything, the essay samples in this book should help calm you down and demonstrate to you that *you can* do it; really, anyone can! Each chapter begins with some advice, but the meat of this book is the student writing that offers you a peek into hundreds of actual college applications. The wide variety of styles, themes, topics, and essays prove that *there is no one right way to go about the essay writing process*. You can write a college essay that works for you. Anyone can. Be inspired and be yourself. And good luck!

—Cynthia Clumeck Muchnick, M.A.

---

[1] *Elizabeth Harlow, "Inside Holistic Admissions: How Does My Decision Happen?" Duke University Undergraduate Admissions Blogs, March 26, 2014, http://blogs. admissions.duke.edu/?cat=14.*

Chapter One

Writing from Your Heart and Mind: A College Essay That Only You Could Write

When beginning to tackle the college essays, most students think that the questions and prompts are pretty fun and interesting and actually look "easy." Students seem enthused to begin to write about themselves and answer the questions that colleges pose. Once they begin to dive into really answering the prompts, though, many are often faced with writer's block, stress, panic, fear, concern, or some combination of these feelings. Since most prompts are relatively open-ended, first decide what you want to write about and then later make your essay "fit" the prompt. Think of writing about a personal experience, and that essay can probably be tweaked to respond to a question.

Questions to Answer: Self-Reflection Activity

Before you even look at the questions that colleges ask, consider making a document by hand or on your computer that answers the following questions about yourself. (My students complete a student questionnaire that asks some of these questions to help me get to know them better and also to help identify possible essay topics.) This activity will help you "get to know yourself better," and often, by answering these questions, you can discover the germination of your essay or small nuggets that you can include elsewhere in your application that are unique to you.

1) What is your favorite childhood memory? (whether you remember it or not, even if it has been told to you for many years)

2) What hobbies do you enjoy outside of school?

3) What games do you like to play or what do you do in your free time?

4) What special talents do you have? (The quirkier, the better!)

5) What is your favorite family tradition(s)?

6) How would your best friend(s) or closest sibling or family member describe you? What words—adjectives or verbs— would they choose? Don't be afraid to ask your friends or close family members this question to collect their reflections of you.

7) What is the most embarrassing thing you have done (within what is appropriate to college admissions readers)?

8) What is the best book you have read? Why?

9) What is your favorite subject in school?

10) Who is your favorite teacher from any grade and why?

11) What struggles in your life have your overcome (if any)?

12) Who is your personal hero/heroine?

13) What activity, which person, what food, etc., brings you happiness? Or, what makes you happy?

14) How would you describe your family, and what experiences have you shared that are memorable to you?

15) What achievements or accomplishments, academic or personal, are you most proud of?

16) What are some "defining moments" in your life? (i.e., experiences, conversations, moments that changed, challenged, or enlightened you in some way)

17) What is your community or neighborhood like, and how do you see yourself or your role in it?

The Essay Questions

Once you have completed your self-analysis by exploring these questions, look at the colleges' essay questions. Below are the five Common Application prompts that over 500 colleges (and counting) use today. The good news is that these questions are meant to guide you and are relatively open-ended, so they leave much to your imagination and creativity. You have 650 words maximum (and 250 words minimum) to answer one of these prompts. Other colleges have similar open-ended questions or allow you to make up your own question and answer it. Some ask you simply to write a personal statement on a topic of your choosing. The Common Application questions provide a good base from where you can begin to formulate your ideas.

Here are the actual instructions from the Common Application (from commonapp.org):

The essay demonstrates your ability to write clearly and concisely on a selected topic and helps you distinguish yourself in your own voice. What do you want the readers of your application to know about you apart from courses, grades, and test scores? Choose the option that best helps you answer that question and write an essay of no more than 650 words, using the prompt to inspire and structure your response. Remember: 650 words is your limit, not your goal. Use the full range if you need it, but don't feel obligated to do so. (The application won't accept a response shorter than 250 words.)

Here are the current five questions or prompts being used:

- *Some students have a background or story that is so central to their identity that they believe their application would be incomplete without it. If this sounds like you, then please share your story.*

- *Recount an incident or time when you experienced failure. How did it affect you, and what lessons did you learn?*

- *Reflect on a time when you challenged a belief or idea. What prompted you to act? Would you make the same decision again?*

- *Describe a place or environment where you are perfectly content. What do you do or experience there, and why is it meaningful to you?*

- *Discuss an accomplishment or event, formal or informal, that marked your transition from childhood to adulthood within your culture, community, or family.*

And then there are the schools with more unusual main essay prompts:

University of Chicago

The University of Chicago, a school that always prides itself on the "Uncommon Application," offers a string of prompts that are quirky and off-the-beaten-path and often elicit responses that involve creativity, humor, and wit. The questions themselves beg for personality in their responses, whether applicants choose to be serious, silly, thoughtful, or whimsical. The annual essay questions are actually written and submitted by current or recently admitted students and even graduates. And the good news: the final question (usually) is entirely open-ended, so if you don't respond to any of these, you can still decide on your own what you want to write about. Here are the 2014–15 University of Chicago questions:

1. *What's so odd about odd numbers?*
   —Inspired by Mario Rosasco, Class of 2009.

2. *In French, there is no difference between "conscience" and "consciousness." In Japanese, there is a word that specifically refers to the splittable wooden chopsticks you get at restaurants. The German word "fremdschämen" encapsulates the feeling you get when you're embarrassed on behalf of someone else. All of these require explanation in order to properly communicate their meaning, and are, to varying degrees, untranslatable. Choose a word, tell us what it means, and then explain why it cannot (or should not) be translated from its original language.*
   —Inspired by Emily Driscoll, an incoming student in the Class of 2018

3. *Little pigs, french hens, a family of bears. Blind mice, musketeers, the Fates. Parts of an atom, laws of thought, a guideline for composition. Omne trium perfectum? Create your own group of threes, and describe why and how they fit together.*
   —Inspired by Zilin Cui, an incoming student in the Class of 2018

4. *Were pH an expression of personality, what would be your pH and why? (Feel free to respond acidly! Do not be neutral, for that is base!)*
   —Inspired by Joshua Harris, Class of 2016

5. *A neon installation by the artist Jeppe Hein in UChicago's Charles M. Harper Center asks this question for us: "Why are you here and not somewhere else?" (There are many potential values of "here", but we already know you're "here" to apply to the University of Chicago; pick any "here" besides that one.)*
   —Inspired by Erin Hart, Class of 2016

6. *In the spirit of adventurous inquiry, pose a question of your own. If your prompt is original and thoughtful, then you should have little trouble writing a great essay. Draw on your best qualities as a writer, thinker, visionary, social critic, sage, citizen of the world, or future citizen of the University of Chicago; take a little risk, and have fun.*

University of North Carolina Chapel Hill (2013–14)

1. *Most of us have one or more personality quirks. Explain one of yours and what it says about you.*

2. *What do you hope to find over the rainbow?*

3. *Why do you do what you do?*

4. *If you could travel anywhere in time or space, either real or imagined, where would you go and why?*

5. *Tell us about a time when your curiosity led you someplace you weren't expecting to go.*

These topics, whether straightforward or more creative in nature, all seem reasonable, thought provoking, easy enough to address, and even clever, right? What is tough for you is that you may not have ever written a personal statement before. Instead, you have been drilled in your classroom into writing five-paragraph essays almost all of the time. But here is the thing: you can really write about WHATEVER you want to as long as it loosely answers the prompt and shares coherent ideas and a glimpse of who you are. Do not stress about answering a question exactly the way you think the reader wants you to. Instead, decide what you want to share about yourself and see how it connects in some way to the prompt. Most prompts are rather open-ended and are a means to "get your juices flowing," to elicit a reaction from you that excites you to share a piece of yourself.

Now, imagine a college admission officer with thirty to forty applications on his desk that he needs to get through in the course of his day. Next, imagine that your application is the fortieth and final read of the day. Your reader is a bit tired and bleary-eyed and might not be focused enough to recognize the (dozens, scores, or hundreds of) hours you have put into this application. Whatever you do, do NOT write a dry, five-paragraph essay, or any five-paragraph essay for that matter. When it comes to your personal statement, take most of what you have learned about writing in your English class and throw it out the window. Personal statements break many of the conventional rules of English class—except for the obvious ones of good grammar, syntax, and spelling.

Instead, think about ways you can "speak" to your reader and connect with him or her.

What things can you do to make the reader remember you, want to meet you, and welcome you into the campus community?

- When you write, be sure that you show, not tell. Illustrate experiences and situations that show your reader your topic, world, experience.
- Use your five senses when you write so that your reader can see, hear, smell, taste, and touch your essay.
- Feel free to use dialogue as you write (or even share thoughts going on in your head).
- Consider breaking some structural or stylistic rules (while using correct grammar and spelling, of course), and use sentence fragments or some stream-of-consciousness if it helps set a mood or tell your story.
- Humor is perfectly acceptable. Don't be afraid to use it, especially if you are a funny person.
- Being serious, honest, and straightforward is perfectly okay, too. Being truthful and not exaggerating is best and will come though in your writing by showing you to be genuine and real.
- Take some risks (within reason) to stand out a bit.
- Be yourself.

Where to Begin?

How do you decide what to write about? With the prompts generally in the back of your mind to serve as a framework or starting point, begin to brainstorm ideas as they come to the surface. Go back and reread your self-reflection questions to see what answers you wrote jump out at you that you may want to expand upon. Again, the college essay should ideally be an essay that only *you* could write—not your mom, dad, sibling, or friend. It needs to be authentic, in your voice and writing style, and should come across like a conversation you are having with your reader. If you were to share your finished essay with a parent or best friends, they should say once they have read it, "That essay is so *you*! It sounds just like you."

As outlined before, continue brainstorming by thinking of a variety of ideas that relate to your life:

- Family traditions
- Anecdotes or family folktales that you or loved ones share about your life, childhood, or upbringing
- An interesting or controversial conversation you have had
- A lesson you have learned in either a common or an unusual way
- Challenges you have overcome or risks you may have taken
- How your best friend might describe you in a story that reflects who you are (Consider asking a friend or relative to tell you some things that they think about you or stories that remind them of you, and see if there are any nuggets to be found.)

Keep a journal, or reread one if you have had one. Often, ideas that are personal and recorded privately can be very revealing.

Think of this statement as a peek at who you are, what makes you tick, or an anecdote that is emblematic of how you see the world or view yourself in it.

Here are some things that your personal statement should NOT be:

- Your life story or a string of experiences linked together without a consistent theme
- A repetition or summary of your activities along the way
- A "cry me a river" story that makes the reader feel sorry for you

Don't get me wrong. There is nothing terrible about writing about a setback or misfortune, just be sure you don't play your own violin the entire time. You should make the reader want to root for you or share in your struggle, but you must show your reader what this difficult experience has taught you and how it has influenced you.

Your first draft of writing is never, ever your last. In fact, revisions can go on and on and on until you are ready to upload or input them onto your computerized application and push the "send" button. Make sure that every word of your final essay counts. Use more active verbs than linking verbs. Be sure that your voice is heard and comes through clearly in your writing. Use real vocabulary; don't include words that you would not actually use when speaking to someone. Only use a "$10 word" (that is an SAT® or other big word that might need to be looked up in a dictionary) if that is truly a word in your spoken vocabulary. Read your essay aloud into your bathroom mirror, and check to see if it really sounds natural and genuinely like you. Don't try to be someone you are not, or someone who you think an admission officer will like. Be yourself.

When you write from your heart and show real emotion, your reader is welcomed in and enters your world more easily and seamlessly. When you write from your mind, you share your thoughts and intellect and the way your brain works in processing and connecting ideas.

Final Word of Warning: Plagiarism

And a final word of warning: Don't even **think** of using any of the essays in this book (or any book, Internet source, relative's essay, or any other person's essay, for that matter) as your own. Plagiarism is a serious offense and can jeopardize everything you have worked for! Colleges can verify that your work belongs to you by using simple Internet search tools and programs to identify sentence strings that might not look like your own. And, you will be asked to sign a waiver electronically for your colleges indicating that the work contained in your application is solely your own. Don't blow it by being dishonest.

The essays in this book are meant to inspire, stimulate, and demonstrate to you the wide range of possibilities and options that have worked for other students. The rules you follow in this process can be invented (and dictated for the most part) by you. I hope you will enjoy the process of writing your successful college application.

Chapter Two

Dos and Don'ts in Writing Your College Application

Dos

- Do be honest and genuine in what you choose to write.
- Do use vocabulary and a voice that is distinctly your own.
- Do write about a topic that is meaningful to you or offers your reader a glimpse into who you are, how you think, and what is important to you.
- Do use humor, if you are a funny person.
- Do be serious, if that is your style.
- Do brainstorm many ideas. Even if you don't use all these ideas in your main essay, you may find yourself coming back to your brainstorm list when you write your supplemental essays. As you know, you usually have to write more than one essay for your applications.

- Do proofread, proofread, and proofread again. Spell check does not know the difference between "from" and "form" or "and" and "an." Only human eyes can make those changes and catch those mistakes!

- Do read your essay out loud to yourself before sending it. Does it sound like the way you speak?

- Do show, not tell. Do use your five senses when you write, showing your reader how things look, taste, smell, sound, and feel.

- Do use dialogue, sentence fragments, stream of consciousness if applicable or to help get your tone and point across.

- Do make sure your first sentence offers a hook or opening that grabs the reader's attention.

- Do get to know yourself: ask friends, relatives, and others who know you well how they would describe you.

- Do go back and read your journal (if you keep one) to remember details about your mindset from earlier times in your life.

- Do peruse old photos or photo albums in search of special moments, memories, and traditions that you might weave into your writing.

- Do prepare your essays in a word processing document before transferring them to the Common Application or other online application. That way you can better edit, spell check, and complete your work before pasting it into the online version.

- Do, if possible, convert any file or attachment to a PDF before sending to preserve your font and eliminate the unsightly "colored squiggles" that can appear under words for grammar or spelling.

- Do double check that any uploads you import are formatted in the correct way. You should print out a full draft of your application before sending it. Sometimes

Firefox works better than Safari to import or copy and paste essays, so try both (or any other browser) and see.

- Do keep a complete, printed draft of your application from your "print preview" screen. Having a hard copy on file is never a bad idea as pages can sometimes get lost in cyberspace.

- Do seek help from a trusted adult: a private college counselor, your school's college counselor, a teacher, or a parent, sibling, or older friend who has applied to college.

- Do be prepared to write multiple drafts of your essay.

- Do save your old drafts until you are done. Sometimes an earlier version said something better than a later one, and you may want to refer back to it.

- Do treat every piece of writing with the same level of importance. While your main essay or personal statement may seem more significant to your intended reader, remember that ALL pieces of writing are closely evaluated and considered by the admission office.

- Do take some time away from your essay and reread it with fresh eyes several hours, a day, or a week later so that you might have a new perspective. Sometimes, being in the grind of writing for hours does not offer you the distance to gain an objective perspective on your work.

- Do spend your time. College essay writing is a process that is not meant to be completed in one weekend. Thoughtful planning, shaping, reshaping, editing, and proofreading will ensure that when your essay is finally done, it's done! Do spend time creating writing that you are proud of and that genuinely reflects your voice and who you are.

- Do try to have some fun in the process if you can!

Don'ts

- Don't choose a topic that could offend your reader. Avoid overly political or religious essays that could be misinterpreted or viewed as extreme by your reader.

- Don't even think of using an essay or any part of an essay that is not your own. Plagiarism is a serious offense.

- Don't jump in and write about your first idea. Let it simmer. Chances are good that many other people might write about a similar idea, and you don't want to sound like everyone else. Seek out essay ideas that could only come from you and are not generic in theme or topic.

- Don't try to write your life story in one page; choose an experience, conversation, or idea that offers the reader a sense of who you are.

- Don't be too colloquial or casual. No curse words or slang.

- Don't write about your experience on a sports team. If anyone else could write the same type of essay as you, avoid it. Most sports themes (it's not all about winning, what it means to be a team player, the time I got injured, leadership and being the captain, and so on) are generic for any athlete. Writing about the generic sports themes won't reveal anything unique about you. (If you do want to write about sports, perhaps write about coaching, refereeing, or a conversation you had with a teammate that somehow changed the way you look at things, etc.)

- Don't write your essay as an expanded and more detailed summary of your activities. Your reader will read your activity paragraph and see your student résumé/brag sheet elsewhere in your application.

- Don't "throw away" short-answer questions. Don't mistake shorter-length writing as somehow less important than your main essay(s). The activity paragraph, academic paragraph, "why this school" question, and other short answers are just as important as your personal statement.

- Don't have too many people offer feedback on your essay. The more eyes that see it, the more opinions and edits you will consider, and the more changes you will make. Then your essay may sound less like you and more like another person's voice.
- Don't write about a topic just because you think it will impress your reader. Write about something meaningful to you.
- Don't write a five-paragraph essay with a thesis and supporting paragraphs and conclusion. This essay is your personal statement and those rules of structure do not apply here. (Check for proper grammar, spelling, and syntax though!)
- Don't use too many linking verbs (any form of "to be" and other exceptions) if you can avoid them. Instead use active verbs.
- Don't procrastinate. Begin your college writing the summer before your senior year or, in some cases, sooner.
- Don't feel compelled to write about some drastic or dramatic event in your life. Oftentimes, the most mundane and simple topics reveal the most about you.
- Don't make yourself crazy or panicked about your essay. The work you have done and grades you have earned in school—your transcript—is the most important part of your application. Your essays are just more ways for your reader to get to know you better as a person.
- Don't tell. Show.
- Don't use the thesaurus too much.
- Don't try to be someone you are not, or someone you think an admission officer will like. Be yourself.
- Don't include the actual name of the college in your writing unless it is in a supplement that is exclusively for that college. This means <u>no</u> names of colleges should be included in your main essay.

Questions and Answers

Q: How do I know if my essay represents my authentic voice?

A: If a close friend or family member were to read your completed essay, he or she should say, "That sounds just like you!" or "Your essay is totally you." If there is questionable vocabulary or expressions that you would not use, take them out.

Q: How do I know when my essay is finished?

A: Read your essay out loud while looking into a mirror. Does it sound like you? Is your voice and essence coming through? Is every word in your essay essential? Can any words be cut out? Then, put down your essay (or pencil), and save the document on your computer. Push "send" when you cannot find one extraneous word or idea that needs changing. At some point you just have to let it go.

Q: How do I write about someone I admire, a hero, or someone who has influenced me without the essay being all about that person?

A: Be sure your essay demonstrates how you admire or emulate that person and how you have been influenced by that person. If you are sure to tie the essay into YOU, you will not risk it being just about that individual.

Q: How do I write about myself without sounding too "braggy" or pompous?

A: If your essay reads in an authentic way, if it sounds like you, then unless you are a pompous person by definition, it will not come across that way. Remember: your personal statement is not the place to hold back and show too much restraint. It is okay to "toot your own horn" as long as you don't do it in every sentence. It is also nice to reflect and appreciate the talent or life experience you have cultivated. Essentially, in your personal statement, you have some degree of "bragging rights." Use them.

Q: Is it important to use big vocabulary words in my personal statement or any college application writing for that matter?

A: If you use those kinds of words when you speak, then yes, by all means throw them in. Don't insert a word that you would just never say when you speak. And certainly be careful that you don't use a big word incorrectly!

Q: Can I use different fonts, boldface words, or italicize for emphasis in my writing?

A: Often, the online applications and those on the Common Application predetermine the font you are using, both its size and style. This also makes it easier for your readers to view each application more objectively (and also will induce fewer headaches!). If there is a word you need to emphasize, try to write it in ALL CAPS or <u>underline</u> it or put it in "quotation marks" if your computer or formatting allows. If not, (parentheses) are a great way to offer more detail and speak to your reader about ideas going on in your head or to define the emphasis you are trying to incorporate into your work.

In addition, the website for the Common Application states:

Due to errors in the text-to-PDF conversion process, you may see essays with odd formatting, including inconsistent fonts and errant paragraph breaks. We understand that students have no control over this formatting, and admission offices will not penalize students for a technical problem that is out of their control.

So don't stress. Glitches in the Common Application and other online applications are always being worked out, and you will not be penalized for how they may impact the formatting of the "look" of your essay. If you are overly concerned about something, read the FAQ page, send an e-mail to the individual school, or, as a last resort, call!

Q: Do I need to completely fill in every section of the application?

A: If there is a space to fill in on the application, use it as an opportunity to share even more about yourself. Don't under-write or supply a response that is significantly below the allotted space or word limit. Try to fill the space since your reader is prepared to read all that is contained there. That doesn't mean, however, that you should fill your application with unnecessary fluff of extra words just to fill space. Make each word count, but use the space you are given. View it as an opportunity to share a bit more, even if it is just a few sentences.

Q: What are some ideas of topics or content that could go in the "Additional Information" section of the application?

A: Information that you want to share that is not addressed or sought elsewhere in your application goes here. Examples could be a concerning grade that might be out of sync with your transcript in general; an explanation for why you might have moved levels in a course (down from AP to college prep for example or from Honors to non-Honors); a break in your education, such as a gap year or time off due to illness or a personal family issue; some "good news" that you haven't noted yet, such as an award, honor, additional activity, or unique talent; any other explanation that you feel you need to share with your reader to offer information that you believe is important in clarifying who you are or adds to "making your case."

Q: How strict are the word limits on applications?

A: "650" seems to be the magic number for the maximum word count for both the main essay and the additional information sections of the Common Application. For those colleges or universities that are not part of the Common Application, you should always check to be sure you're complying with their particular application's word limits.

Q: What is the best way to ensure I don't have typos on my essays?

A: Do ALL of your application writing in a word-processing document where you can edit, spell-check, and grammar check, and still read it aloud to be sure you have caught all of your mistakes. For example, the computer cannot tell the difference between "from" and "form" and therefore may not catch those words as mistakes if they indeed are. Then copy and paste your FINAL version into the Common Application or other online application form. Check in "print preview" that no words are cut off or formatted strangely in translation.

Q: How can I protect my application once it is complete and be certain it does not get lost in cyberspace when I am finally ready to push "send?" How can I be sure that it arrived at the college?

A: There isn't a 100 percent foolproof way to protect everything on your computer. Obviously have backups of all your work and what you've saved on your computer (in case it crashes), and it's a good idea to print out hard copies of your work every once in a while so you don't have to solely rely on your computer or cyberspace to hold onto your work. Also keep in mind that the Common Application gets very congested and can even crash close to the deadlines, so try to submit your application at least a week in advance if you can. And, be sure to PRINT OUT a final copy of your application before sending it. In addition, print out any confirmation pages you get from the school or Common App site stating that your application has been submitted. While it may waste some trees, printing out hard copies is never a bad idea when it comes to the application you have worked hours and hours completing.

Q: Is there any way to get around word limits and include more words than suggested or recommended?

A: The best advice is to follow the word limits as closely as possible. Changing font size or margins in a college application is not really an option. But, if there is a space or option to upload a PDF or document in lieu of pasting text into an existing space, the word count of your upload is pretty difficult to enforce. In other words, an admission officer or application reader will not take the time to physically count your words on an upload. If the text does look too long, it might annoy the admission officers. They may stop reading your essay if it gets too long, but if it is "close enough" and reasonable in length, you should be okay.

Q: How are arts/athletic supplements handled? Are they still in the Common App or are students supposed to send them in separately for each school, case by case?

A: Some schools still use Common App for the arts supplement, and some schools have their own arts supplement. As of 2014, the athletic supplement no longer exists in the Common App.

Q: Should I mention the name of the college I'm applying to in my application essays?

A: In some shorter answers that are supplements (not main essay/personal statements), you may feel compelled to name the college you are writing for in your piece. That is perfectly fine— as long as you can remember to change that reference should you reuse or recycle the answer for another school's supplement. (See Chapter 9: How to Recycle Your Writing for more details on this topic.) It is not recommended to use the name of a college in your main essay unless it is for a school that has its own application and does not use the Common Application. Instead, it's better to just refer generically to "college" than to specify the school's name in your piece. To reiterate: Never name the specific college unless that piece is only going to that school, such as in a supplement. If, however, a school you are applying to is not on the Common Application and has an individual online application of its own, then you can certainly name the college since the work you send will only be going to that school.

Q: What do I need to submit for a portfolio for my school?

A: Check with each school as to its specifications, but many colleges allow supplemental portfolio information to be submitted with applications for studio artists, musicians, and sometimes actors. Portfolios include the best samples of your artwork or some sample music pieces as well as a separate résumé for that discipline listing your deeper involvement in your art form. Also, it is helpful to include a list of any awards or recognition you've earned in your art. This is your college application, so pull out the stops and don't be too shy about your accomplishments. Also, the Common Application has an arts supplement, which you can complete if your school requests it as part of your application. Again, check with each individual school about this.

Q: Do I have to go to the campus to audition for dance, drama, music, or other disciplines?

A: As mentioned before, check with each school and department as to the audition requirements. Many schools offer off-site locations in or near major cities, enabling applicants to audition or display their artwork closer to home; sometimes more than one date will be offered. Keep in mind that some schools will not see an audition until after your application has been submitted. Check with each school to see if it allows for submissions of videos or web links in lieu of a live audition if you are unable to visit the campus or attend an off-site audition before the application deadline. If you have the means or the time, a live audition is always preferable to make the experience more "human" than a video submission.

Chapter Three

50+ Sample Essays

E ssays come in many shapes and sizes, themes and styles. The 50-plus personal statements selected for this book come from students of every academic level and from a variety of communities and histories. When you read each essay, imagine that you are an admission officer. What does this essay tell you about its writer? What did you learn about the student from the story he told? Would this be someone you might want to see join your college community and classroom? Has the writer shared enough with you to allow you to "know" her through the essay, to hear her voice?

The essays are grouped in the following categories:
- Taking Risks and Conquering Fears
- Role Models, Teachers, and Heroes—Learning from Others in Unexpected Ways
- Pursuing Passions and Hobbies
- Family Reflections, Traditions, and Influences
- Personal Setbacks and Self-Reflection

- Work and Community
- Academic and Philosophical Aspirations—The Thinking Essay
- Cultural Identity and Personal Identity
- Humorous and Miscellaneous

Read on to better understand the range, breadth, and depth of writing you can explore to find your authentic voice in your own personal statement. Hopefully, you will be inspired and maybe even a little less intimidated by this process once you read what your peers have written.

Taking Risks and Conquering Fears

Essays that tackle this theme offer your reader a window into you as a human with faults. By recognizing your fears, showing your reader how they concern you or how you have tackled or conquered them, you provide insight into how you approach the world and the concept of failure. Don't be afraid to take risks and expose some of your weaknesses when you write your personal statement (or any of your other supplemental writing pieces for your college application). In the following essays, you will see that each writer dug deep to share personal fears or challenges that were conquered and learned from.

Essay 1: Taking Risks and Conquering Fears

"I would rather take a 10-hour-long calculus test." "I would rather eat a million ants." "I would rather go three days without eating." These were just some of the thoughts that ran through my brain when my theatre teacher, Mr. S., announced, "All Theatre III students are required to study musical theatre. In order to pass the course, each of you must perform a song for the class." Although I realize that most people would view it as only a minor embarrassment, singing—in front of my whole class and my teacher—was the worst thing I could possibly imagine.

Where did my extreme fear of singing begin? Maybe it was when I was traumatized in eighth grade when the music teacher forced the entire grade to audition for a musical. I stood to perform my song, but no actual human sound came out; all I produced was a scratchy and unrecognizable noise. My eighth-grade mind had no doubt that the entire class discussed my horrible singing in detail as soon as I was out of the room. Or maybe I am afraid to sing because of my younger sister, who is capable of bringing tears to people's eyes with her voice. I most definitely do not have the ability to make an audience cry, at least not in a positive way.

Admittedly, I am accustomed to succeeding in everything I put my mind to. I have always done well in school, and I am a talented runner. I can stand at the starting line of an important race, and, regardless of how nervous I feel before the start, can overcome those feelings and win. But I have never been able to overcome my fear of singing. This was the first time I ever thought I would fail a class, because I truly believed that when the time came for me to perform my song, I would just sprint out of the room. I tried to tell Mr. S., but he just kept saying "Everyone can sing." "Nope, not me," I replied. "I would rather get hit by a bus."

We started out slowly. Mr. S. gave us each the lyrics and music to a song, and also had us prepare the song to be performed as a spoken monologue. My assigned song was "So in Love" from the musical *Kiss Me Kate*. I learned in class that the higher the stakes of my "story," the more compelling my performance would be to the audience, so I decided to create a good story behind my song. I imagined what it would be like if someone I loved was leaving me forever. What would I say? How would I feel? I convinced myself that, while I was singing, the most important thing in my world was getting my feelings across to this person through the music and lyrics of the song.

The next step was hearing the music and putting the words and my story to the notes. The first few times I sang aloud, my teacher and I were the only ones in the classroom. I started out timidly, almost whispering the notes, even though I was singing to one, very supportive person. Gradually, I became louder and more confident, but I still didn't think I would be able to perform in front of the entire class.

The day arrived, and it was finally my turn to sing. As the opening notes of my song played, I concentrated on my story and transferred my fear of singing to the sadness I was supposed to feel. I focused on a spot on the back wall, and as loudly and compellingly as possible, I sang. My voice emerged strong and clear. I was able to put myself in that "place," and for a brief two minutes I was so involved in my story that I forgot I was singing, forgot that there was a classroom of people watching me.

When I came out of my imagined world, I noticed that Mr. S. had tears in his eyes. I had done it. I had sung in front of an audience and survived. I know there will be much greater challenges ahead, but this simple success has me truly believing that I am capable of doing anything.

Essay 2: Taking Risks and Conquering Fears
My Running Paradox

The gun fires, and I'm off, running almost haphazardly (the only way my uncoordinated body allows). I've never been able to pinpoint what drew me to cross-country as a freshman. I am not an athlete; I can't throw a ball, hold a racket, or tackle an opponent. It seemed like the only sport I could do. As expected, I've never led the team to any state championships; in fact, I've never even competed in a varsity race. Regardless, I remain committed to and engaged by this foreign and unnatural activity called "cross-country."

Here arises the paradox of running that has defined my four-year "career" in the sport. I'd never tell somebody that I love to run because, most of the time, that would be an outright lie. But, on a few good days, running is my portal to a world without the everyday pressures of life. On those days, my awkward body falls into a rhythmic movement, and my mind is free to wander. Only one mile out in the race, I wipe mud off my face after other runners, all ahead of me, kick it behind them; at this moment, running is about the satisfaction in even the slightest improvement in my time—it becomes a race of me against myself. Cross-country is a place where I know I'll never be the best, but I'll never be able to live with being the worst.

Make no mistake: my body is not built for running; my legs pronate inwards, and my feet have high arches. So, by the time we reach the second mile of the race, I'm usually at the back of the pack. I watch as people fly around turns and up hills while I struggle to move on a flat stretch meters behind them. Still, I try to chip seconds off my 5K-race time, and, over the past four years, I've made some small progress. I've accepted the fact that I'll never be a good runner, but I haven't accepted the fact that running is hopeless. It's a humbling experience for me—I am not the best, and never will be, but how much can I improve? That unanswered question always pulls me back to the sport.

I see the finish line, and I dig down for that final kick. I keep running, getting ever closer to that elusive white line. My cross-country career has now come to an end, but my running career hasn't. It never will. I'll never be a marathon runner or a professional sprinter, but running is part of who I am. Even though I won't qualify to be on your school's cross-country-team, I'm still bringing my running shoes with me to college. No, I won't be the fastest and definitely not the most graceful, but I'll be on your campus running, perhaps to the amusement of other students, but, more important, to my own satisfaction.

Essay 3: Taking Risks and Conquering Fears

I want to learn to take risks. I want to change my attitude about taking chances. Assessing my academic and extracurricular achievements, I am proud of my accomplishments. I see myself as an open-minded, goal-oriented person who achieves and succeeds through hard work and determination. How much of that success is a result of staying on comfortable ground?

I began wondering about the range of my abilities when I attended Northwestern University's Theatre Arts Program last summer. The theme of the institute, announced by the director, was: "Dare to fail gloriously." This idea encouraged participants to take bold risks on the stage. Over time I applied this philosophy to my acting and my life. I began the Northwestern program as a quasi-accomplished actress with a hunger to absorb all I could about acting. I emerged not only a well-rounded thespian, but also a more secure person with a new outlook. I knew that there was something about my life that I wanted to change and could change. Now, as I approach college, I am committed to continuing successes and occasional glorious failures. The first day at Northwestern I was asked to choose among three subjects in technical theatre, ranking them in order of preference. Set Design was my first choice, followed by Costumes, and finally Stage Lighting. Much to my dismay, I was assigned to the lighting crew. Though disappointed, I tried to stay open-minded. I knew nothing about lighting, but I followed the slogan that kept repeating in my head: "Dare to fail . . ."

By the third lighting session, I had discovered a new passion: I was eager to learn everything I could about lights. Having always been a performer who enjoyed the limelight, I had never realized the skill required to create it properly. In my free time I climbed the catwalks, memorized cues, circuited lamps, or changed gels. My competence was recognized when I was selected head light board operator for the final production of the summer.

If the choice to study lighting had not been made for me, I would have missed an enriching opportunity. The experience taught me to take more risks, rather than to follow the most certain path to success. The exposure made me realize how limited my perspective had been in approaching new situations. The choice that was made for me, undesirable as it seemed at the outset, taught me to embrace new experiences and ideas.

I believe that "the past is prologue." In college I will take more risks, convinced that the potential rewards outweigh my fear of failure. I have stopped trying to select a major and am committed to studying in many academic disciplines before deciding on a field of concentration.

Accepting the possibility of failure is a new concept for me. While I have had the recognition for academics, performing acts, community service, and athletic achievements, perhaps I have missed some enriching experiences because my certainty of success was doubtful. I will not avoid such opportunities in the future since I am changing my philosophy of life: I am learning to take risks.

Essay 4: Taking Risks and Conquering Fears

Nervously, I picked my first candidate: my roommate. I began the conversation, "So, where do you live?" She answered, "Seattle." Luckily, Seattle is one of my favorite cities in the world. The conversation was easy and flowing and before I knew it we had been talking for over two hours. This encounter may seem like no big deal, but for me it was a very big deal. Overall, I have many strengths. I am unique, carefree, driven, and intelligent. One of my biggest downfalls, however, is being extremely shy when I meet new people. My shyness is my comfort zone, but it limits me by preventing me from experiencing new things. After this conversation with my roommate, my nerves were eased. A growing sensation of excitement developed in me. Learning and practicing this new trait, overcoming my shyness, was difficult but rewarding.

My eyes were opened to broaden myself as I sat in the lecture hall at Fordham University while attending the Lead America Journalism and Media Conference. I was proud to be nominated as one of the 100 high school students across the country that attended. There I heard the words of an inspiring speaker, Dr. Gilbert M., "To be successful in this life you must be more diligent and innovative than ever before. You are the most privileged young people in human history. . . . The power of the individual to change things will result in the ability for your generation to solve worldwide problems." Although American teenagers make up 4.7 percent of the world's population, my personal influence, according to Dr. M., is astounding. Hearing the reality of what my generation can become I wondered, "Am I aware of how privileged I am? Do I know my responsibility in this world? How have I influenced the people around me?" I began to analyze myself, and I realized that I was not fully the person I had the potential to be. After Dr. M.'s talk, I came to the conclusion that being shy is the ultimate form of self-absorption. From then on I worked hard every day at Fordham to try to be more outgoing. Fordham provided the perfect environment. When I arrived at the ten-day conference I knew no one, and by the end, everyone knew who I was.

I believe that my shyness has stifled me from growing into a powerful individual who can change things. I used to take myself out of conversations in big groups by just standing silently and listening. I tried to blend in and look like I was doing something by text messaging on my phone. It was difficult for me to start conversations with a new person so I only spoke to people when I was approached by them. I now realize that being so self-absorbed and not allowing new people to come into my life stunted me in many ways.

Once I identified and focused on changing my downfall I saw immediate results. Now, my voice is heard in group discussions, my opinions are made into reality, and I have become a more powerful person. I automatically feel more in control and comfortable when I meet new people. I feel confident in my conversation abilities and truly interested in what people have to say to me. I now enjoy discovering the different ways others live their lives and take their outlook into consideration when I form opinions. Changing my downfall I am now perceived as more outgoing, and my new peers have no idea that I used to be terribly shy.

In college I plan to develop into an even more powerful person by speaking my mind in my class, making new friends every day, and taking on more leadership roles in campus clubs or organizations. I will no longer stand silent, focusing inward. Now, my confident voice from here forward will be heard.

Essay 5: Taking Risks and Conquering Fears

For most of my life, I was the nervous kid. Whether I was crying before the first day of kindergarten, hiding behind the piano in the second-grade concert, or not wanting to get on the bus to Sea World for the fourth-grade trip, my nerves seemed to always win.

Fast forward to eighth grade—I am backstage at the Los Angeles Galaxy game, eyes closed, visualizing the task at hand: walk on the stage and deliver a flawless performance.

The butterflies in my stomach are so fierce that I struggle to stand up.

"Now on stage we have John Farnworth, world champion soccer freestyler from England!"

Just my luck, I'm following the world champion.

John pulls off some of the greatest tricks ever seen. The crowd is in awe. But I'm just a 13-year-old boy getting ready to make my first freestyle soccer performance in front of crowds coming in by the hundreds. All the work will define this moment; the times my mom came into the garage and said, "Time for dinner! You've been going at it for 3 hours!"

"No, mom!" I would retort, "I have to keep practicing!"

One drop of the ball, and my nervous mind would certainly panic as it had always done before.

My name has been called. It is like going into a battle: Performer vs. Emotion.

I head up to the stage. It's only five steps, but feels like a hundred. The heavy bass of the DJ resonates through the audience. I center myself on stage, getting an aerial view of the massive crowd that has formed.

A hard swallow, a deliberate exhale. A loosening shrug of the shoulders, an acknowledgement of the crowd.

I perform the various tricks I have spent hours practicing, and after a successful few minutes on stage, I kick the ball up and catch it, give a wave to the crowd, and take in the moment. The emcee yells, "Woooooooooow! Anything is possible!"

I exit the stage, and the other performers congratulate me.

As I sit back in my chair and breathe a huge sigh of relief, an uncontrollable smile stretches from ear to ear, and people ask me for my autograph. Dedication and self-belief really do pay off.

The performance was more than a show to me; it was the conquering of nerves and facing the fears that had plagued me for as long as I can remember. Had I never walked those five steps to the stage that night, I would not have gained the maturity to challenge myself throughout high school. My heart still pounds when I present an argument during an AP Government debate, and my knees still shake during an AP Economics presentation. I still get nervous, but now I have the experience to channel those nerves into productivity.

Those five steps were much more than a path to the stage; they were the path away from a shy boy toward a confident man.

Essay 6: Taking Risks and Conquering Fears

Red lights illuminated the dark room as the violin and guitar began to blend together. I held my best friend's hand in mine as my heart began to beat faster and faster. As the song progressed into the chorus, the entire crowd began to sing aloud together and I closed my eyes: "Keep your head up, keep your love." Hundreds of voices chanted the same beautiful words with more energy than I had ever felt before in my life.

For as long as I can remember, I'd stay up nights listening to music and taking comfort in writing songs. Even when it seemed as if nobody else was there, music always was. Music allowed me to break out of my shell, although, for a long time, I kept my passion within the confines of my room.

In the middle of my junior year, I finally pushed myself to audition for my school's Academy of the Performing Arts, a prestigious arts program ranked first in the nation. Hesitant and insecure, I listened to Bob Dylan's words of wisdom: "You better start swimming or you'll sink like a stone." I needed to take my chance.

I rehearsed for months and then, in the blink of an eye, it was audition day. About 60 of us restlessly waited for our turn. My hands and legs were shaking as my lyrics ran through my head continuously.

"Ms. A., you're up."

My heart sank, my palms sweat, and I thought to myself, "Don't you know it's gonna be alright?" The Beatles always calm me down.

I was soon standing in front of the 3 program directors, with their clipboards in hand. My hand trembled as I gripped the microphone. I took a deep breath and gave it my all.

Then, after a mere 2 minutes, my fate rested in their hands. Although there was no way to know what they were thinking, I knew I had done my best and that I had finally put myself out there. That was more than I ever dreamed I could do. Coldplay had it figured out all along: "If you never try you'll never know just what you're worth."

Less than a year later, I found myself in that room again, in awe of how far I'd come. With 30 of my peers, we closed our eyes and sang harmonies to The Beatles' "Because." With each note, my smile grew wider. I looked around at my classmates and heard the Foo Fighters in my head: "I wonder, when I sing along with you, if everything could ever feel this real forever, if anything could ever be this good again." I knew right then that, because I took that chance, I had become part of something extraordinary.

That audition changed my life as much as my favorite concert in that red-lit room did. My relationship with music is indescribable. It's like trying to put one's faith into words. It's not something you can explain; it's something you feel. Music is how, in my lowest of moments, I'm able to make sense of the world. Music is the reason I will always have the strength to tell myself "keep your head up, keep your love."

Role Models, Teachers, and Heroes—Learning from Others in Unexpected Ways

Teachers come in all shapes and sizes, from the adults who lead your classrooms or coach you in athletics to those younger than you are who you might mentor or tutor. Be on the lookout for people who influence you, challenge you, and help you to grow. You may be surprised to have them all around you, even in the most unexpected scenarios. Be sure to connect yourself into this topic, and keep it about your relationship to and with the person(s) and not just observations and comments about this person. How has this person influenced you? What have you learned from him or her? What have you applied to your life to emulate that person or those individuals? Read on to see who the following writers selected and how they learned from these (sometimes surprising) influential people in their lives.

Essay 1: Role Models, Teachers, and Heroes— Learning from Others in Unexpected Ways

---

I love quotes. I hold on to them for years. But I hate cheesy quotes. I only allow cheesy quotes into my life if they are the cream of the crop: the havarti among the spray cheese. So here is my havarti:

> *"I've heard it said that people come into our lives for a reason, bringing something we must learn. And we are led to those who help us most to grow, if we let them." —Glinda, Wicked*

Mr. B. came into my life for many reasons. When I met him, he was my 26-year-old charismatic English teacher. However, over the past four years, he has become a director, editor, mentor, friend, and role model. As an athletic 14-year-old, the girl who met Mr. B. her freshman year had not discovered dance, acting, or herself. But I attribute who I am today—artistic and unafraid—to the things he taught me. He once claimed, "Holden Caulfield is not crazy. He just needs somebody." And today, I try to be that person for anyone in need of that "somebody." He convinced me to try acting, and on a whim, I did. If it hadn't been for Mr. B., I would not be looking at acting opportunities in college. Moreover, he taught me the most important thing I learned in high school—the thing that made me grow the most—once I eventually auditioned for, and joined, my high school's Acting Company.

Being utterly wrong is miles better than being mediocre, forgettable, or hesitant: this is how he taught us to act both on and off of the stage. To my former self, a perfectionist, the concept of imprecision made me cringe. Years of gymnastics and dance training instilled this phobia in me. Thus, acting forced my personal character to do a 180° turn. My first Company production, Eugene Ionesco's *Rhinoceros,* tore me mercilessly out of my comfort zone. From its upbeat tempo to its strict comedic timing, the play made me struggle. One night, sensing my uneasiness, Mr. B. gave me my favorite quote of all time. "Take a risk," he said. "Worst case scenario, you find out exactly what *not* to do." And risk I did. I screamed, whispered, wept, and exhausted my impression and accent repertoire from *My Big Fat Greek Wedding*'s Gus to Elizabethan English (though my director described most of these as painfully inaccurate). But I persisted, experimenting until I hit it right. After that rehearsal, my cast mates and I came down with horrible cases of sore stomach due to laughter. Walking out of the theatre, I realized that acting, and life, are about risk and reward, and sometimes what feels downright wrong creates a comedy that is downright perfect.

Mr. B. left my school last year to take risks and follow his personal dreams. I wrote him a note when he left, and I told him, "You came into my life to make it a better place. You taught me so much more than who Pisistratus was or what the heck Holden did in his hotel room. You taught me actual lessons that are infinitely more important. You taught me that even if I don't think I can do something (i.e., acting company, honors math, applying to University of Nobody Gets In Here, etc.), it is always worth a try."

Essay 2: Role Models, Teachers, and Heroes— Learning from Others in Unexpected Ways

I remember it as if it were yesterday—a hot, long week in the middle of last summer. I was attending my first day as a counselor at Special Camp for Special Kids. All of the counselors were in a big group eagerly awaiting our camper's arrival. I had been through an extensive training program on what to expect and what to do in every possible problematic situation. To be honest, however, I was still petrified. What if something happens to my camper while she is with me and I do not know how to respond? What if she doesn't like me? What if I say something that makes her mad? I signed up for this camp to challenge myself and go outside my comfort zone. I liked kids, but I knew very little about special kids. This was my first time interacting with a special needs person, and all I knew about my camper was that her name was Elise E.

When we first met, Elise was so quiet and shy and never wanted to say what she was feeling. Of course I thought it was just my luck to get a camper that will not even talk to me! We had a choice of four activities: dress up, arts and crafts, reading, or a room that contained sensory experiences to explore. I asked her, "Elise what do you want to do?" There she stood silently, her big brown eyes looking directly into mine and did not say one word. I thought, "Perfect. Does she not know how to speak?" Finally, I selected the exploration room for us. Elise immediately ran to a table where she spread shaving cream all around. She used the entire can of cream and played with it smiling, giggling, and asking, "I want more." In my counselor training clinic the teachers urged me to be strict and structured with my camper, "There is no more, Elise. You have to play with what you have." Soon she got bored, however, looked up at me with her devilish smile, and asked, "Can I put this on your face?" I told her seriously, "It has to stay on the desk, Elise." Suddenly she jumped up and threw a huge pile of shaving cream at me. She was laughing so hard it was contagious, and then we both broke out into uncontrollable giggles. My cheeks hurt and tears came to my eyes from all the laughter. This experience began our bond.

From then on, Elise was not quiet at all. We became "best friends" for the week. Elise also loved to hear scary stories; she was actually obsessed with them. Her favorite ones I told her about were about mummies in a graveyard. Anytime Elise did something wrong I warned, "If you keep doing that, I will not tell you anymore scary stories." Of course she immediately stopped when she heard my "threat," and looked directly into my eyes, pleading, "Lauren, will you tell me another scary story?" By the end of the week, I racked up an endless amount of "ghost stories" that I made up for her. I had found another way to connect and build a strong bond.

During our week together Elise taught me important life lessons: Even though she suffered from Down syndrome, she had an ambition to love life. She always put a smile on my face, even when she was doing something inappropriate. Elise is my hero. My opportunity to have spent time with her has changed my perspective on life. Even though Elise had a disability, nothing seemed to stop her from doing what she wanted. Her positive demeanor made everyone smile around her. Elise gave me a new confidence that I had never had before. I became more comfortable with who I am, and more sure of myself and my actions. I still write letters to her to see how she is doing. Who would have ever thought a little, 11-year-old girl could have impacted my life so much?

Essay 3: Role Models, Teachers, and Heroes—Learning from Others in Unexpected Ways

---

I always saw tension amongst the people as they fought for a position in line, and when someone cut, a fist fight usually followed. By eight in the morning, a line about a mile long of homeless people awaiting their meal wrapped around the building. Every Saturday for a year I volunteered at Loaves and Fishes, a local soup kitchen. I spent most of my time in the kitchen preparing dozens of the 800 meals produced each day. Only with obvious signs of dedication to coming every Saturday, did I earn the most coveted job, the ice cream scooper, but it was no easy task with Bea at the helm. In the beginning, I slaved cleaning the kitchen because the "kitchen staff" labeled me as the "newbie". I cleaned off the tables that they didn't clean after preparing one type of food, I picked up the trash that they left, and worst of all cleaned every pot and pan that looked like it could serve a giant. As I wiped the oil-greased, black-tarred pans with all the elbow grease that I had, I admired the other jobs in the kitchen. My favorite, though, was the ice cream scooper.

The other jobs looked appealing but always seemed to end in a mess. But Bea, the lady in charge of the ice cream, always exited Loaves and Fishes spotless and smiling. Eighty-seven-year-old Bea was an expert ice cream scooper, an ironic job for someone who appeared so fragile and weak. Yet a solid-as-a-rock block of ice cream was no challenge for her. She scooped almost effortlessly, proud of the role she played. She was strict: one scoop per person, and only one scoop; this is something I learned after many weekends of watching her processes. The same girl always worked alongside Bea. Amanda was consistent and reliant, so Bea trusted her to be her helper every weekend. But one weekend I noticed that Amanda was not there, and so instantly I took the chance of picking up a spoon and heading over to Bea's direction. Bea accepted, as there was no one else to help her.

The following weeks, Amanda did not show up, and I continued to work with Bea and strengthened our relationship. One Saturday as I walked through the kitchen door I noticed that Amanda was alongside Bea with a spoon. I froze up as I saw them working together but realized there was nothing I could do, so I headed toward the dirty pots and pans. Once Bea saw me she took the spoon away from Amanda, and tapped on my shoulder lightly, with the spoon in her hand and smile on her face. It took work to become her friend, and that bond we developed made me return each Saturday. Feeding the homeless was of course satisfying, but the challenge to make my way up in the "kitchen staff" chain, work the most coveted job, and make a bond with someone unexpected was very rewarding.

Essay 4: Role Models, Teachers, and Heroes— Learning from Others in Unexpected Ways

"Our deeds determine us, as much as we determine our deeds."
—George Eliot

It appeared to be another normal Tuesday night at the Sawdust Art Festival concession stand, until Jon didn't show up to work. So I offered to take over the task of working the ice-cream cart all by myself, propped in a corner on a sluggish weeknight, leaving the warmth and excitement of the more social concession booth I usually occupied with my friends. I now faced, with slight reluctance, a 7-hour shift spent in solitude perched over the humming ice chest sitting upon a hard wooden stool. There was little to do but watch the few tourists and art lovers pass by with no interest in an "icy treat." So I sat alone, gazing at the various vendors: from the creative pottery workshop to the hand-made Beanie Booth, while trying to enjoy my night of quiet meditation.

Around the fourth hour, I looked up to see a little boy, no older than 7. He was standing timidly by himself next to the blue and white Nestle ice-cream umbrella hoping to catch my attention. Little did I know this boy would be able to teach me a life lesson and help me to appreciate the meaning of a 'random act of kindness'.

"Can I help you?" I asked, leaning down to his level.

"I want a red pop for my sister" he simply stated.

So I searched through the mess of chocolate ice creams, frozen cookies, and vanilla drumsticks, but couldn't find a red Popsicle.

"We only have orange, is that okay?"

"No, she wants red!" he insisted.

"Orange is just as good," I remarked, hoping to persuade him.

"I promised I'd get her a red one. It's what she wants."

And thus, we began the search. He eagerly helped me sort through various flavors with only one goal: to make his sister happy. The freezing cold ice biting the tips of our fingers as we dug deeper into the chest did not seem to bother him as much as it did me. I then realized that I only took the time to search for the Popsicle because of the sheer boredom I had faced before. But, after seeing how genuinely sincere his need for the Popsicle was, I felt a surge of importance in this mission, and caught his contagious kindness bug. I began shifting and opening and sorting through boxes as if my life depended upon the one red Popsicle.

"Here it is!" I yelled, a little frightened from the excitement the situation had instilled upon me.

"Oh, thank you," he said, and handed me a crumpled dollar bill.

"Do you want anything for yourself?"

"Not really. I got this for my sister."

And with the red Popsicle proudly in hand, he skipped away. This brief encounter left the mark of the one customer I had helped, who acted completely out of selflessness. How surprising that a young boy I barely knew taught me a life lesson in compassion, a boy who only wanted to make his sister happy, no matter how small the act was. In awe, I sat and felt my tingling fingers slowly thaw out. All that work for a red Popsicle, a promise made by the boy for his sister, which I helped him keep.

I now approach life a little differently, realizing that a small gesture can really make a big difference. So whether it is holding the door open for just one more person or putting extra change in the expired parking meter, the small things affect those around you, and a simple good deed turns into the embodiment of compassion.

Essay 5: Role Models, Teachers, and Heroes— Learning from Others in Unexpected Ways

---

My ASL (American Sign Language) journey began with a bilingual musical. When I first met Alana, the only deaf girl in the cast, she appeared lost among the loud, chatty musical theatre students. Wishing to break her isolation, I went to introduce myself. Within minutes of our conversation I mangled several deaf manners—don't shout, don't speak at the translator, etc. It became obvious that Alana was not the one out of place. I was the outsider to deaf culture—an outsider who desperately wanted to come in.

My fingers immediately took to the concept of painting my intentions, and Alana and I became knit together by our "secret code." Antsy fingers could spread a joke silently across a rehearsal room and incite laughter that, from the director's perspective, seemed to come from nowhere. ASL was like no language I'd ever encountered—it was a language, yes, but also an art form and a culture all wrapped into one. It opened a burning desire within me to learn—more, more! I went from knowledge-base-zero to semi-fluent in weeks. It was rapid-fire learning: thrilling, invigorating. And then it was over.

I felt like I'd been thrown out to sea without a lifeline—no school within a 70-mile radius offered ASL classes for children. I attempted to maintain my speaking ability through online instructional videos, occasional Skype conversations with Alana, and solo review of my vocabulary, but I could still sense it slipping through my fingertips. After a few months, I contacted an interpreter to come and coach a few friends and me. Soon I started a school club to share my knowledge with my classmates.

A year later, Alana invited me to her birthday party. As one of the only hearing girls among a slew of talkative signers, I was fairly timid. However, they quickly engulfed me into their conversation, delighted that I was even attempting to communicate in their language. As we sang/signed happy birthday and giggled over our cake, I knew I was an outsider no longer.

Essay 6: Role Models, Teachers, and Heroes— Learning from Others in Unexpected Ways

Rafe. To most, this name is merely a "different" name, but to me, Rafe is a boy who altered the way I have looked at life for my past seventeen years on this Earth. This one-of-a-kind boy stands as tall as a playground tire swing and at age 6 is still trying to determine whether or not the Tooth Fairy exists. He is also my new hero.

Working as a summer counselor at my local JCC, I expected to meet my fair share of eager, runny-nosed, squeaky-voiced, and wiggly-toothed first graders, but the day I met Rafe, I'm not sure if I realized how drastically my perspective on life was about to change. Rafe wasn't like the Richards or the Rebeccas, the Johns or Jessicas. Rafe was Rafe, and nobody was going to change that. On the first day of camp, "Mr. G." as he liked to be called, confidently galloped into the auditorium where all of the other campers had already gathered. While a majority of the boys and girls poked their heads out of the window hoping to lure their mom or dad back in for a final hug, Rafe looked straight forward and never turned his head back once. From that second on, I knew I had a jewel on my hands.

Rafe was certainly far different than the rest of the campers; instead of baseballs and action figures, Rafe preferred flowers and fairy wings. He definitely moved to the beat of his own drummer. A bond between us began to develop, and, although I was trained not to play favorites, I simply could not help myself when it came to Rafe. I admired his independence and surprisingly found myself trying to learn to be more like him.

A turning point came one Friday just as camp was ending. The campers were picked up by their minivan moms and dads one by one. Suddenly, a nicely dressed man in a red and yellow sports car approached me. "You must be Jacob, Rafe's counselor," he exclaimed. "I'm Rafe's father and I need you to help me with something." My mind was racing with possible outcomes of this conversation, but none of them were positive. "Make my son more into a man. When you see him wearing those fairy wings, take them off and give him something more manly, will ya?" I was speechless.

For the next couple of days at camp, I did my best to follow the request of his father, but it was like trying to make a cat bark or a dog meow. It just wasn't meant to be. One day at the lunch tables I observed a boy approach Rafe with a question, "Why don't you like sports like the rest of us, Rafe?" While most kids would have curled up into a ball or burst into tears at a question like that, Rafe proudly said, "Why should I like something just because everyone else does?" Right then and there, I felt as if Rafe should have been wearing the camp counselor shirt I was wearing with the words "Role Model" printed on the back. I truly admired him and wished that I had his confidence and view of life about everything. At 6 years old and even 16, everything that I did and all the things I thought I liked were mostly based on what was "in" and what others had influenced me to enjoy. My biggest nightmare was to stand out and be different. Peer pressure or my own lack of confidence prevented me from always being my own person, but to Rafe, there was no being different or the same, he was just being himself.

That night, I wrote a letter to Rafe's father explaining what a special child he had and that he should be very proud to have such a unique son like Rafe. I also told him that Rafe was going to be whoever he wanted to be and that if others, including myself, carried themselves the same way he did, the world would be a much happier place. After reading the letter, Rafe's father thoroughly thanked me for my kind words and explained that he certainly appreciates how lucky he is.

Some might think that since my days with Rafe are now over, the things he has taught me will be forgotten, but nothing could be farther from the truth. As I move forward into the next chapter of my life, Rafe will always be my reminder of how much better my life can be if I am able to show my true colors to the world. I will never again follow in the footsteps of the majority but instead try to begin charting my own path. Never again will I underestimate the power of my 6-year-old hero named Rafe.

Essay 7: Role Models, Teachers, and Heroes— Learning from Others in Unexpected Ways

Coach S., my running coach, gave me a pep talk after a really tough practice one day. "Failure to prepare. . ." he began, "is preparing to fail," I finished for him. Those are the words that I have heard countless times during practices and meets. Those are the words that keep me going when I am ready to give up.

Picture a goofy 60-year-old man with an extremely short attention span who runs every day despite his two replaced Achilles' tendons. Most people who do not know him think he is crazy; however, those who do have more respect for him than I have ever seen anyone have for a person. I am proud Coach S. is in my life. I admire his persistence, determination, focus, dedication, good personality, and sense of humor; he instilled these values in himself in order to achieve a better life. He has been through so much in his lifetime: he almost did not make it to adulthood; he was shot; he lived on a roof for a year; he fought in the Vietnam War; and I am sure much more that I do not know. All of these life experiences make him an amazing, motivating, and inspiring teacher whom I admire. He not only teaches me lessons, but he *is* a lesson. He learned all of his lessons the hard way, so he makes it his job to see that I learn from his example. He is extremely sharp. He has my entire plan (my workouts, where I am going to be, and the lessons I need to learn to get there) laid out one year in advance.

My coach has helped shape me into the person I am today. He refers to our team as a class, "AP Cross Country and Track" and also "Life 1A." His goal is not just to train me and my team to win the State Meet, but to teach me life lessons along the way. He "hides" these lessons, so I have to find them on my own through my workouts or the questions he asks me. I have found myself on numerous occasions unable to stop reading a bad book because I hear Coach's words in my head, "Don't stop doing something just because it's difficult." I have also found myself being very persistent in finding a summer job, after all of the college students had come home, or getting the input that I needed to complete a challenging assignment because Coach has said, "Never stop working and trying until you reach your goal and what you came there to do." Going into my fourth year of practices, I now realize that Coach S. wants me to apply the concepts and values he teaches in practice to my everyday life.

I will never forget the Laguna Hills Invitational. It was pouring down rain; I was freezing cold and covered in mud, and I was not having a good warm up. I walked up to Coach with a sad look on my face and said, "Coach, what do you want me to do?" He put his hands on my shoulders and told me as he has done many times in the past and as I am sure he will do many times in the future, "I know what you are capable of and you have proved me right before, so go out there and want it and prove it to yourself. I am not the one out there running the race. You are. So it all depends on whether or not you are going to use the resources you have."

"Failure to prepare is preparing to fail." Those words will forever ring in my ears as I grow up, keeping me motivated while I continue my life-long class of "Life 1A." Coach S. started me out on this road with the lessons and values he instilled in me: determination, persistence, drive, and loyalty to oneself as well as others. This is the road I will follow.

Pursuing Passions and Hobbies

Doing something you love serves as an example of how your heart and mind works. Writing about your true passions and your experiences with them offers readers a clear view into what excites you outside of the classroom and what makes you tick. Be careful if you choose to write about your involvement in a sport. You need to do so in a way that is unique and specific to you and not in a way that could be generic and seemingly written by any another applicant.

Essay 1: Pursuing Passions and Hobbies

"Guam," I answered confidently as a hush came over the entire auditorium. Breaking the piercing silence, my teacher Ms. I. announced, "Correct!"

To be truthful, I cannot recall the question, but "Guam" was my winning answer in the all-school National Geographic Geography Bee. Ever since I was a little girl, obsessed with maps and my dad's stories about the Civil War, I have had a passion for history and geography. Naturally, I set my goal and decided in Kindergarten that I would someday win the all-school Geography Bee and now, as a seventh-grader at Harbor Day, I had accomplished what I set out to do. As Ms. I. awarded me my momentous certificate, I beamed with pride, overjoyed by the fact that my long-time dream had at last come true. The following week, my picture was on the cover of the school newspaper for my achievement. I recall being amazed that something that I truly enjoyed could bring both recognition and pleasure.

Since early childhood, my love for history and geography has grown. As early as preschool, my placemat at the dinner table pictured the United States and included the names of all of the states and capitals. At age 8, I acquired the ability to read the *Thomas Guide*, a detailed map of the Southern California area. Since then, I have always been the designated "navigator" on all road trips. Even today, I have an atlas placed on the nightstand next to my bed for any late-night or early-morning inquiries, as well as history books scattered throughout my room to sift through just for fun. Although I often hear many of my friends claim that history and geography are "boring" and "useless," I always retaliate vociferously to such comments. To me, history is not merely about memorizing a meaningless list of dates, nor does geography consist of just looking at maps. History is the feeling I get when thinking about George Washington's anticipation as he took office as America's first president, leading a nation in its infancy. History is sensing the torturous heat and thirst, which Ibn Batuta experienced crossing barren wastelands to spread the culture of Islam. History is attempting to understand the state of mind of Roman soldiers as barbaric groups ultimately took them over. Similarly, in my eyes, geography is visualizing the people and natural phenomena of a certain region, and understanding how the varying landscapes impact those who live here in this relatively small world in which we live. Each morning, I run downstairs to review the front page of the *LA Times* to read about history in the making, and at school, my heart thumps with increasing rapidity as history class approaches. In the evening, I turn on CNN to learn about the ever-changing world, its people, and its climate.

History and geography are my passion. I look forward to absorbing all that I can in college, so that I may not only expand my own knowledge, but also instill my contagious love in others.

Essay 2: Pursuing Passions and Hobbies

When I was 3 years old, my aunt and uncle sent me a Flamenco dress from Spain. Instantly becoming my favorite piece of clothing, I wore it on any occasion I could: performing for my parents, while eating dinner, and as my Halloween costume (two years in a row).

This red, black, and white polka-dotted Flamenco dress marked the beginning of my love for all things Spanish.

I discovered my favorite place in the world when I went to Spain on a class trip in seventh grade. My classmates and I traveled through Barcelona, Granada, Seville, Toledo, and Madrid, where we finally got a chance to meet our Spanish pen pals and spend several days and nights with their families. My pen pal was Laura Hernandez, and her father offered me a glass of red wine with dinner. Being 12, that was very exciting. At Laura's school her classmates crowded around me, asking me what kind of music I listened to, if I had a boyfriend, and how to say dirty words in English. We got along perfectly. All of the boys were extremely impressed when they discovered that even though I couldn't beat them, I held my own against them when playing soccer. (To beat a Spanish boy at *futbol* would be truly impressive indeed.) We toured plazas, palaces, cathedrals, open-air markets, and museums.

Though these were *all* impressive sights, the most amazing spectacle I have ever seen was the Semana Santa parade in Granada. Priests wearing pointy-hooded robes in white, purple, red, and black slowly marched barefoot through the narrow streets as almost sinister-sounding drumbeats throbbed steadily. Enormous floats displaying ornately decorated altars to the Virgin Mary and Jesus were carried through the city on the heads and shoulders of the faithful, who were only visible where the cloth from the float ended to reveal their bare feet. Young girls in black lace mantillas scattered flower petals as they walked in the procession. The air was thick with incense and the only light came from the thousands of flickering candles adorning the altars. By being present at this foreign ritual I was given a privileged glimpse of something simultaneously beautiful, solemn, mysterious, and intense. Though not a Catholic, I remember thinking to myself that night that I had just witnessed something sacred, and I knew that I would never forget it.

Though I have no Spanish ancestry, there is certainly something in me that connects with Spanish culture. The food, language, customs, and people all greatly appeal to me. It may sound cliché, but I know that it is the passion of the country that attracts me so strongly. The passion for love and beauty and music and art! It's the unique combination of intensity and relaxation. The people's enthusiasm for life is contagious. It is a culture that is deeply emotional, yet at the same time is characterized by a "don't sweat the small stuff," easygoing attitude. The pace is slower, the lunch breaks longer, and the parties later and louder. When I entered this passionate atmosphere so many years ago it seeped into my bloodstream and became a part of who I am.

Though Spain *is* a lengthy airplane ride away, I'm lucky to live in Southern California where I can put my love of the Spanish language to good use. I listen to Spanish radio and converse with the waiters at Mexican restaurants in their native tongue. I volunteer with Hispanic children at nearby elementary schools, and I am planning to make my upcoming Senior Project about working with these children and the effects of bilingual education. My high school ran out of Spanish courses for me to take, so I have begun an internship at the Orange County courthouse, which involves translating to Spanish-speaking victims and witnesses. And even though at first my friends groaned whenever I would play my favorite "Latin Groove" CD, after all these months they have eventually grown to enjoy it, too (though not as much as I do).

I'm not sure I can explain why it is that I am so moved by Spanish culture. I get the chills when the opening chords to a song are played on a Spanish guitar. I feel every stomp and clap and snap of the castanets in a Flamenco dancer's routine. I close my eyes in deep appreciation at the first bite of *paella*. A good friend of mine and I have made a pact to spend a semester of college abroad together in Spain or another Spanish-speaking country, and I know that whether or not she keeps her end of the bargain, I'm definitely going. Who knows? Maybe I will meet a handsome Spanish *hombre* and not come back, like my aunt did thirty years ago. And since my old Flamenco dress has long become too small for me, I plan on buying myself a new one. However, I know that I will keep my first memento from Spain with me until someday I can give it to my daughter or niece, and perhaps spark in her a curiosity for a beautiful, foreign culture.

Essay 3: Pursuing Passions and Hobbies

"Are you blind?" "What game are you watching?" "That's a penalty!" These are normally not the comments that a high school lacrosse player hears when he is running up and down the field. That is unless that high school lacrosse player is also a referee.

It all started when my brother and I decided that we should try to get a fun easy job that interested us. I assumed refereeing would be very easy because I had practically been born with a lacrosse stick in my hand and had been playing since third grade. I thought I knew lacrosse inside and out. I was definitely wrong about that. In the 8-hour training session, I realized the technical rules and learned every little nuance of the game that I love so much.

As I walked to the field before the first game I was about to referee, I looked around at the two teams and all of the spectators who would all be focusing on my calls during the game. I began to sweat, my heart was pounding and I panicked; I tried to compose myself and began to review all the different hand signals in my head. And I thought *playing* in a big lacrosse game was nerve racking! It is certainly nothing compared to refereeing! That first game felt like the longest 40 minutes of my life. Every time I blew the whistle somebody yelled at me, not to mention the game was a very hard-hitting game. Any minute I thought there might be a huge brawl, which could be entertaining for a fan but is a referee's worst nightmare. There were many instances where I felt helpless. For example, a few times in the game I forgot the hand signal for the penalty I was calling. Many times I internally questioned myself, unsure if I had made the right call. When the time finally ran out and no bones were broken, I was so relieved. The ref that I was working with was one of the more experienced referees in Orange County. He commented, "That's the hardest game you'll ever ref." It was quite an introduction into the harsh and unsympathetic world of a referee.

I had many learning experiences during that first game. Some of the parents on the sidelines were people I knew through other lacrosse events. In those outside contexts they seemed like perfectly normal people. The competition during the game, though, changed them into completely different "animals." They got so caught up in what was happening during the game that they turned into ruthless, crazy people. Unfortunately, much of their negative attention was directed towards me, the referee. I tried my best to not play sides but the losing team will almost always use the referee as a scapegoat. That negativity has taught me to have a thicker skin, and also reminds me as a fan to not take the game too seriously.

I now understand that a referee's job is to control the game; without a referee there would be no game. I used to think it was the other way around, that the players controlled the game. I tried my best to keep a cool head and not play sides. When the game got more hectic I tried my best to get calmer. Refereeing taught me to block someone or something out and focus on the task at hand. Not everything about refereeing is bad; I learned many lessons not just from that first game, but from the whole season. Before I became a referee I was extremely judgmental of them when I was a player. Since becoming a ref I have an entirely different outlook. I realize that sometimes I just need to cut the ref a break; it is impossible for them to see every play that occurs. Refs are a "team" without any fans; they never get cheered; they are only blamed. On the other hand as a ref I enjoy the power of making "unbiased" calls. Although I also feel a lack of appreciation for the job I do, a player or parent rarely takes the time to thank a referee. As a result, I have learned as a player win or lose to thank my referee. Most important, I learned that without a referee the *game* is just chaos.

Essay 4: Pursuing Passions and Hobbies

Frantically I rushed, hiding in a shadow, down the ominous alley and ducked into the building. It was dark, and I was alone in Los Angeles for the first time. Suddenly there was an explosion and a burst of light; Victor Wooten took the stage. It seemed as if he had ten fingers on each hand, all coming alive with their own individual spirit—running up and down the fret board of his Fodera bass as if being chased by the music. Although he played with such immense passion and love, his style was deceptive as he beat the strings and body of the guitar with a powerful slapping and pounding motion as if it were a drum. Victor Wooten's innovative style of creating music was a revelation to me. Just when I thought there was no other way to play a guitar, I witnessed new ground.

On the long drive home from the smoky jazz club that night, my head burst with the overwhelming events that had just occurred. I had the kind of flashbacks people who have died and come back to life experience; this single performance made me reflect on my entire music journey to date.

I thought back to my seventh birthday. I am in a music shop with my dad choosing my first guitar. It didn't seem as important at the time, but from the moment I first held that marked-down, Japanese-made, Fender Strat, I forever lost the feeling of being bored. I always had something to do with my time: a playmate, a pet, my guitar. I immediately packed my life with music lessons, learning instruments ranging from piano to cello to saxophone. By the fifth grade I focused in on the instrument that has molded my life, guitar, and primarily jazz guitar and intensive jazz theory.

At the same time that I got my first guitar, I lived next door to 2 preschool-age sisters who had just gotten hearing implants. Before that day, their lives were silent. Every buzz of a bee or honk of a horn that I took for granted was finally something they could experience with the rest of the world. I ran next door with my new guitar to give the girls their first live music show. From the moment the sound reverberated out of my cheap amp and into their ears, my fumbled open chords seemed to flow through their bodies, and they exploded with joy. Their pure human emotion was a defining moment for me. Looking back at that day, I was their Victor Wooten, and I will never forget the excitement on their faces.

During my junior year, my guitar skills were crafted more substantially to give back. I wanted to teach. From this urge came the birth of Hearts@Harmony, a group that I co-founded with a like-minded friend, in hopes of passing along my passion to the less fortunate. I paired up musically talented high school students with special needs children to teach them the art of music. My first students were the hearing-impaired girls from next door, now in fifth and sixth grades and ready to learn their first instrument, which resulted, for me, in a hard-earned lesson in patience. Then came the ebullient adventure of Bradley.

"Mr. Ben! Mr. Ben! I'm going to work hard for my goal today!"

We both know this isn't true. Bradley gives me a giant hug and we get down to business. The next hour consists of a few minutes of intense concentration. I give Bradley tokens toward his goal for the day. The rest of our time is spent with me running around the house preventing him from choking on guitar picks or breaking his instrument. A variation of this same routine has occurred with autistic 8-year-old Bradley every Sunday for the past year. I look forward to these "lessons" as much as he does. In the car, I think about how Bradley's mother told me he played "Happy Birthday" on the guitar for his family all on his own. I am so proud. I think about how hard it is for him, yet it is so natural for me. And then there is the brilliance of Victor Wooten. His show brought a culmination of feelings that made me realize how much more there is for me to achieve. My work is not done. He gave me a forever-lasting goal: I want to impact others as he did me.

I return home from the magnificent concert and crash onto my bed. I look up on my wall and there, hanging, is my first, beaten up Fender Strat that started the chain of events that led me to this day and every day to come. I know what I want to do with my life. I guess I have always known. Music is my journey, and no matter where this passion takes me, I am confident that it will create new memories and life experiences that will shape my future. My job now is to continue learning and creating them.

Essay 5: Pursuing Passions and Hobbies

Hiking through the ground of fallen leaves of the jungle, I silently inched my way into a dark den to hide from the treacherous T-Rex that was headed toward me. I ducked under the canopy of a giant banana tree and looked for a weapon with which I could kill the savage prehistoric beast. When I found my bow and arrow, I knew the monster was as good as dead. I hit the ogre twice, and, like a recently severed redwood, he swiftly fell to the ground.

Unfortunately, the falling of the "dinosaur" commenced the descent of many other objects in my closet. A couple of books from my encyclopedia set came crashing toward me, as did a rack of hangers that was once my banana tree, a box from my remote controlled monster truck, and finally a crimson rectangle with knobs. My 7-year-old eyes peered closely at the foreign object and read the title of the toy from the top of its plastic outer frame. It was called an Etch-A-Sketch™.

I started slowly with my recently discovered activity, but gradually I became more efficient and eventually gained speed and control. Soon enough I was copying simple pictures out of cardboard picture books and other easy geometric figures onto the screen. Then one day, I was introduced to X-Box™, and suddenly I was no longer amused by ridiculous, childish games of imagination. After all, who needs Etch-A-Sketch and "Dinosaur Hunter" when you have FIFA Soccer and Madden? Over the next few years, video games took their hold upon me and that once adored, burgundy Etch-A-Sketch floated further and further away from my mind.

But then it happened. Ten years later while sitting on a bus to a MUN Conference, I was reacquainted with my first love whom I had met in the jungle so long ago. The kid who I was sharing a seat with had a Travel Etch-A-Sketch, and I began to recall the magic of how it once felt to hold that half-pound plastic rectangle. The knobs seemed so familiar and, just like riding a bike, I never forgot how to use the simple-on-the-outside but complex-on-the-inside apparatus. I was filled with joy all through the day, and after the conference I scavenged through my closet to locate my old friend. It seemed ancient when I finally found it on the top of my cabinet. I wiped away the dust that had accumulated on the screen over the decade and sat down in my closet and etched for 3 hours.

Etch-A-Sketch and I traveled everywhere together: from Florida to Hawaii to Texas and to Maryland. The things we could do together were endless. With my "imagination machine," I went from drawing pictures of dinosaurs and rocket ships as a 7-year-old to portraying entire works of Baroque artists and fashioning detailed etches of teachers and friends. I earned the nickname "Mr. Etch" and introduced masses of people to "another creation by Ohio Art." I can remember walking through the locker halls at school and having random kids ask me to show them drawings and looking around school seeing kids sitting down during snack and lunch so zoned into their magic screens that their mouths would involuntarily be gaping, wide open. I was even rumored to be the founder of the "Laguna Hills High School Underground Etch-A-Sketch Movement." We went through millions of shakings and really became buddies. I actually realized that this 8- by 10-inch box meant a lot more to me than any other material possession. Not many things can be bought for only $10 yet give unyielding pleasure for over a decade and teach someone so much about himself or herself. Even through my toughest times of carpal tunnel, I was always kept entertained by this masterpiece of a toy directed to consumers of ages 3 and up. Today, I am fourteen years older than the toy's recommended starting age, yet I continue to be captivated.

Through years of trials with the toy, I learned that I am a pretty simple, artistic person. I am a guy who tries to put my best and my all into everything I do. Deciding to turn the Etch-A-Sketch screen upside down and shake it after spending 3 hours on a drawing is not something easily done by most people, but I think it is that aspect of my personality that makes me unique. The swishing of the aluminum beads is a difficult sound to hear for some, but to me, the whisper of the powder is a sweet sound of starting anew, doing my best, and just having fun.

Essay 6: Pursuing Passions and Hobbies

A church is not a place one would typically look to find a rock band. But attendees of the 5 o'clock youth mass at Saint John Fisher would have their choir accompanied no other way. Guitar, bass, drums, piano, and electric violin: these five instruments converse in a perfectly synchronized musical dialogue. If Brian, the bass player, begins the tenor line, I, the violinist, will jump to a floating high note up the octave. If I grab a descant, Joe, the guitarist, will relax back into strummed chords to let me cut through "the blend." Each performance is mixed preparation and improvisation—no two masses are alike.

I used to watch this musical discussion from the vantage point of the choir. Enthralled as I was by its smooth, perfected nature, I knew my classical viola would never fit in the ensemble. So I went in search of an alternative—an electric alternative.

The resulting purchase—an electric violin—seemed completely incompatible with me. It is a shocking pink, with small black tiger stripes and an extra string that makes it stick out even among other electric instruments. I, on the other hand, have the demeanor of the viola, a maker of rich harmonies that add to the orchestral mix yet are indiscernible to the average listener. In the first few masses, I played the melody along with the choir, afraid to do anything that the congregation might actually be able to hear. My fingers felt slick on the slim, black fingerboard, my bow awkward in maneuvering the fifth string. With each mistake, I turned the volume on my amp down a little more, even as the other instrumentalists encouraged me to do the opposite. I abstained, determined not to let my fumbling ruin the group I had been so eager to join.

I practiced diligently at home, but soon learned that jazz and improvisation cannot be drilled to perfection like the state capitals or a multiplication table. Musical spontaneity is developed through trial and error, however painful those "errors" may be. The notes on the page were a guideline—not an instruction manual. In music as in life, I realized, the best approach is often the one you create for yourself.

The day when I first really came "off the page," my fingers seemed to move of their own accord. They soared above the melody to sing along with the choir like a gospel soloist, with the richness of a classical violin accented by the metallic edge of an amplified instrument. True to the forgiving Catholic spirit in which we played, my flaming pink violin and I had finally made our peace.

Essay 7: Pursuing Passions and Hobbies

The air is cool and crisp, the ground still wet from rain. I take off quickly and feel the breeze whip my ponytail around my head. Goosebumps dot my arms, but I know I'll warm up in a few minutes. Soon, sweat will bead on my forehead and drip down the back of my neck, burning stress away with each drop. I breathe in the smell of wet grass, feel the soft gravel beneath my feet, and enjoy the warmth radiating from my body with each step.

I feel most content outside, running. My perfect environment is not so much a place as a state of action. I run to connect with my world, with others, and with myself. I cannot describe one particular place outside because I like to run on all different trails in all sorts of environments: down by the beach, near my high school, and through various neighborhoods close to my home. Although some of my friends have a favorite trail or loop that they run again and again, I prefer to try new trails and places; if I run the same one too many times I become bored. I thrive on variety in my running trails and in life. My interests range widely from acting out ridiculous and hilarious improv scenes in acting class to debating serious issues on the Senate floor in Sacramento. As a runner and as a student, I love to challenge myself with new things.

I also run to connect with others and build new friendships. I enjoy jogging along at a nice, slow pace, chatting with a friend. Running is universal. During the summer I took a writing class at Brown University, running proved to be the perfect activity to share with my new friends. I forged friendships with students from all over the world as we laced up our shoes and explored Providence on foot. I find that it takes some of the pressure off because no one is just standing there, unsure of what to do with his or her limbs. Instead, all legs, feet, arms, and even hands are engaged. And when those awkward silent moments sneak up, we simply catch our breath and focus more on the task at hand. Naturally reserved in large groups, I prefer to run with one or two people. I joined the cross-country team but found that although I enjoy the spirit of competition in other activities, the intensity and the large group took the joy out of running for me. Instead of providing an outlet for stress, competing created superfluous pressure. So I stick to running with friends on my own time, instead.

I don't always run with a partner, however. Sometimes, I like to go out by myself to spend time alone with my thoughts. It aids me in my creative process; while running I spend a great deal of time thinking about new story ideas or how to add to and improve existing ones. Or I simply contemplate life, while at the same time taking a break from the stress of my busy schedule. After a run, I am often so filled with energy, both creative and physical, that I accomplish some of my best work for both school and my own writing. Running awakens me like no cup of espresso can.

The best part of running, though, is the ability to find my "happy place" anywhere. I know that no matter what city, country, or even continent I am on, I can put on a pair of running shoes, tie up my hair, and head outside. Although the locations and routes may vary, I am perfectly content as I feel a cool breeze in my face and drops of sweat trickle down my neck. Whether I'm alone or with a friend by my side, I connect with my world, with others, and with myself when outside—running.

Essay 8: Pursuing Passions and Hobbies

As I chase my basketball down the court, every bounce sends a resounding echo into the expanse of the empty gym. The memory of my last shot bouncing short off the front rim repeats infuriatingly in my head and will continue to do so until I get my next shot up. In those moments, nothing is more important than making my next shot, erasing the unsuccessful attempt from my mind. I catch up to my ball, set my feet, and let it fly, the swish of the net pushing me to chase the ball down again and repeat the action.

No one will ever know how many shots I make or miss while I'm there in the empty gym. No one will ever know the frustration I fight through when shots don't fall, or the gratification I feel when I've finally hit my tenth 3-pointer in a row and the pressure I've put on myself dissolves. When I'm alone on the court, the only thing that matters is how hard I work while I'm there, when it's just the game and me. There is no one there to tell me when I should take a break or if I'm doing something right or wrong. It's my choice to push myself past my limits. It doesn't matter where my future opponents are, and it doesn't matter that my coaches and my teammates don't know I'm there. I am putting myself in a position where I know I will have controlled everything in my power up to the time when the ball and the game are in my hands with 10 seconds left in our last league game.

There is a deep sense of assurance that comes with that knowledge, because once I have that, everything else is out of my hands and I can simply enjoy the game I love. The empty basketball court gives me the chance to attain that knowledge. Every time I walk onto the vacant court, I feel the presence of possibilities and opportunities. Of course, part of that feeling comes from the chance to improve my skills. But more than that, this court becomes for me what would be the equivalent to an empty studio for a musician or a blank canvas for an artist. It becomes a place where I can do something that I love for however long I wish and in whatever manner I wish. It's important to note, however, that while I do love the game, there are those days when I lace my shoes up and still do not have an intense desire to push myself. The luxury of the empty gym, however, is that it allows me to switch the lights on, step onto that faded paint on the low block, and start warming up anyway, because I know that the work I put in here, even when I don't want to, will soon allow me to do the things I truly do want to.

I know that, at least for basketball, a place like this won't exist forever. I've heard many wise coaches say that basketball is not the be-all, the end-all, but rather a means of learning how to be a successful person who can practice discipline and devotion to something that he or she chooses. So, while I am working tirelessly on the court, I can think to myself that all of this work is leading to something greater, something that will allow me to chase down opportunities in the future, like misses and makes in the empty gym. And when I've finished for the day, sitting on the red bench changing my shoes, I relish the feeling of the rest I've earned as sweat drips off me, knowing that my eagerness to return to this place will grow inside me until I arrive tomorrow.

Essay 9: Pursuing Passions and Hobbies

I remember my 4x100 freestyle relay team was swimming the last event of the varsity season regional meet. Every second of training, every pill of Motrin, and every ounce of determination came to this one moment, this one race. My competition dove in before me; I had to catch up. By the end of my first 50, my heart threatened to explode, my muscles screamed bloody murder, and my lungs protested collapse. As I flipped to finish my 100 free, I heard my teammates (or should I say sisters?) shout one thing: "Go!" Energy and adrenaline flooded my veins; I did not train to finish second-best. I gave my swim my all, beat the girl in the next lane, and finished with my best time all season. For the rest of that night, I felt so elated because I had conquered my goals.

As the old saying goes, "Winning isn't everything." When I first joined the school swim team, I barely spoke a word. My natural shyness predominated, and the upper school classmen intimidated me. I continued to swim, and that decision has been the best choice I have ever made. My times steadily improved; I transformed from one of the slowest into one of the fastest members of the team, and I won races. Even though winning was nice, the competition itself could not begin to compete with the relationship I developed and continue to share with my team. The older swimmers who had frightened and awed me so much my first few days became my older brother and sisters, mentoring me in every way possible. My coach always supported me and pushed me to reach my highest potential. Throughout my middle and high school years, these amazing people have influenced me so much; their positive attributes are now engrained in my being. I hope I can influence the younger swimmers I lead now just as much.

Why would I put myself through the physical pain, lack of sleep, and headache over school? I can never really explain. My friends cannot understand the early morning practices, broken pool heaters in November, or the amount of plastic, latex, and nylon I go through. They can't comprehend the joy I feel when lactic acid builds in my muscles, the songs that run through my head during a distance swim or the battle between lungs and brain when I fight the urge to breathe in a sprint. They can never truly appreciate the bond I share with my teammates that became a family, my coach who encouraged me, and the pool that became a home. They'll never share the long bus rides to away meets or the inside jokes. They'll never get the feeling that builds inside me when I touch out my competition by a tenth of a second. Even in writing, I can express only one hundredth of the intensity of the hold swimming has on me. So in the end, I tell them that I simply live for the competition, live for the countless friends, live for the practice, live for the pain: how swimming is just a part of me.

I have learned to see life as one long race, and what I do determines how I reach the finish line. Ready? Definitely. Set? Absolutely. Go.

Family Reflections, Traditions, and Influences

The people with whom you live and share your life deeply influence and shape who you are, how you think, and your overall being. Celebrate the experiences and what you have learned from these people in your personal statement. Just as in an essay you may have written on role models, teachers, and heroes, if you choose this topic, you should also be sure that you connect yourself into this topic and keep it about your relationship to and with the person(s) and not just your observations and comments about them. How has this person influenced you? What have you learned from him or her? What have you applied to your life to emulate that person or those individuals (or not)?

Essay 1: Family Reflections, Traditions, and Influences

All eyes were focused on me. This was it. The tension had been building up to this point, and I knew there was no way out. I had gotten myself into this predicament, and I was the only one that could get myself out of it. There was nobody to turn to, for they were all waiting for my final move. I had never felt so alone, so isolated.

I thumbed through my cards for the fourth consecutive time, and I could still not decide which one to throw. I glanced up from my cards and caught a glimpse of each player. I immediately felt the intensity of my brother's eyes glaring at me from across the table. He did not provide me with the support and reassurance I was looking for from my partner. I shifted my eyes to the right. My mother, having just discarded a five of clubs and seeing that it was of no use to me, was sipping coffee with a carefree grin of relief. Then I peered directly at the most intimidating canasta player I have ever encountered. Great Grandma Rose was calmly humming a tuneless tune, which added to her enigma. As this crafty 88-year-old lady squinted at her cards through her bifocals, I knew that time was running out; I had to make my decision. The most obvious choice was to discard the king of spades for which I had no use, but I was afraid that she was waiting for this card. My alternative was to break up my meld and throw the six of clubs, a card which I felt somewhat safe in throwing.

In the midst of my despair, my great grandma delivered the final blow. She stopped humming and uttered these dreaded words: "It only hurts for a minute."

She could not have dug a knife any deeper. My brother's eyes were flaring with tension, I had complete control over his fate, and I knew our team unity was riding on the outcome of my decision. I therefore decided to play defensively and throw the six of clubs. No sooner had my discard settled on top of the pile than my great grandmother's hand darted out to snatch up the stack of cards, and my brother simultaneously belted out a scream. "The six of clubs? How could you throw the six of clubs?!"

I wanted to ask him if the king of spades would have been any better, but I knew a rebuttal was useless. I knew he would get over it soon enough, and, like Grandma Rose says, "It only hurts for a minute."

After my great grandma laid down her meld and sorted her cards, the game continued (and so did her humming). Although we lost that particular hand, my brother and I miraculously came back to snatch victory from the jaws of defeat. As we reveled in our triumph (my brother had now forgiven me for discarding the six of clubs), I could not resist directing my newly acquired quote at our opponents, who were mulling over their defeat. "Well, I have only one thing to say." My smile was so big that I could feel my cheeks stretching. "It only hurts for a minute."

Although my great grandmother had no intention of being profound, this quote actually embodies an important concept. Many people spend so much time worrying about the infinite possibilities that may result from any decision they make that they actually never make a decision at all. Although it is necessary to weigh the options and consider various viewpoints, excessive deliberation can often be detrimental. From personal experience, I have found it usually better to think about the choices and come to a firm decision rather than to prolong the problem and perhaps create a new one by avoiding a commitment one way or the other. The best course of action is to make the wisest choice possible with the available information and then to make the most out of your initial decision. Even if in retrospect you see a better alternative, you can always pursue a new direction based on what you have learned through this experience. Surprisingly, what may at first appear to be failure may often spark an unforeseen success. I have learned not to let undue hesitation hinder my ability to take advantage of opportunities. After all, as my great grandmother so eloquently remarked during those heated canasta games, "It only hurts for a minute!"

Essay 2: Family Reflections, Traditions, and Influences

Many people are blessed with one loving family for their lifetime. A family that loves, cares for, is always there for them. But for me it's different. I don't have that *one* family. I have *two*. The Mallon family, though not genetically related, is more family than not to me. They have been a part of my life since I was born.

My father wasn't born into a wealthy family. I've heard stories of how he and his 5 siblings had to survive an entire week on only $20, which they almost lost in a street gutter but thankfully later found. But the wealth he did have was in his next-door neighbors, The Mallons. They took him in and raised him as if he was their own son. Now my dad's relationship with this amazing family has been passed down to me, and I could not be more honored to continue this legacy.

The Mallons are as Irish as Irish gets. Mr. and Mrs. Mallon came over from Ireland sixty years ago with all of the customs of the homeland and aspirations of the American Dream. As an "honorary Mallon," I partake in festivities. Our most heralded is the "Sunday

Roast Beef Dinner with The Priests." These dinners were also my dad's favorite childhood memories. Almost every Sunday, 2 or 3 priests came over, and Mrs. Mallon made a roast beef dinner, complete with heaping mashed potatoes, and three kinds of vegetables. The conversation was always lively and the wine flowing. Nowadays, our gatherings only happen once or twice a year because the hosts are in their eighties, but when it does I am excited for this dinner. Most of my teen friends would probably not really appreciate the amount of knowledge one can gain from these older people.

I'll never forget the one fateful dinner when I exhibited my adolescence in all my glory and I did something no one else in the family has ever done or dared to do. I asked three trivia questions of the priest. Eager about my new knowledge from Catholic school, I decided to test it against someone who I believed would be the best to answer. My father sat cringing in his chair as his 14-year-old son rattled off to the priest, "Who is the first apostle of Jesus? What year was the Council of Trent? What book of the Bible forbids the eating of rabbit?" The priest, an old Irish born regular of the Mallon dinner, was a person everyone respected and feared just a little. The room fell silent. My mom glared at me, and I received several kicks under the table. I just had no idea of the gravity of my actions. Luckily though, Father Tom, with a smile across his face, answered all my trivia correctly. Who knows what would have happened to me if he got one wrong? You just don't mess with someone who can communicate with God.

So over the years we have had our laughs, rivalries of sports, enjoyment of the meal, and enjoyment of each other. With some of our members growing old, the ambiance of the dinner has become much more about savoring the moment. On our most recent Sunday meal, Mrs. Mallon called me into the kitchen to "help with the ice cream." This ploy was a way for her to get me alone, to tell me in private, "Soon you're leaving for college and beginning to start your young adult life. You should never forget your family or your loved ones 'cause you are family to us. Without family what do we have?" So though I am not her grandson and she is not my grandmother, the Mallon and Sandfer families share a relationship that I will help continue for generations to come. I look forward to the moment that my son becomes an honorary Mallon, too.

Essay 3: Family Reflections, Traditions, and Influences

Friday. That simple word evokes thoughts of freedom, relaxation, rejuvenation, celebration, and a sense of accomplishment after a hard week of work. Friday is a slightly earlier dismissal from Jewish Day School, followed by some stress-relieving exercise before our family's Shabbat dinner. But our Shabbat dinner is especially meaningful to me. At approximately 4 o'clock in the afternoon, Grandpa Bernie arrives in his wheelchair with one of his devoted helpers. He never makes it earlier in the day despite my dad's persistent reminders to come right after lunch.

I hear the clang of the metal ramp being laid down in front of the doorway while our dog J.J. barks to welcome Grandpa. Shabbat has officially begun.

"The Big Z!" he'll call me, followed by the same question each week. "How is physics class going?" To which I teasingly respond, "Well it was okay when I took it a few months ago!" I don't mind answering that same question over and over again, because I've come to realize that for my grandfather, a former science teacher, my physics class was a reminder of his life before the tragedy. In June 2006, we received a call from Boston, informing us that his healthy, active wife, and a beloved grandmother, had died in her sleep. My parents knew that my grandfather, a stroke victim at age 39, could not live alone without Grandma Sandy's care. After months of arguing over the issue, Grandpa left his friends and cherished Boston Red Sox to join us in Irvine, California. Can you imagine leaving your life behind after 76 years? Not only was life physically hard for Grandpa, now he was emotionally alone. So if there is one time in the week that can bring a smile to the face of a man who spends most of his day in an apartment, sitting in the same reclining chair watching baseball games on television, it's Shabbat dinner at our home.

From the moment Grandpa arrives to the time he leaves with a fresh batch of my mom's homemade chocolate chip cookies, Shabbat means togetherness. Mom lights the candles, and my sister Daisy and Grandpa say the blessing over bread together. His hearty Amen (pronouncing it "Ah-Maine"), is followed by a list of the rest of the New England states that he misses. Friday night is about living in the present and being happy with the people who care for one another the most.

Shabbat dinners with Grandpa have made me even closer to my family. I decline invitations from friends and instead I happily spend Friday nights at home with my family. When I look sixty years into the future and picture a successful life, I see the Shabbat dinner table in front of me, sitting with my grandchildren just as my Grandpa Bernie does, remembering the countless laughs and stories that were told on Friday nights.

Essay 4: Family Reflections, Traditions, and Influences

A snake in the corner of the room—Hector they named him—sitting in a cage next to birds. Sweet singing swallows. A joyous voice awoke me from my daze. I shifted my attention to see my Uncle Lenny turned away from his canvas looking me dead in the eye, with a smile from ear to ear. His curly grey hair was unforgettable, and his big brown eyes seemed always to be ecstatic even when nothing exciting was happening. He was working on a painting of pop star idol Christina Aguilera. She was placed floating in a swimming pool, in an electric pink floatie, wearing a black thong as a bathing suit. This image was purely comical from my 7-year-old mind. Uncle Lenny was one of a kind. I giggled aloud, entertained by his presentation. He got up from his stool to glance at my work. I felt his presence tower over me as his jaw dropped in awe, "Have you completed this?" he asked. I nodded and smiled. His smile grew bigger. He placed my artwork, an acrylic canvas I made of the chateau where we stayed, on a shelf behind his desk displayed for everyone to see, first thing when entering his art studio. Before the clutter and paint splatters distracted anyone's eyes, my painting was front and center. This moment made me proud and gave me inspiration and motivation to keep painting as a hobby, which grew to become a passion.

Every summer, I was fortunate to grow up visiting the South of France. My grandfather owned a large property there that welcomed all of his family and friends year after year. Whenever I visited, I looked forward to the day that Uncle Lenny would grab my arm and take me off to his art studio to paint. He singled me out from all of my cousins and we shared a special bond over our love of art. He inspired me in every way possible. He told me often, "You have real talent. I can't wait to see it grow." Last summer, when I visited at the age of 16, my childhood painting still stood broad. The small canvas depicting our families' special chateau remained in the same place Lenny displayed it years earlier. Lenny had passed, but his presence and happiness still inhabited the room. Even when Uncle Lenny was going through hospice, I never once saw a frown or tear on his face.

Influenced by his unforgettable character, I remember to smile and reach towards the positive aspects of life. Lenny always brought laughter to a room. His sense of humor still makes me smile. He was and remains one of the strongest and most true role models I have ever known. He was a gentle soul and in our times together taught me patience; both patience to finish a piece of artwork and patience to slow down in life when necessary. My childhood painting now sits on my bedroom shelf; its juvenile strokes and flat dimensions are a reminder of lessons learned and the person who gave me confidence to continue painting as a hobby, passion, and future profession.

Essay 5: Family Reflections, Traditions, and Influences

"My life is terrible," I remember thinking to myself the day my mom informed me we were moving. Here I was, being forced to move from the house I grew up in, moving away from my friends, and moving from the memories in the walls of my home. My mother was literally pulling the rug out from under my feet and I was floundering. Now, a few months later, I am sitting by the waterfall in the new home, luxurious compared to the old one, still feeling lost and thinking about my grandfather. My new home is 20 minutes from my old one, but as a boy, my grandfather was lucky to barely escape Nazi Germany to live thousands of miles away in the Philippines. And then, at an age even younger than my own, he was once again escaping for his life, this time from the Japanese, hiding out in the jungles of the Philippines, searching for food just to survive the night.

Ralph P. was born to a Jewish family on October 17, 1930, in Breslau, Germany. By the time he was in grade school, Hitler's denouncement of Jews had taken firm hold of the country. To avoid the stones the other children threw at him, my grandfather recalls, "I had to become a very fast runner." This was a vivid memory he had from a young age, when he was forced to go to a "Jewish" school 20 miles away. His life was constantly altered against his will in ways unimaginable to me. My grandfather's family was lucky to be able to leave Germany after *Kristallnacht*, or the Night of Broken Glass, in which mobs of Germans were encouraged to defile and deface practically anything that was owned by Jews across the country. The Philippines was the only place to which his family could obtain visas.

At age nine, my grandfather was forced to move to an alien island where the people spoke different languages, and he never saw many of his family members again. Once in the Philippines, his journey did not end. Like a story out of our history book, my grandfather found himself on the other side of World War II. The Japanese had invaded his small town just as he started to get acclimatized, and he found himself in a new martial state yet again. And then, when the American forces began their campaign to retake the islands, he and his parents were forced to leave everything behind once again to hide in the mountains to survive until the war in the Pacific was over, returning to a house that had been burned down.

I can't imagine how my grandfather went on to high school at this point, after missing several years of schooling because of the war. Later on, again out of his control, a hurricane blew off the roof of the University where he was currently studying. So when accepted to M.I.T. in the United States, he gladly took a ship to America by himself to once again start anew. There he met my future grandmother and a few years later had a child who would eventually be my mother. And it was this chain of heart rending events, which all had to occur precisely so that one day I could be born. I try to remind myself of this fragile web whenever I indulge in thinking my glass is half empty.

And just the fact that my grandfather lived through all this is not what is truly inspiring to me. When asked what he thinks when looking back over the events of his life, my grandfather says, "I feel I have had a pretty good life." It was only a few months ago that I was convincing myself that my life was terrible because my mother has achieved enough success to move us to a nicer house only 20 minutes away. Yes, my life now has a small dent in it, but nothing in comparison to the torture that my grandfather had to endure throughout his entire childhood. My grandfather inspires me to have the same view of the world that he has. He has told me, "There is no way that I could have survived my childhood if there was not a reason for it." I believe that the chains of events that led to my own life happened for a reason. Grandpa Ralph taught me, "It is your obligation to live the life you were given to the fullest."

I have been born, through no doing of my own, into a fantastic life compared to most people in the world. My grandfather inspires me to be grateful for what I have and what is to come in life. No matter what roadblocks get in the way, things can get better. Now as I sit by the waterfall in the back yard of my new house, thinking back on my grandfather's life and all that he had to endure, I believe that life is genuinely really good. Thank you, Grandpa Ralph, for reminding me through examples as well as your truisms to appreciate and savor what I have been given.

Essay 6: Family Reflections, Traditions, and Influences

Brrrring! 4:30 a.m. For most people, if their alarm clock went off this early they would grumpily pull the covers over their heads and refuse to roll out of bed. For me, that was not the case. I had been waiting for a year to wake up this early. A 4:30-a.m. alarm only means one thing for me: the annual Morro Bay camping trip.

I bound down the stairs into my mom's gold minivan and swing open the heavy door to find Marissa Hoffman already inside waiting for me. My parents have known the Hoffmans since they were in college; naturally, I have known them since I was a few days old. I have always looked up to Marissa, who has been my best friend and "older sister" ever since I can remember. I aspire to possess her sense of individuality, fearlessness, and spunky spirit.

"Hey Min!"

"Rae! How excited are you right now? Want some Bubblicious?"

Bubblicious bubblegum. I don't usually chew gum at 5 in the morning, and I don't really like its taste, but I take a piece anyway. It's a Morro Bay tradition.

Even though the 6-hour car ride seems long, we know how to entertain ourselves. As if I'm not weird enough normally, Marissa really brings out my silly side. We groove to funny songs, take pictures, eat many of my mom's famous, home-made chocolate chip cookies, and play games. One year, we created our best pastime yet by tying Fruit by the Foot wrappers around our heads and lip-syncing to Linda Ronstadt's "Heat Wave."

When we arrive, the campsite looks exactly the same as it has every other year. The fire pit, eucalyptus trees, tire swing, and hiking trails seem untouched as if we have never left them. The Hoffmans engage my family in a tent-building speed contest. Of course my family always wins because we have the "wussy tents" that already had the poles woven through the loopholes.

After we set up camp and the parents wind down with some Coronas (an adult Morro Bay tradition), we start to make preparations for our first dinner around the campfire. It's always the same main course: Cornish game hen. The beauty of this meal is that we all work together. The men start the fire and put the grill together to prepare it. The mothers wash off the hens and we help chop veggies. As we prepare the food, we cringe at the disgusting yet necessary task of sticking a lemon wedge in the cavity of each hen. Then, we wrap up the hens in tin foil and the men grill them.

After dinner, we relax and play games for hours. Mr. Hoffman plays "La Bamba," "Puff the Magic Dragon," and many other classics on the guitar. Through the years, he has taught me to laugh when I feel defeated and how important it is to have a sense of humor. I cozy up to the campfire and read a book with Mrs. Hoffman, the bookworm of the group, who reminds me by example that it's okay to take time for myself every once in a while, even if it means being anti-social. Marissa's brother Chris helps me with my lack of hand-eye coordination in a game of Whiffle Ball and shows me how fun it is to be "one of the guys" from time to time.

What really makes the Morro Bay camping trip so special? Morro Bay acts as a constant in my very chaotic and busy life. After running from school to practice to rehearsal to family dinner, I am exhausted by the end of each school year. The simplicity of our Morro Bay trip gets me in touch with who I am and the people that I love. The slow pace and relaxed vibe allows me to take time to glean insight from the people around me. With the opportunity to engage in casual conversations with both adults and kids at the campsite, I make deeper connections with them, learn from their experiences, and grow from their advice. My Morro Bay family reinforces the importance of education and encourages me to chase my dreams. Their achievements and values inspire me to work hard and have fun at the same time. Through our annual camping trip, they emphasize the importance of tradition, a value that has now become essential in my life. Morro Bay also serves as a way to document my life year by year. Even though I return to the same campsite annually, my experience is different each time because *I* have changed (the site somehow seems smaller to me year after year, too). Morro Bay witnesses my awkward phases, biggest laugh attacks, and fondest memories. It assures me that although change is good, some things still stay the same, and that gives me comfort.

Essay 7: Family Reflections, Traditions, and Influences

The raw chicken hits the cast iron pan, sizzling and crackling with excitement, spurting oil all over the stovetop. My dog, Chester, crowds the pan trying to get a sniff, and I accidentally step on his tail. He lets out a yelp in our tight kitchen quarters. My mom glares at me, noticing the mess I am making. Five minutes later, the chicken is placed in the oven, and for a short time the kitchen is still. Not for long though, as my dad grabs a pot, fills it with water, and starts preparing the string beans. Meanwhile, my younger brother carelessly plops glasses and plates on the stone-topped table, and mom chops tomatoes and carrots for our salad. From the sounds of our noisy kitchen, one would think we were cooks preparing a meal for an army.

Ever since I can remember, we have had family dinners. It's a time when the world around us stops and we all get a chance to check in. Not only do we eat together, but we also prepare the meal together. Each person has a designated job to do.

"Ding, ding, ding!" The kitchen timer rings, and all four of us are now crowded in our small kitchen. I get the roasted chicken out of the oven, and as soon as my mom smells the garlic-infused aroma, she forgets her earlier complaints about the oil splatter.

We all sit down with full plates while Chester eagerly peers over the edge hoping for any scraps. What follows next is our signature family banter as we discuss our past week and the one ahead. "Did you hit them straight today, David?" "Yeah, I did. Did you manage to stay out of the water?" "How was your business trip? Eat a lot of meals out?" "Mom, did you buy anything new for Chester today?" To survive in my family, I need to be quick-witted and roll with the punches, as we constantly pick and pry at each other.

As much as we enjoy our communal meal, we all can't wait for our "dessert": dominoes. We have played dominoes as a family since I could count. It's how I learned my fives-times tables, trying to add up all of our points. There are not many things that we compete in, but when we play dominoes, all bets are off. The teams are always the same—my brother and dad against my mom and me. We can't just quit after one game; one game turns to two out of three, and then three out of five, and so on, for hours on end.

We have fostered a unique rhythm in our family, a sort of peace within chaos. When I'm back in the real world, working on a tight class-project deadline or dealing with crying campers at work, I sometimes pause and think: This is real chaos. It is then that I yearn to be back around my family table in the comfort of our own organized chaos, at home and at peace once again.

Essay 8: Family Reflections, Traditions, and Influences

Several years ago, my family had just finished eating dinner at a local Chinese restaurant and our waitress brought the bill and four fortune cookies. I eagerly grabbed one, cracked it open to read my fortune: "Try new things." I immediately thought of all the changes I had recently been forced to make as a fifth-grader: finding new friends, starting a new school, and even playing a new sport. Although at first glance these obstacles appeared to be rather difficult, I realized that these challenges would ultimately help me adjust to my new life in California. For me initially, change instilled a fear that I had to continually work to accept in order to overcome it. On that "fortunate" day, however, the thought of change began to thrill me. That fortune served as a catalyst for change.

My father's job had recently transferred my family from the small, quaint town of Washington, Pennsylvania, to the booming, vibrant surroundings of Southern California. The students at my new school were less inviting than those back home, and many had already known each other for several years. I tended to remain quiet and constructed emotional barriers to separate myself from what I saw as different, making the befriending process even more complicated. Angry with my parents, I constantly begged to return to Pennsylvania where I felt at home and fit in, but they tried to calm me down and convince me that all of this change was ultimately for the better. Doubtful and reluctant, I tried my best to fit into a new environment.

My fortune gave me new insight and perception not only into my life but also the world around me. Whenever I tried to avoid any sort of change, I stopped myself to remember that fateful fortune cookie's message. Starting out slowly, I began by expanding my typical diet of pizza, macaroni and cheese, and chicken tenders to explore new foods such as sushi, guacamole, and others that I once rendered inedible. I moved on to bigger and more difficult challenges such as opening myself up to my classmates to a point where I finally felt accepted. I also enjoyed being the first person to welcome any new students to our class. Today, I am proud to say that I continue to enjoy new opportunities and now challenge myself to scuba diving, a sport that to some seems dangerous, but to me is exhilarating. Recently, I completed a daring dive in Hawaii with manta rays bearing wingspans of up to 15 feet encircling me.

Looking back on my life, my father's decision to move my family to California was one of the greatest transitions to happen to me. That initial change in the norm coupled with the fortune cookie I received years ago inspired me to do things I once deemed impossible. Now whenever I am confronted with change I embrace it, and moving on from high school to college is no longer an overwhelming hurdle of feared anticipation; rather I look forward to experiencing this new chapter of my life and welcoming all of the change that comes with it.

Personal Setbacks and Self-Reflection

You are only human. Bad news can impact anyone. What do you do with that bad news? How do you process it? How are you changed by it for the better or worse? How do you look at or live in your world differently once you have this news or have a challenging or life-changing experience? Many of the examples in this section have to do with major health issues that a student has had to deal with. You don't need to have suffered physically to write a great personal statement, though. Some students chose to write about other bad news or complicated circumstances they encountered or experienced. What these essays have in common, though, is that each of these students took their personal suffering and learned valuable lessons from it.

Essay 1: Personal Setbacks and Self-Reflection

People often talk about those life-changing moments after which nothing is ever the same. We watch them unfold in movies. We read about them in books. We usually think about them as happening to other people. I remember the day I became one of those "other" people.

Only a few weeks earlier, my friends and I were welcoming the start of the summer before our senior year with beach volleyball, bodysurfing, and campfires. After spending countless hours in my second home, the ocean, it came as no surprise when I woke up one morning with a clogged right ear. At first, I thought nothing of it. I probably had water in my ear, and at worst, a small infection. But, when the hearing loss got worse, even the optimist in me had to admit that it was time to see the doctor.

The ENT confirmed the hearing loss but not the cause. When he recommended an MRI, he phrased it as precautionary and based on the off chance that there may be something else at play. At this point,

I was much more convinced by Web MD's diagnosis of "random hearing loss" common to frequent ocean-goers than the ENT's statistic that there was a 1-in-a-1,000 chance that I might have something more serious. The odds seemed to be in my favor, but as anyone who has won the lottery or gotten struck by lightning could tell you, odds don't matter when you're that one.

I came home from a July 4th fireworks celebration to find my parents waiting for me at the kitchen table. Either I had done something wrong or someone had died. That evening, they had gotten a call from Hoag Hospital with the MRI results and were anxious to tell me the news. The MRI detected a golf ball sized tumor on the right side of my brain. A future for a normal life depended on having it surgically removed as soon as possible.

The 7-inch scar around my right ear reminds me how lucky I am to be alive and well. After a 10-hour surgery on August 1st, I lost all hearing in my right ear, could no longer taste on the right side of my mouth, and would never again produce tears in my right eye. But, I was also tumor free.

My recovery took place one step at a time. The first week, I could barely walk up a flight of stairs because I couldn't find my equilibrium. Despite my physical fatigue and difficulty finding balance, my mind committed to an unrelenting sense of optimism. Sometimes you don't really appreciate what you have until you're face to face with the possibility that it will be taken from you.

In many ways, this experience makes me feel like I have re-entered my own life. With each breath, I am filled with gratitude. Gratitude for the friends and family who stuck by my side. Gratitude for the surgeons who removed 100 percent of my tumor when a millimeter of wrong movement would have meant permanent facial paralysis. Gratitude for my ability to think, problem-solve, and articulate my thoughts.

For me, this was one of those life-changing moments after which nothing is ever the same. French novelist Marcel Proust once said, "The real voyage of discovery lies not in seeking new lands but in seeing with new eyes." I now see with new eyes.

Essay 2: Personal Setbacks and Self-Reflection

I've never wanted to be a statistic. While I don't consciously fight conformity, I like that I'm not always part of a group, such as the "typical teen." But this past December, I didn't have a choice. That's when my family became a statistic, part of the growing percentage of unemployed Americans.

I never gave much thought to my dad's job or the economy before-hand. I knew he worked and that we were able to live comfortably, but I never thought he'd just be let go.

My family has always been thrifty, even before the recession made it "cool." We don't try to live beyond our means, and I've always valued that. It's given me an uncommon amount of common sense. That's partly why being hit by the recession was so difficult. We weren't part of the problem, but we were still affected. We also weren't the only ones, and being in the same boat as so many other families helped widen my perspective. While my dad was unemployed, we continued to live fairly normally. My mom had worked part-time before, but she took on more hours and their roles in the household flipped. Dad was the one who was dropping me off and picking me up from school now. Dad was the one home during the day. And while he was far from doing nothing—always actively seeking networking opportunities and freelance jobs—it was frustrating for him. I got to see how hard he was working when, in eighth grade, instead of participating in Take Your Child to Work Day, I went with him to his networking group. There, I met other kids like me, with at least one parent out of work.

We were fortunate. Our struggles weren't as bad as those of other families. But my dad's three-year period of unemployment did teach me some things. It taught me that sometimes, no matter how smart you are, or how secure you feel, life happens. I never blamed my dad for being laid off, nor anyone else. It just happened, and even if you think you're prepared for anything, sometimes entirely different things occur. This experience also helped me see how a family can persevere. We stuck it out. We didn't know what the future held, but we just had to get through it together. When he applied for a job and didn't even get an interview, or actually was interviewed and then nothing happened, it hurt. But we didn't have time to have a pity party each time, because the rest of life was still going on. We just had to roll with it and look at what was coming next.

My dad has been working full time again for about a year and a half, and he enjoys what he does. Finally, everything feels more stable. Though his time of unemployment was long and frustrating at times, I learned the importance of determination and perseverance and the strength that can come from your family.

Essay 3: Personal Setbacks and Self-Reflection

Some people are born with silver spoons in their mouths. I was born with an extra hole in my head. As a toddler, I enjoyed a blissfully benign relationship with the genetic anomaly. However, our relationship became strained when this hole—a preauricular pit— began misbehaving. When it saw fit, it collected bacteria and swelled in a rage of pus and pain, only to erupt at the most inopportune times. Like precalculus tests.

Preauricular pits affect less than one percent of the American population. The chance of the mutation being as sporadically and severely infected as mine is even slimmer. Perhaps mine was just as motivated to succeed as I am. As my otolaryngologist described it, this "skin tunnel" planted itself in front of my right ear and burrowed its way into my cranial tissues. The grosser the entity became, the more engrossed *I* became in the science of its existence. Still, no matter how attached we were, it had to go.

As I frequented the hospital for check-ups during the summer of 2012, my ear endured its final days of bacterial bullying. I never feared the hospital. Instead, I grew captivated by the idea of one: a medical microcosm bustling with people whose common purpose is to heal others through the seemingly antithetical forces of pure science, human creativity, and personal empathy. As my specialist investigated my preauricular pit, I interrogated him about the oddity's origins and treatment methods. But information wasn't enough—I wanted to *perform* the medical analyses. So, I requested a release of the excised portion of my ear. My specialist declined, but counter-offered *another* way to get the experience I craved, making up for my loss of specimen custody. Almost.

With my specialist's encouragement, I applied to Joe DiMaggio Children's Hospital's volunteer program. Once accepted, I was overwhelmed with work opportunities from oncology to imaging. I soon learned that the pediatric intensive care unit had no volunteers. Mentors warned me that volunteers avoided it because of its emotionally and medically traumatic environment. But I saw it as an opportunity. Against cautionary dissuasion, I committed to the PICU. Immediately, the grateful and hard-working staff welcomed me and taught me the cold, hard facts about illnesses and medical equipment. But I quickly learned the softer side of medicine: I spent Friday nights singing to a show-tune-obsessed toddler; quickly replacing a tracheal tube during bath-time; running from playroom to patient room to retrieve a fresh oxygen tank; and cradling an infant whose sternum was cracked from cardiac surgery, while monitoring his consciousness and breathing.

Although many of my schoolmates shared my fascination with medicine, my school provided no organized means of exploring this passion. So, I founded a Pre-Med Club and gathered medically inclined students to join me. Before long, we hosted teleconferences and speaking engagements; physicians and medical professors eagerly shared their experiences with us. We even created educational programs with homemade presentations and member-specific volunteering.

And good news travels fast. Administrators from the Lucanus Center for adults with disabilities noticed my work and recruited me to help reform national healthcare for intellectually and developmentally disabled (IDD) people developing dementia. Here was an opportunity I could not pass up, to provide meaningful assistance locally and globally to underrepresented and often mistreated people. Through the National Task Group on Intellectual Disabilities and Dementia

Practices, I joined international leaders in IDD specialties and geriatrics. Together, we are transforming the diagnosis, treatment, and prevention of dementia-related health problems in IDD patients.

Although my preauricular pit took a behavioral turn for the worst, its plans backfired: Its outbursts brought me into the medical community. I committed my life to medicine as a student, mentor, researcher, and caretaker for everyone from pediatric patients to special-needs adults, and from classmates to physicians. All I needed was a miniscule hole to open me up to my future as a medical specialist.

Essay 4: Personal Setbacks and Self-Reflection

It was the final night of my high school's senior retreat, Kairos. I glanced around the candlelit room as I tried to discern the faint silhouettes of people who I never realized were so similar to me. I once heard, "Everyone has a story behind every mask they may hold up towards others." Well, tonight was the night we pulled down our "masks," and I learned these "stories" from my peers. Classmates I merely pass in the hallway each day, but never had the chance to talk to, or students from other cliques who never seemed to want to look me in the eye before tonight would now be revealed to me.

My nerves started to rise as the intimidation of being the only junior with the seniors sank in. (I had been nominated by teachers to attend out of my entire junior class based on leadership and character, so that I would be prepared to lead next year's retreat.) Stories continued to be told by each person about their most difficult journeys in life. My eyes were opened wide as life stories unfolded. Struggles through parents' divorces, a lost loved one, sibling rivalry, or just the average high school problems. I felt my stomach start to knot up when I noticed it was my turn to speak next. Would I have the strength to tell my story?

My hands felt a little shaky, but the adrenaline kicked in as I commenced, "Seven years ago, my life took a drastic turn. As my mother, sister, and I were walking the streets of Long Beach looking for an apartment for my sister to live in when she was to attend college that fall, my sister collapsed as my mother struggled to pin her against the wall. Kristen suffered from an AVM, which is similar to a brain aneurism. After undergoing a 9-hour surgery, she was left a quadriplegic." The whole room sat completely motionless, mouths agape, eyes astonished. An acquaintance from across the room asked, "What exactly is a quadriplegic? I've only heard of the term." I explained, "It's almost like someone is paralyzed, only they have some limited movement in their limbs. You never realize how much we really take for granted. A simple common cold to us spirals into pneumonia and a two-month hospital stay for my sister. Instead of coming home and bickering with my brother and sister, I arrive to a chaotic house filled with medical equipment. But none of that compares to seeing her smile every time I walk through the door." My voice broke down and my eyes teared up. I looked at many others who were also crying. Members of my retreat group approached me, and we joined into a group hug. I had never felt such support in a group of newly made friends before.

The next day we loaded onto the bus to return to school. I now had 40 new people who had seen me without my "mask," who could understand my background better and offer support. They had never known before what went on in my life beyond school. Furthermore, their stories helped me to grow and also overturned many of my misconceptions of them. As the wind from the bus blew through my hair, I pondered these stories I had heard. Many classmates had lost a parent or friend, which helped me realize how grateful I should be that my sister is even still living. Other feelings and thoughts went through my head. Anger filled my veins as I thought, "How could this happen to my sister when she was so innocent?"

Guilt struck as I pondered, "Why didn't this happen to me, and not her, or anyone else in the world?" Then I deliberated, "Looking back, I would not pick to avoid this life-altering incident. Although it causes much pain to the loved ones around me, it helped us grow together and closer to our faith. Was this the real reason it happened?" The question of "Why?" now began to be more comprehendible. My classmates' stories helped me become more proactive with my incident as well. I developed an even stronger inclination to help people like my sister, which is why I chose to work in the medical field after college. We arrived back at school where we had all originally stepped onto the bus as individuals. But now we stepped off as one.

Essay 5: Personal Setbacks and Self-Reflection

Nobody asked me to this year's homecoming dance, and I believe that the United States should maintain a strong nuclear arsenal. Correlation? Maybe.

Last year before the homecoming game, my high school brought back an "old southern tradition:" mums. To clarify, a mum is composed of a set of 4-foot long streamers exploding out of a gift-wrapping bow the size of my face, given by a boy to a girl after asking her to accompany him to the homecoming dance. As a non-invitee, my "all-inclusive" school still encouraged me to attend the homecoming game and dance even without a date, and I obliged. I cheered at the game; I put on a pretty dress for the dance. I smiled and laughed alongside my friends, though I was one of few girls without an obnoxious, glittery ribbon fastened to my chest. I consider myself a connoisseur in art of social defense: I never divulge too much about myself, I am reluctant to trust, and like I did on that homecoming weekend, I can slap on a convincing grin even when I am devastated.

I often say that my high school social life began two years later than that of my peers. This in itself made me an unlikely homecoming date candidate. After devoting thirteen years of my life to competitive gymnastics, things like fashion, gossip, and homecoming had little space in my carefully calculated regimen of a life. I devoted myself to gymnastics with every fiber of my being. For most people, gymnastics is a dumbfounding spectacle that appears once every fourth year during the Olympic Games. Gymnastic fever grips the planet for two weeks, and then everybody quickly cools back down to 98.6°. But gymnastics was my hourly alibi that devoured my life—every meal, every workout, every ice bath. Thus, when my competitive career came to an end, and I began devoting most of my time to school-related activities instead, I entered a totally new realm. Suddenly, I found myself befriending strangers at school instead of relying on my teammates: my support system. I started talking to boys and (making feeble attempts at) dating. I wore mascara and learned to subtly shift my hips as I walked. I found myself fighting to be valued in this new world, to be invited to study groups, parties, and dances.

You are probably wondering where the nuclear weapons come into play. I firmly believe ballistic-missile-launching submarines (SSBNs) and long-range bombers are both important and necessary, unlike most of my fellow Obama Campaign volunteers. As a Democrat growing up in a conservative atmosphere, my *"flaming liberal!"* views have often defied the norm. However, while I support the passing of *Roe v. Wade* and oppose Proposition 8 through and through, my firm belief in nuclear possession and proliferation cracks my leftist armor.

I believe this because the United States has far and away the strongest military on earth. We hold this title largely because of our massive nuclear arsenal, one capable of devastating any other nation within seconds. I would NEVER encourage such an action. I DO wish I could argue against nuclear weapons entirely. I wish we lived in a la-dee-dah world where Al-Qaeda didn't set the civilian-filled sky ablaze and Hamas didn't station suicide bombers at schoolchildren's bus stops. But reality is exactly that. As Middle Eastern nations illegally and unsafely build such weapons every minute, the United States must not simply keep up—it must also dominate the field to prevent such horrors. It often has been said that the best offense is a strong defense, and I think this quote applies perfectly to national defense. The United States is a connoisseur in *national* defense.

My painted-on grin couldn't harm a fly. To compare my closed-off nature to the military is bombastic at the least. But in faking a smile, I too can defend myself. In recent months, I have become a much more open person. Instead of simply hiding my true thoughts or feelings, I make them known. My smile is no longer a shield, but an indication of happiness. I now question why I feel the need to defend myself in social situations where little is at stake. This newfound self-awareness allows me to make outrageous connections between petty dating mishaps and hot-button political issues. I am proud of myself for adjusting my personal defense policy, but I am glad the United States holds strong to its.

Eight short months after homecoming, a boy rang my doorbell to pick me up for the prom. But I still believe the United States should maintain a strong nuclear arsenal.

Essay 6: Personal Setbacks and Self-Reflection

Toilet paper leaked out our pants as our laughter awakened the quiet street. The moon illuminated the night sky. Showers of hose water rained on us as we ran down the dark paved road. This wasn't some ordinary activity children experience occasionally. Toilet papering became our lives. The adrenaline rush cleared our minds of reality. For those hours spent painting lawns with toilet paper were the hours we could escape pain, agony, and tears. Despite the agony, we never stopped mummifying houses. As I looked at my partner in crime it was difficult to distinguish between him and my brother. Our closeness radiated.

Rhabdomyasarcoma. Who knew one word could alter the life of two best friends. Rhabdomyasarcoma, neighbors gossiped. Rhabdomyasarcoma, doctor explained sadly. Rhabdomyasarcoma, families cried bitterly. Hospital visits, blood transfusions, and balding hair engulfed our world. We became more comfortable building Legos® within cold hospital walls, rather than kindergarten classrooms. Walking alongside my friend, I tried to fight his battles for him. Witnessing IVs, seeing pain and feeling afraid, I just wanted to make Zach smile. I decided to rise to the challenge. I began learning to be a trusted friend, who listens with courage and faces difficult circumstances with cheerfulness. I pressed forward, trying to be a normal boy while death followed like a long winter's shadow.

Life-threatening moments ceased, while miracle upon miracle occurred. Ten years passed and sickness was now behind us. Even though our toilet-papering days seemed childish now, they were a part of our seal as boyhood brothers in life. Suiting up for my routine surf, I watched the sun's rays gleaming off the ocean's glassy surface. My picture-perfect evening did not prepare me for my mother's phone call minutes later. "Zach has been diagnosed with cancer a second time," she choked. Tears, pain, agony, all came crushing back into my life. It was going to take a lot more than courage and friendship to walk the road less traveled once more.

Peace, serenity, dark chilled pavement runs along the soles of my feet as I walk down memory lane. The moon continues to illuminate the night sky, however silence remains, toilet paper only found beside the toilet. As I look to my side, I see emptiness—no more partner in crime. The houses we once plastered with bathroom tissue I cherish. My identity is now clear. I learned not to let sickness or struggles define who I am. Instead of worrying about pain, I now love, encourage, and cherish those around me. Step by step I walk down that dark paved road eyes on the future prepared by my past. No more does one word bring hospital visits and blood transfusions; all that remain are the memories of two partners in crime. I continue my journey alone with courage, loyalty, love, and friendship being my compass, navigating my way through life.

Essay 7: Personal Setbacks and Self-Reflection

I entered the dilapidated farmhouse through its rustic, worn out door. As I pushed it closed, the handle hung lifelessly, tilted out through its place of original attachment. I heard a shuttering echo bounce wall to wall from the heavy door closing. I felt a slight nudge from behind.

"This way to your room," she spoke hesitantly, hoping that one day I would feel comfortable in her house. She didn't step ahead of me. In fact, she didn't even point to the direction to my new room in my new home. She stood motionless and studied me, completely unaware that

I was watching her. We caught glances and she instantly threw her face back to the direction of my room. She danced carefully in front of me making sure that she didn't touch me.

I stepped through the doorway. Propped on my new bed-to-be was a poster inscribed in messy crayon that read "Bienvenidos Hope." The worn edges of the strictly white poster matched the rest of the stark room: old, used, and isolating. The only form of light, coming from a small barred window, gave access to a view and the smell of cows grazing.

I was a foreign exchange student in Chazon, Argentina, for five months during my junior year. I left my privileged environment in Orange County with dreams of an exhilarating and adventurous experience, and what I got in return was the complete opposite.

I would not classify myself as the farm type. I love cities and bright lights, not cornfields and paper lanterns. The smell of the farm made my eyes water, and often I put a t-shirt over my mouth to breathe. The farm rooster was the worst. The bird nagged 'ka-ca-doodle-doo' at different times throughout the night, not just at sunrise. He sung a range of clucking tunes from midnight until 6 a.m., making my patience run low. Unfortunately, like the rooster, my Argentine "brother" was just as irritating. He made sure that I was always annoyed. He loved to poke, taunt, push, scream in my ear, and pester me until I ran to my room for safety. His parents didn't intercede, expecting me to deal with him. Furthermore, every meal, as my whole family sat down to eat, I was questioned incessantly by my Argentine "dad" on any topic involving money. I felt awkward and uncomfortable. My "mom" often retreated, too, since he yelled a lot.

After a month of depression full of long and expensive phone calls home, many tears, and absolute homesickness, I realized that I needed to pull it together. I could not quit and go home, and I had to figure out some way to make the best of my situation. It took every ounce of my mental strength to stay positive and begin to seek out opportunities. I started to form a bond with my Spanish teacher, Sylvia. As we grew closer, she invited me to travel with her family. I also built a strong bond with her youngest daughter who was my age. Fernanda participated on her local basketball team, so I began traveling 45 minutes by bus to her town three times a week to have an athletic and cultural outlet. When I wasn't at Sylvia's, I took long bike rides and walks with my "sister" after school. We found a secret lagoon where we snuck out to see the sunset whenever we had the chance. I also committed myself to the study of Spanish to make communicating with my friends at school easier. As my Spanish improved, my relationships with my new friends strengthened.

I grew from this unfortunate experience in Argentina. I struggled to become a better person, and I was put to the test. If something similar happened in the future I know I would react differently. I would go into the foreign place and know that I was there for an experience whether good or bad. No matter how hard the circumstance, from that moment forward, I would try and be open-minded, knowing that this experience would only be for a little while. If something in the future happens that I don't like, I will not let it bother me, and I know I can move on more easily. With the strategies I learned from being away, I will use my new skills and be successful in any new situation or challenges that I encounter in the future.

Work and Community

Working a job demonstrates commitment and an understanding of responsibility, and it implies that you have applied for and been hired to do a job. Any job! The more appropriate the job for a high school student, the better. Bag groceries. Work at a shop or store. Host at a restaurant. Babysit, walk dogs, wash cars, or scoop ice cream. Understanding the value of a dollar and needing to be somewhere on time and ready to work are important results of having had a real job.

At the same time, volunteering and giving back to your community demonstrates an awareness of needs outside of your own. Sharing your time, talent, and personal resources or being willing to roll up your sleeves and volunteer speaks to the humanitarian in you. Those who give back recognize the value of their lives and the true importance of community, and they appreciate the blessings of life. In the following essays, students share their work and community experiences in an effort to have their readers understand what it means to give back.

Essay 1: Work and Community

In a swift motion, I skillfully extend my right arm across the adjacent wooden beam, hanging onto the questionably stable rafter like Spiderman, and scrub the last bit of cruddy black mold with a bristle brush. My feet are dangling 10 feet off the ground in a suffocating and blisteringly hot attic. Beads of sweat drip from every pore of my body at an alarming rate. Pushing aside the plastic gas mask that protects my eyes and airways, I wipe my face repeatedly with my already sweaty shirt, wishing I had a nice clean, cool washcloth—or maybe an air conditioner. As I climb back down the shoddy attic ladder to take a drink from my precious water bottle, I take a glance at myself in the reflection of the kitchen window. I am a frightening mess drenched in perspiration and coated in strange black residue.

It is my summer vacation, and I am helping with mold remediation in a house in the Ninth Ward of New Orleans, Louisiana. The home belongs to a gentleman who lost everything in the floods that followed Hurricane Katrina and is now trying to rebuild his home as well as his life. Along with other high school students, I am there to do my small part to help repair his world three years after that catastrophic event. From his home to others in the surrounding neighborhoods, I find it inconceivable that the devastation can still be so great and that my humble efforts can mean so much—especially in this man's life.

His name is Bud. When others evacuated, he stayed behind and watched as Katrina's storm surge destroyed his home—leaving him stranded on his rooftop for days. Bud not only lost all of his belongings (including his dentures), he also lost his faith in the government and the agencies that were supposed to offer help. Apparently, the National Guard never came for Bud despite his frantic screaming and yelling. Luckily, he was rescued by a neighbor's boat before hypothermia set in.

As we munch on turkey hoagies and Sun Chips (not easy for Bud without many teeth) on what once had been his driveway, Bud shares details about his survival and his quest to restart his life in New Orleans. With a toothless grin and tears in his eyes he thanks us repeatedly saying, "Y'all may never fully understand what ya' did for me and others here in New Orleans. You volunteers are the ones making the difference, and I'm truly grateful."

These simple yet heartfelt words, in Bud's thick Southern accent, continue to resonate in my mind. He makes me realize that I have the power to make a difference, to repair the world a little, and to make someone's day just a bit brighter. During my two weeks in New Orleans helping in the clean-up efforts, I have the opportunity to meet many compassionate and caring people, who despite their frustrations, are grateful for "the kindness of strangers" and who always take a moment to share their story with a warm smile and a genuine "thank y'all so much for coming here."

I begin to realize that my very presence here means even more to these residents than the manual labor of remediating mold, weeding, or painting. Instead, I am scrubbing a sort of mold that has accumulated in their lives since Katrina hit the Gulf Coast three years ago. Little by little as I listen to their stories, I "scrub" and clear a part of the black burden and ache from their hearts. Their wooden spirits become stronger and more resilient with a gleaming new coat of protective varnish and they begin the process of starting life anew. My brush now becomes filled with a sense of purpose and leaves New Orleans with a perpetual yearning to find new moldy places to scrub again.

Essay 2: Work and Community

Line 1:"Good morning Dr. M.'s office, this is Madeena. How may I help you?" "Okay, let me go grab your chart." Line 2: "Thank you for holding; this is Madeena." "Okay and your name and the date of your appointment?" Line 1: "Thanks for holding, I will call the insurance and give you the breakdown of your benefits." And then from a hygienist in the back, "Madeena, can you come and help me with probing?"

I never would have guessed how much work, time, and effort it takes to run the front office of a dental office. As a patient, I simply walked in the office, checked in with the pretty ladies in front, and waited patiently in the waiting area for my appointment to finally be over! If I waited 5 minutes past my 2 p.m. appointment, I wondered what could possibly be taking so long. Ten minutes past my appointment, I got frustrated and observed how easy these women have it, just sitting at a desk, staring at a computer all day, and glancing in charts in a well-decorated, air conditioned office. Now as an employee, I realize it is much more than that.

Working has also made me more aware of money. Before I had this job I would typically be heard saying, "Mom I need to buy this shirt at Nordstrom's—it's so cute!" "Okay, how much do you need?" "I haven't checked. Just give me a fifty." Looking at a $50 shirt now, I think of all the hours of hard work it would have taken me to earn that shirt. Now I think twice before I purchase anything.

Teamwork, I have learned, is the key component in the success of any business. What I find challenging about my work is that I am like a pillar holding up an unstable structure. Every pillar is needed, but if one breaks, the others have to work together in order to sustain the structure. I especially know I am needed when I return from a day off or occasional sick day. My coworkers welcome me with, "Madeena, thank goodness you are back! The charts were overflowing the office while you were gone!" Usually I have a pretty big "mess" to clean up.

Yes, it is hard waking up at 7 a.m. during my summer to go to work, but when I arrive, a rush of excitement overcomes me since I can confidently handle any situation. It feels good to know that I am needed and valued. Working at a dental office is more than just answering phones, helping patients, and checking insurances. I am part of something bigger, an office that creates "genuine relationships" with real, live patients who have real problems.

Essay 3: Work and Community

A balloon pops putting everyone in temporary shock. A woman bends down to hush her crying child. A man complains that his order is running late. A little girl spins around in circles knocking an entire rack of greeting cards to the floor. The cash register slams shut as it is closed once again. The bells on the door jingle constantly as a consistent flow of people move in and out. "Welcome to Party Land, how may I help you?" I ask.

When I began as an employee at Party Land two years ago, I was expecting to do a job completely different than what I do now. I wrongly assumed that everyone who came into a party store was happy and cheery because a party usually is a fun event. I also thought that every day I would come to work and help people plan the party of their dreams and that everyone would be accepting and open to my advice. Furthermore, I incorrectly presumed that customers were regular people, too, and sometimes they could be wrong. I quickly learned none of my assumptions were true.

It was during my first few days at Party Land that I started making small, unexpected changes from my perception of the job. It was usually just simple things like realizing that kids in a party store weren't always the best mix and that a free balloon couldn't solve everything. I also realized that customers expected *me* to be the cheery one instead of the other way around. It wasn't until a few weeks into my job that I made a change that not only affected my work, but also other aspects of my life.

I will never forget the day when an impatient woman came storming through the door. She pushed a stroller filled with 2 children and several bags of groceries while a bouquet of flowers hung in her arm. As she struggled to make her way to the register, the woman furiously looked around.

"Where are my balloons?" she demanded as she handed over her receipt. I looked down at the order form that had been neatly written weeks before, noting that the pickup time wasn't for another 2 hours.

"We haven't quite finished them yet, but I would be happy to get a start on them now," I replied.

"No, they were supposed to be ready by now! How am I supposed to get my party set up on time?"

"Well, you wrote a different time on your order form. They would have been done if the time was correct," I honestly replied without thinking.

The woman stared at me for a second as if she was almost shocked and responded, "I am sure I wrote the right time on there. I'm positive you messed this up."

"I'm sure you're right," my coworker jumped in, "Sorry about the misunderstanding."

This is when it first hit me that my sometimes argumentative nature wouldn't work in all situations. That sometimes I would have to hold back what I was really thinking just so that I could please someone else. The customer is always right. It seems cliché to say, but for some reason I thought that it only worked if they really *were* right.

Over a long period of time, almost two years, I learned that I have to be accommodating and flexible not only with customers, but also with other people in my life. I realized that even though I may think people are wrong, I have to consider other people's viewpoints. Immediately shutting out other's perspectives will get me nowhere in life. This job has taught me tolerance, patience, flexibility, and openness. Now it wouldn't be a surprise to me if I had to completely redo a balloon order because the green was a shade darker than expected. I also don't get shocked anymore when a man comes running in, desperate for balloons and a card to make up for a forgotten birthday. It seems that I have become accustomed to dealing with people's so-called emergencies just so that the customer can always remain happy.

Essay 4: Work and Community

At a first glance, I probably wouldn't present myself as your typical house painter. Usually in this business you see us clothed in full body suits that used to be white that are now dappled with paint, sporting beards or some kind of fascinating facial hair and a red bandana, and smelling so much like paint thinner that one might think we're wearing the new "Eau de Turpentine." As a clean-cut high school student, I never really viewed myself as a painter and didn't think it would be very difficult until one day when my friends and I were in desperate need of some extra money. What started as a quick way to make some money, however, turned into a full-fledged entrepreneurial enterprise.

What most people don't realize is the amount of time and artistry that goes into painting one simple slab of wood, let alone an entire door, porch cover, or garage. My crafty grandfather once stated, "Preparation is the most intricate aspect of painting," a statement that I can completely vouch for. From laying down a mat to masking to sanding to cleaning to priming, at times it seems like the job will never be finished. As a rookie painter, I would come home from a 7-hour day of work, my hair stained with oil-based white paint, sawdust caught in my eyes and on my skin, spackled shoes, and a hatred of the awful profession that some called "painting." Many times I thought to myself,

"What kind of an Orange County kid is slaving outside in the brutal 90 degree sun getting unintentionally high off of paint fumes and feeling dehydrated for a measly few dollars?" In the beginning, the painting seemed to be a chore with no end: a swirling, sucking whirlpool of hopelessness. But over time, I discovered how much of an art form painting really was. Gradually I improved, and it hit me that there was a method to the madness of painting. Since the first arduous summer of painting, I have been volunteering myself to paint anything, realizing it's a way to show my artistic abilities and seeing that with practice and a little knowledge anything can be made enjoyable.

I know now that the ability to paint is a life experience that I have mastered by discovering my rhythm and my routine. Even at the times where I felt underpaid and underappreciated, the feeling of peeling off the tape around windows once the painting is finished, walking back a few steps, and admiring a striking new coat on something that once looked irreparable and ancient, was always worth the toils and discouraging effects that came with painting. Now that you know my knack for a new coat of paint, what color should I paint my dorm room?

Essay 5: Work and Community

"Coleman, give yourself a break. You wanna watch the fireworks?" Larry asked.

I nodded and finished unloading plates into the bin of dirty dishes that I would soon take down to the kitchen. Larry, the waiter, was standing on the deck of the restaurant patio, which he had commandeered from all of the other waiters for the summer. He had wanted me to be his busboy up there as well, and he constantly told me not to work so hard: "You're too conscientious." But this night was the Fourth of July, early in the summer; I walked toward the railing of the patio and stood behind Larry. The fireworks glared hotly in the summer night, lighting up the throngs of vacationers and partiers coming out of restaurants and bars up and down the street that led to the beach. I wiped the sweat off my forehead with my apron and looked at my black boots that were wearing down from trip after trip up and down the stairs from the patio to the kitchen and at my white-collared sleeves that were becoming gray with the grime of Italian food, perspiration, and sloppy stops at gas stations. I was disappointed that I was spending the night of Independence Day at work, and the fireworks quickly triggered a stream of memories for me.

Each time I see the fireworks in the summer, I feel a connection to the fireworks from the year before. I pictured myself in Ketchum, Idaho, with my grandma, last summer; I remembered walking up and down the streets of the small town looking for companionship, and always returning back to my grandma's condo, where I read Kerouac and listened to Tom Waits. In the mornings, I would watch and listen to the stream outside by the deck and sit in the hammock—just my grandma and me. Then I'd walk into town for lunch and sit on a bench to watch the girls go by. There were the bike rides on trails along the stream in the crisp dusk and my wanderings into the outskirts of town, near the mountain, in the unlit darkness, on the Fourth of July, listening to the sounds of drunken parties in the hidden backyards of houses with rusted broken down pickup trucks parked on the lawns.

After I went back to the condo and got ready for bed, the fireworks began going off, and my grandma got me into the car and we drove across the dinky highway to a clearing where we could somewhat make out a few explosives in the dark sky behind the thick trees. And the next night, on the fifth, I stopped my downtown wanderings on a corner with a king-sized Coke in my hand when I heard more explosions. I looked to the east, and fireworks were going off again as the scattered pedestrians on the corners, including myself, stopped and watched the lights in the sky. A prank? A continuation of the celebration? Everyone shrugged; no one knew for sure, but they chuckled anyway.

So as I stood with Larry in Villa Romano, I wondered where I would be a year later on the Fourth of July, and so on and so on for the rest of my life. I felt proud to have begun accumulating a stock of different experiences, so that at the end of each year I could look back on all of them and evaluate my life in terms of drastic changes of sights, feelings, and even identity.

But I had to fold the night's tablecloths. I returned home at midnight, kicked the boots off my sore feet, and read.

Essay 6: Work and Community

I was silent as we drove slowly down Normandie Avenue in South Central Los Angeles. The only sounds I heard were the barks of dogs and the cry of a siren from somewhere not too far away. Passing block after block of tract houses, separated by rusted chain link fences littered with plastic bags and empty soda cans, I reminded myself that I was only a short drive from my home. I felt uneasy as I stepped from the car and approached the faded pink door.

I first heard about the Susan Burton House when my mom and I were looking for a place to volunteer together. Desiring to learn more about the lives of women in the inner city, I thought this opportunity would be ideal. But now, standing in front of the house, the prospect of volunteering with ex-convicts was a little scary.

Then the pink door opened . . . and everything changed. I was engulfed in the warm hugs of women and the invigorating pulse of their excited greetings. As I worked, cooked, and chatted with these women, the labels that would have defined our relationship fell away.

Perhaps what initially drew me to the house was a belief that I was going to be serving in a culture markedly different from my own. Growing up, some of my fondest family memories came from service opportunities, particularly when we went outside of our comfort zones. But meeting women like Jasmine—a single mother escaping gang life—I saw that while our backgrounds and choices had been different, our hopes were remarkably similar. Seeing this, I knew I would be coming back.

Over the years, my visits to the house erased many of my preconceptions about people who've found themselves at the end of their rope. I've heard stories everyone should hear. Stories about the consequences of "small" compromises, falling to peer pressure, or unwisely choosing one's friends. I don't think the women were trying to scare us; rather, they were simply being honest about how easy it is to end up in a really hard place. I began to realize the strength and value of my social support network, where friends, family and community encourage me to make better choices.

While my involvement started as a mother-daughter project, the cause has become my own. The more I learn, the more I am motivated by the women of Susan Burton House who, by my age, have been labeled addicts, thieves, prostitutes or victims, women navigating a society that often fails to lend a hand. And I am disheartened to acknowledge that the majority of women who are incarcerated will likely fall back into the system.

The realities of the Susan Burton House caused me to spend a lot of time wondering what resources might have kept these women out of trouble in the first place. Why are jobs so hard to find in these neighborhoods? What creates strong family and social support networks? Why do social welfare programs seem to be so ineffective?

These questions made me curious about alternatives to traditional philanthropy and sparked my interest in areas like microfinance and social entrepreneurship. Moved to make a difference, I've been leading an effort at my school to create awareness of poverty and raise support for innovative solutions to combat it.

My emotional connection to the women of Susan Burton House has evolved into a passion for better understanding the economic and social causes behind their tragedies. I know I don't have the answers, but I am committed to searching for them. And I don't want to do it alone—I hope to be part of a community of people who are interested in questions like these. People who will challenge and inspire me to think differently. A community of those, like me, who are dissatisfied with the status quo.

Essay 7: Work and Community

I was born into a world of privilege. I live in a small, seaside community located in California, where profligacy is brazen and ostentatious wealth is accepted. A majority of the population is accustomed to always getting what they want, without so much as lifting a finger. The rest of the world looks upon residents as spoiled and ungrateful, and to some degree, these people are right. Fortunately, I have been lucky enough to come from a family that has kept me grounded and instilled me with morality. I learned the value of a dollar when I was required by my parents to get a job to pay for the ever-increasing price of gas. My family has not only taught me to appreciate the life I have been blessed with, but simultaneously to give back to people who are perhaps less fortunate.

One afternoon, my mother handed me a copy of the book *Three Cups of Tea,* explaining that it had deeply touched her. As I flipped through the gripping pages of the novel, my blessed life was put into perspective. The novel chronicles a mountain climber named Greg Mortenson's failed attempt at climbing Pakistan's K2 Mountain, to his establishment of numerous schools for the impoverished children of Pakistan and Afghanistan. After befriending the compassionate people of Korphe village, Mortenson founded the Central Asia Institute (C.A.I.), a nonprofit organization with the mission to promote community-based education, especially for young women, in this remote part of the world.

Mortenson's unbelievable persistence and courage inspired me beyond words. I learned that one person can truly make a difference, and I decided to join the fight. Driven by the vivid detail depicting the hardships of the Afghani and Pakistani children, I arrived at school determined to find a teacher sponsor willing to support my new club, the C.A.I. I submitted a final proposal, created flyers, and advertised an on-campus presentation to solicit members. In front of a group of 20 curious students, I detailed the accomplishments of Mortenson and the often-misunderstood culture of the tribal villages he encountered.

I noticed the interested expressions of my classmates change into looks of compassion as I told of the gentle ways of the villagers and their overwhelming desire to learn. I shared an example of village girls using sticks as pencils to practice multiplication tables in the dirt. Imagine our fancy white boards replaced by sticks and dirt! Through bake sales, carnivals, and holiday fundraising, we raised $782 to donate to this organization that promotes peace through literacy. Although our donation may seem trivial, a teacher's salary in a Central Asian village is a mere $365 a year: students of my high school donated over two teachers!

What now? The *Three Cups of Tea* has ignited a lasting fire within me. The sharp contrast between my life and those Mortenson writes of reminds me to reach out to the world outside of my little bubble. Besides gaining a new understanding of a culture entirely different from my own, I have developed leadership skills from organizing a group of teenagers. I have learned to lead in a more relaxed manner, breaking from my usual perfectionism in order to reach the antsy members of the C.A.I. The persistence of the young children of Central Asia to learn and mentally grow also encourages me to be thankful for the educational opportunities I have and not to take my schooling for granted. I plan to continue my club into my senior year and college and constantly advertise Mortenson's inspiring book and organization to whoever will listen. My goal is to double our membership and raise $1,000 my senior year. Greg Mortenson's story has opened my eyes wider to the world around me and taught me that one person can truly make an enduring difference. I am proud to contribute in my small way to an organization and experience much larger than my own and to assist in providing a tangible gift to villagers half way around the world. "Of all the things you have, learning is the one we most desire for our children." —Urkien Sherpa

Essay 8: Work and Community

"Hey! What's up?"

"Oh my god, I had so much fun the past few days. I swallowed a zipper. Hahaha!"

I freeze. What do I say to something like this? Is it a joke? I somehow stutter out, "M-Melanie what are you talking about? What happened?"

"I tried to kill myself, duh! I swallowed the zipper so it would cut my stomach. So it was really fun. I got to ride in this like ambulance thingy and then they gave me a shot in my butt to calm me down and I had to be like held down because I was kicking and screaming and stuff. I kinda want to go again. I spent four days in a mental hospital! The people around me were freaks though. But yeah it was super fun!"

I knew Melanie was unstable when I met her. When Ian, the tutor coordinator, told me that I had been paired with the most difficult girl at The Children's Center, I wasn't sure what I was getting into. I soon learned that Melanie was a dramatic 11-year-old girl stuck in the body of a 16-year-old. During our first meeting, my eyes immediately fell to the scars on her arms, and I realized that we came from completely different worlds. Over our weekly sessions, I found myself developing an older sibling protection of Melanie. I would intentionally shrug off her occasional outrageous stories, making it clear that I wouldn't want to do something that risked my safety or my dignity. She usually listened, wanting nothing more than to be thought of as mature, my friend.

This is different. She explains this to me as if she were talking about new clothes or a boy; as if taking her own life was amusing, a joke. I can't force myself to laugh and say, "Dude, why? That's not really cool. If one of my friends did that I totally wouldn't think it was funny." I look at her without a smile. "Melanie, why would you ever think of doing that to yourself?"

"Um, why not? It's not like it would matter anyway. It's not like anyone would miss me or anything."

I am heartbroken. Sitting in front of me is not the boisterous 11-year-old who pretends to be older than she is to protect herself. Melanie sits here looking at me with deep brown eyes that reflect vulnerability and anguish.

"Melanie, I cannot even begin to tell you how much I would miss you if you were gone. You can never think about doing that again." My eyes fill with tears. "Please. Never do that again."

The look in her eyes changes. Confusion turns into understanding; hopelessness turns into optimism. She has heard me. She knows she matters. She promises it won't happen again.

While I sit at school fearing that I won't get a certain grade to get me into a certain college, Melanie walks around fearing that she will be living in group homes until she is dropped right at 18 and left to fend for herself. This girl needs my help. She doesn't just need help listening to adults and following directions; she needs help understanding that she matters. She needs a mentor, and there is nothing in the world that I want more to accomplish. I alone cannot save a child who has been jumped with a knife, repeatedly abandoned, betrayed, and abused, but I can help.

That day, Melanie hugged me for the first time. As I said goodbye, she whispered the two words this child never says, "Thank you."

Essay 9: Work and Community

The doors stood opened to welcome the day's warm breeze as shy children eagerly peeked into the new computer lab. There I stood, uncomfortable and nervous, in the company of the Bahamian Deputy Prime Minister. The island's relentless heat caused my buttoned-down shirt to cling uncomfortably to my perspiring body; however, the children who eagerly eyed the computers had no interest in my appearance. All they wanted was a chance to get their hands on the computers. As the room filled with almost 100 children and their proud parents who crowded against the walls, I realized that I had accomplished my goal. I looked around and saw the faces of parents, thrilled that their children had been selected for my first class.

My dream began when I realized that not all children have access to fundamental technology that could improve their quality of life. The day I met Diane C., a missionary who runs an outreach program in Nassau that ships dictionaries and educational supplies to schools in impoverished areas, I knew this dream could finally come to fruition. Up until then the norm was dated textbooks and worn tools that barely functioned until her efforts drastically changed the educational dynamic for the better. Diane told me about Urban Renewal Centers that provide safe havens and vital resources for at-risk students. These centers host after-school programs with a focus on computers; however, the centers did not have computers for the children to use. I could not imagine children lacking access to technologies that would provide them with the potential to escape poverty and enter into the global workforce. I knew that these children deserved the same opportunities that I had taken for granted all my life.

I decided to provide the children of the Bahamas with computer labs. Being a high school student with limited resources, I began shopping for refurbished computers using capital that I raised on my own and repairing old computers that others no longer wanted. Diane facilitated the shipping of the computers, and after a few months, and battles with customs agents, the computers reached their destination.

I have returned to the Bahamas several times to set up the computers, teach workshops to students, and help the program grow. I designed the curricula and brought the equipment. Four computer labs have been established with thirty-seven computers total, and more are on the way. The programs are so successful that I also wanted to provide this service to my community at home. So I created a partnership with the Lauderdale Lakes Middle School, which is located in an impoverished region, in configuring its own computer lab for local children. I trained teachers for both the Bahamas and Lauderdale Lakes so that efficient computer lessons will continue long into the future.

I had always noticed that many people visit developing nations to provide food, build shelters, or care for the sick, but very few provide them with the tools necessary to succeed. I strived to be the one to provide the struggling communities with these essential tools. The joy, the smiles, and the responses from the children encourage my resolve to continue this journey. It is not hard to realize the importance of ensuring that these children join the twenty-first century, as access to computers and necessary technology impacts students' futures significantly. All people deserve a chance to achieve their goals rather than being hustled into minimum wage jobs. With this basic access to technology comes a brighter future for every child involved. For me, it is just another day in a world I want to be a part of.

Academic and Philosophical Aspirations—The Thinking Essay

Some students choose to show their reader how their mind works and what academic or philosophical ideas excite them. Writing about your academic passions and interests demonstrates to your reader a bit more about what you might be like in a college classroom setting. If academic ideas excite you, the essays below might also resonate and speak to you. Academic and philosophical passions can be contagious!

Essay 1: Academic and Philosophical Aspirations—The Thinking Essay

For the past seventeen years I have had a burning question that no one seems to be able to answer: Why does chronological age serve as a barrier for innovation and ideas? At the age of 2, my developing brain could not grasp the reason I had to slurp my orange juice out of a sippy cup, yet my 5-year-old brother had a full-sized cup of fresh orange juice without the lid. I was a bit jealous of my older brother who seemed to me an equal. Fortuitously, I found my perfect solution to a seemingly nuanced problem: electronics.

Considering that at the age of 7 I wired my own speaker system in my bedroom based on an old home theater setup, I began thinking that I just enjoyed the art of electronics. The concept of being able to construct a modular system of electronic components initiated a natural dopamine reward mechanism in my brain. Tinkering around with any wires, bulbs, or broken capacitors I could find excited me. While my peers were still happy to build towers with wooden blocks, I quickly got bored and advanced into robotic Legos. I felt good mentally and physically whenever I unscrewed the chassis of an old amplifier or precisely crushed light bulbs to collect filaments. After constructing my speaker system, I was hungry for more.

In response to the Y2K virus, my parents decided to upgrade our home computers to a more stable form. Though I don't recall too many details from my childhood, I vividly remember Paul, the computer guru. As he walked into the family room for the first time to upgrade the network interface card, I naturally gravitated towards him. I don't know if it was his long, chalky-white hair or the fragrance of fermented food remnants on his shirt that lured me. During Paul's numerous visits to the family computer, I sat by him silently as he worked through levels of MS-DOS and configuration screens. On one visit, Paul informed me he was going to replace the motherboard on the computer. Though I had no idea what he meant, I sat quietly engaged and took careful notice of the replacement procedure. After his few trips, it became apparent that we shared a very unique relationship. Paul taught me how to think critically and how to troubleshoot. It seemed that all those hours spent drifting off into the innards of my family computer metaphorically initiated a wireless data connection between me and the computer system.

I spent my middle school years self-learning various topics such as computer building, network design, and infrastructure. In high school I took Advanced Placement Computer Science as a freshman to learn programming and completed my Comptia A+ exam, an accomplishment that established my credibility as an experienced IT technician. I became an entrepreneur with my credential and moonlighted as a tech support for a distribution warehouse company servicing twenty-five workstations and three mainframe servers. Not only was I surprised by how much I had learned on my own, I never really thought of the sippy cup phenomena again.

What I thought would take most of my life to achieve only took a few years. No more would I be toiling in the face of adversity. No more would I be mindlessly growing up. No more would I not be taken seriously because of my youth. With knowledge, I realized I could gain power. This meant that I was important to those around me and that my ideas were valid. My thirst for and acquisition of knowledge serves as an organic device that merges generational differences and has allowed me to mature beyond my years. My ongoing quest for knowledge is validated.

Essay 2: Academic and Philosophical Aspirations—The Thinking Essay

---

"I'm back." With two words, she alerts her mother that she is lucid. It is brief and fleeting. And unpredictable. These respites from her self-proclaimed "La-La Land" become rarer by the day. For a few moments, she knows her mother, knows her brother, knows herself. But try as she might to cling to reality, she knows she'll soon be taking a detour back to her *own*, less-familiar world.

She is one among many intellectually and developmentally disabled (IDD) people with whom I work. She is among many *more* in America who endure severe dementia caused by Alzheimer's disease. Her risk and manifestations of the diseases are significantly heightened, simply because of an extra chromosome. It is nature's mistake—but one I have pledged to combat.

Interning at the Lucanus Center for adults with disabilities, a forerunner in special-needs day programs, I joined a major force in battling dementia's effects in IDD people. For years, I received groceries packaged by IDD adults and practiced karate with the same sensei who taught the center's clients. Yet, this was the first *real* contact I had with this community.

And it all started with a salad. As I taught a life-skills course on healthy eating, I asserted the importance of appropriate lettuce-to-crouton ratios; my sous-chefs raised their hands to debate the chronology of spells that Harry Potter cast or sing tunes from *Grease*. Quickly, I realized the lesson was more about relating to the center's clients than about denying them the extra shredded cheese for which they notoriously hankered.

Intrigued and infatuated with my new cohorts, I sought to understand the genetic relationship between Down syndrome and the disconnected thoughts and attention-lapses I witnessed at the Lucanus Center. While researching, I uncovered horrors in American healthcare: many IDD patients are *denied* medical treatment or are misdiagnosed because of a general lack of education in IDD care, and a culture largely intolerant toward the challenges of special-needs people affected by dementia. Too often, caretakers immediately attribute IDD patients' medical symptoms and irrational behaviors to dementia—when mainly, they suffer common, though intensified, health issues.

Emotionally driven yet intellectually empowered, I joined the National Task Group on Intellectual Disabilities and Dementia Practices, collaborating with international IDD specialists, geriatricians, and advocates to reform IDD healthcare. As the group's newest—and youngest—member, I wrote new guidelines for recording IDD patients' medical histories and assessing their dementia-related sensory, intellectual, and developmental issues. However, this writing needed action. I used these tools with the Lucanus Center's clients in their *homes*, intimately experiencing late-life care for dementia-stricken IDD adults. After witnessing one client declare "I'm back!" as she fought delirium, I continued battling where she could not. I now work to establish special-needs care teams and educational programs in hospitals and help the Lucanus Center develop the first sensory-diagnostic and treatment center *specific* to IDD people. I know that with each advancement I make, IDD people move farther away from "La-La Land," *toward* the lives they deserve.

Essay 3: Academic and Philosophical Aspirations—The Thinking Essay

It's 11 a.m. on a Thursday. The swell is pumping, and the sun hangs high in the flawlessly blue California sky; yet I sit in a college classroom listening to my professor explain *le subjonctif*. Why am I spending this perfect summer day in French class? And why am I thinking about fiscal policy?

My high school had cut French classes due to California's budget issues. And why shouldn't they? It was a purely rational balancing of student demand versus government resources. My own philosophy, which champions free markets and prefers personal empowerment over hand-outs, would produce the same conclusion.

But this was French, one of my favorite classes! The melody of the words, the drama of the history, the grace of the prose—everything about French is beautiful. And it was gone. I was angry and frustrated. All at once, I was experiencing the reality of what I had so easily recommended for others.

I had worked to maintain my skills by reading French novels, but continuing to improve my grasp of the language was difficult. Despite my best efforts, I could feel the language slipping from my mind. I enrolled in summer school to retain my fluency.

It turns out that budget cuts really hurt when one is on the receiving end. The cuts took away something about which I was passionate and turned a portion of my high school plans upside down. For sure, this was hardly a life or death issue. But the surprise "punch in the gut" gave me a very personal appreciation of the disappointments and setbacks that the women I try to serve experience all too often in this age of austerity.

I spend a lot of time thinking about solutions to social problems, especially those concerning poverty. I am learning that quick-fixes and "one-size-fits-all" solutions rarely exist. I don't think that tough economic problems are insoluble, but I do know that simplistic one-track thinking is part of what makes them a problem in the first place.

Which brings me back to French. The summer class was a great experience and helped me improve my grasp of the language. But the real lesson of my summer was a more subtle understanding of the impacts of government policy and, perhaps more importantly, a more critical look at my own preconceptions. I still lean conservative. I still think spending cuts are a healthy way to trim a budget when used moderately and effectively. But I also have an appreciation for the real personal cost these solutions entail. I found perspective through my experience.

Essay 4: Academic and Philosophical Aspirations—The Thinking Essay

"The world as revealed by science is far more beautiful, and far more interesting, than we had any right to expect. Science is valuable because of the view of the universe that it gives."
—George Greenstein, Sidney Dillon Professor of Astronomy, Amherst College

My favorite animal is the kakapo. And it is my favorite animal because it is, quite simply, the most awkward species of creature that has ever been.

Kakapos are large green parrots endemic to New Zealand. They are fat, round, wobbling birds that, like many species on these predator-scarce islands, have lost the ability to fly. Instead, they waggle their way across the underbrush of the country, blinking their big, sleepy brown eyes and casually ambling their way through life, cheerful and content. What makes them so particularly wonderful, though, is that every single feature they possess just happens to be so heartwarmingly clumsy—from their back-and-forth waddle to their absurdly inefficient mating rituals to the tragic, yet undeniably hysterical, way that young kakapos sometimes scrabble up trees and, forgetting completely their last million years of evolution, leap off the highest branches, pumping their useless wings in bewilderment as they hurtle back down to the forest floor. I read that fact, and I fell in love with kakapos forever. I mean, seriously, what kind of animal forgets that it can't fly? They are hopelessly silly creatures, and for a long time this suited them just fine.

Then came Europeans, and with the Europeans came cats, and rats, and ferrets. And the kakapos simply did not understand what was going on. Nowhere in their collective consciousness or genetic memory was there anything to give them the slightest clue as to how in the world they were supposed to handle this new set of circumstances. It is, I know, misleading to use human frames of reference to describe animals, but even so: kakapos are saints. They are innocent, in every way. Because of this, there are only eighty-four of them remaining on our entire planet.

Science is a lens through which we can attempt to grasp the vast wonder of life on our planet. Science is the comprehension of who we are, where we are, why we are. It is the awareness of what we are, as individuals, as a species, as a part of a planet in which every aspect of life is connected to every other. Science is understanding that every species must live in a balance with its environment in order to survive, and it is realizing that, as a type of animal no 'higher' or 'better' or more 'chosen' than any other, humans are no exception to this rule. Science is the appreciation for just how beautiful, how awe-inspiringly, heart-stoppingly, delicately unbelievable our world really is. And this appreciation is necessary, because if we don't make ourselves look around and see the marvels that surround us now, we won't ever stop destroying them. There aren't many chances left—if we don't open our eyes soon, we'll have already missed our shot.

Two weeks ago, I read an article that contained a more depressing statistic than I could have ever imagined—every hour, three species become extinct due to human activity. The average rate of extinction for the planet before the rise of humanity was one species every century. This year, 26,000 will disappear. That's 26,000 irreplaceable forms of life, each with its unique evolutionary history spanning thousands or millions of years—gone forever.

What angered me even more than this fact were the reasons given for why this loss of biodiversity is so terrible. The article listed the usual evidence arguing that such destruction of life really harms our own: that biodiversity is important because of the benefits—chemical, medicinal, and economic—that humans can derive from it . . . that the reason we shouldn't destroy other species is because we are not sure how worthwhile they may be to us.

This logic just refuses to make itself clear to me. I can't understand how we as a species can still believe that we are above our world, when science has revealed again and again and again that we truly are a *part* of it. We are built from the same basic elements, we have evolved from the same common ancestors—we exist in the same global system. Every step forward in the evolutionary sciences shows more and more conclusively that we are on a level with every other species on Earth— we possess no inherent 'right' to life any more than anything else on this Earth. So then how can it be alright to drain an entire wetlands environment so we can have another strip mall, to burn a stretch of rainforest to make way for more grazing grounds, to over-fish a population to nothingness so we can keep our cheap seafood?

And if that's not enough reason for us humans to stop, then fine, don't do it for the wetlands or for the rainforest or for the fish—do it for us humans. We have to change how we interact with our world, if not for the world, then for the millions and millions of us who are starting to understand just what it is we may be losing.

We live today in a world that has kakapos. I have no intention of ever living in a world without them.

Essay 5: Academic and Philosophical Aspirations—The Thinking Essay

---

Medicine incorporates all of the intellectual components I am passionate about: science, ethics, philosophy, engineering, information systems, and interpersonal skills. The medical field will allow me to use technical knowledge I have and will acquire to help others in the most meaningful way possible. This is my ultimate purpose.

Certain relationships and experiences in my life have led me to medicine. First, my grandfather, "Nono," loved practicing medicine. In 1958, he made the trek from his hometown of Ceres, Argentina, where he was the town doctor, to Providence, Rhode Island, where he began to establish himself and learned psychiatry in a residency program at Miriam Hospital. That next year my mother was born. The experience at Miriam must have been meaningful because he named my mother after this hospital. Nono was always excited and wanted to share the latest prognosis of his patients with me from when I was first old enough to comprehend. He instilled his passion for using medicine to help others to me. He continued to see patients until the week before he died of cancer two years ago.

By end of third grade and three unsuccessful handwriting classes later, I was certain I would become a neurosurgeon. I also had the unfortunate experience of breaking my femur when I was 11. As I was being treated by the local paramedics, orthopedist, and air ambulance personnel, I discovered that my curiosity about the particulars of my treatment (as well as the morphine) distracted my mind from the pain. Understanding how systems work, technological or physical, fixing broken things, and inventing new solutions are what I love to do.

Since the age of 12, I have been administering subcutaneous injections to myself to treat my growth hormone deficiency. During my junior year, I found a mentor in my pediatric endocrinologist. After some phone calls to the Children's Hospital of Orange County Volunteer Office and two TB tests later, I shadowed Dr. D. every week. Since I was just a high school student, I could not give any advice to the patient, but Dr. D. often asked for my opinion on certain issues to get a patient perspective.

During high school, I created a microcosm of what I think medical school may be like. To better prepare for my medical passions, I undertook other effective experiences outside of the traditional classroom, such as the Forum on Medicine at Georgetown, Brown Psychopharmacology summer experience, and Alzheimer's research at University of California at Irvine.

Last summer, I participated in Georgetown's Forum on Medicine. The Forum whet my senses for all aspects of the medical field. I spoke to the Director of the FDA, watched live surgeries, participated in medical ethics caucuses, and proposed new ideas to conquer the deficiencies of public health, such as the AIDS epidemic. I also toured different medical schools, including University of Maryland, Johns Hopkins, and the Georgetown facilities. Witnessing these campuses as well as listening to the medical school students and deans affirmed my conviction that medicine is the right field. While at Georgetown, the student-run EMS group held an informative program about how to get involved in EMS. Many universities offer this program, which to me is invaluable because it ties theoretical knowledge of biology into first-hand treatment of a patient. I returned home and took the prerequisite classes to become an EMT so that the day I turn 18, I can begin directly helping those around me. So, after my junior year of high school, I understood the perspective of a specialist as well as the skills needed to care for anyone in any state of health. In college, I hope to contribute to the EMS team.

Essay 6: Academic and Philosophical Aspirations—The Thinking Essay

---

I have 3 brothers, 4 sisters, 1 dad, and 1 mom. This is my family; but, more important, these individuals have influenced me to pursue a career in medicine. With a large family and an even larger extended family, I rarely experience a quiet or dull moment. Apart from my large number of relatives, my exciting familial environment consists of a byproduct of the convergence of distinct personalities, experiences, and beliefs. Coming from a family of immigrants who speak two languages, practice two religions, and celebrate three ethnic traditions, I cherish Friday family dinners that commence with *challah* and conclude with *tres leches* because, like the distinct flavors that cross my palate, diversity is an integral part of my life.

Like my family, my South Florida community encompasses an increasingly culturally and ethnically varied population. Just as Friday dinners engender companionship among my family on a communal level, it is vital that members of the community engage in activities that foster a sense of camaraderie irrespective of anyone's religious or political belief, ethnicity, language, economic class, or any other distinguishing factor. As an active member of my community, I mentor young boys in their Jewish studies, I volunteer at the hospital, and I organize and mobilize beach cleanups. Through my community service, I have discovered the value of volunteer work for both those serving and those being served and its effect on building and strengthening communal bonds.

A major distinction in most communities exists between those who can afford health care and those who cannot. The schism is socially constructed, specifically dependent on one's economic class. Unlike the differences that make up my family and my community and the differences that I often celebrate, I am unwilling to accept or promote this distinction in the accessibility of health care. As a doctor, I will strive to break down that barrier and thereby bring people together. My mission will involve providing access to health care for those in need regardless of insurance coverage or the ability to pay. Ultimately, I want to study medicine because of the potential impact that I will have in my community as well as other communities.

In pursuing my career in medicine, I believe that the Case Western Dual Degree at the School of Medicine offers the perfect fit. I am primarily committed to pursuing a career in medicine, and Case provides a special opportunity to start my studies as soon as possible. Notwithstanding its opportunities to pursue a career in medicine immediately, Case leads in the focus on telehealth, a vital tool that breaks down barriers of geography and promotes access to health care and education. Aligned with my personal mission, the dual degree program will prepare me to perform medical services effectively in diverse communities while helping me to develop a solid foundation for my ongoing education in medicine.

Cultural Identity and Personal Exploration

Understanding, appreciating, or studying your heritage demonstrates your effort to self-reflect and your awareness of your personal history and family roots. Your life's legacy extends back many generations in history, and your family traditions often reflect or include pieces of your parents' and grandparents' pasts. You are a part of your history, so exploring it can be both rewarding (when you embrace your past) and also a struggle (when you challenge or grow in a new direction from your heritage). These writers delve into their own histories by exploring, investigating, or analyzing their cultural identities. These essays represent students who are trying to find out more about who they are in this world, as young adults who are part of a collective history yet charting their own individual paths as well. Personal exploration essays allow you to self-reflect; writing an essay on this topic shows the reader how you see yourself and paints a picture for them of who you think you are.

Essay 1: Cultural Identity and Personal Exploration

"Guys, it's time for kabeli! Come upstairs!" My aunt calls in her Farsi/English combination language. Instantly, we all dropped our pool cues and video game controllers. Within 2 minutes, the once-filled room was empty. My cousins and I couldn't wait to get to the boorani, kabeli, and dampoukht first, but we were always disappointed to wait for the elders—the men first, then the women, and finally the children. We all stood in line and waited patiently for our turn to serve ourselves at the eclectic homemade buffet. I, however, was always lucky to have my mom sneak me food before all my favorites were gone. This was the beginning of a typical "maymonee," or a family gathering, which was hosted by a different aunt or uncle each weekend.

I am proud to have my large family part of my life. My parents came to America in their teens to escape the war in Afghanistan. My dad is one of 4 children; my mom is one of 13. Altogether, I have 48 cousins ranging in age from 3 weeks old to 45 years old. My "Big Fat Afghan Family" is the most important thing to me. With them, I have a support system that I know will always be there. I glance at my mom sitting with her sisters laughing at past times, despite the many hardships she unfortunately had to go through, such as losing her parents at a young age and moving from a completely different country where she had everything to the United States where she had to start anew. My father also had to begin a new life after losing his father at a young age; Bobah worked four jobs simultaneously while still attending school and managed to graduate from Oxford University. It is because of my strong family history that I inherit a drive to work hard and succeed in life.

Where do I fit into this huge family of mine? I am now considered one of the "older kids," although to the even older kids, I will always be a "younger cousin." But in that same way, that is how I view my cousins younger than I. My older cousins played a role in disciplining me, and now I do the same with my younger cousins. In a good way, we are always looking out for each other. My cousins are family through blood, best friends by choice.

After eating far more food then I really needed, all of us ran back downstairs to the game room, while the men upstairs played cards, the women drank tea and watched Bollywood movies and laughed about fond memories. Later that night, my aunt tried to round up some of us to dance with them. She successfully gathered a few. The rest of us followed to see the entertainment. Upstairs, the furniture was rearranged to make room for a dance floor. We all watched my aunts and uncles dance Afghan style, hands up in the air, to Ahmad Zahir's traditional Afghan music. Soon my cousins and I were caught in the radar of our parents, and we were immediately dragged onto the dance floor. I tried my best not to show it, but I was always excited to participate. As much as we don't like to admit it, we all enjoy the dance, including the older boys that think they are too cool for it. These are the kinds of moments I live for—waking up early to help my mom prepare a traditional meal, learning to play card games, talking with my older cousin about a problem, and even dancing to classical Afghan music. I end my night by saying goodbyes, a hug and three kisses on the cheek, until my next maymonee the following weekend.

Essay 2: Cultural Identity and Personal Exploration
Roots of Value

Snap, pop, fizz! This is the sound coming from the frying pan in the kitchen as I make my way to my seat for lunch, giving my grandmother a kiss on the cheek as I walk by. "Que tal, joven?" my Uncle George greets me as he sees me stroll around the oval-shaped, wooden table, and I reach to shake his hand. As I begin to sit down my Aunt Hilda walks in the room, surprised to see me, as if I hadn't seen her the day before, but months earlier. "Como estas, hijito?" she asks. "Bien bien, y tu?" I respond as I give her a big hug. She complains about her eyesight, her teeth, and also about how forgetful she has become.

I then take my seat at the end of the table for our daily lunch. This is a tradition that began shortly after the death of a close uncle, who was like a father to me. Then, months later only to be struck by another family tragedy, my mother died. Since I was young, my parents always stressed respect for the family. They drilled it into me until they did not have to remind me anymore. I can always hear my mother in the back of my head telling me, "Saluda!" Every time I would walk into Aunt Hilda's house, the first thing I had to do was say "hello" to everyone.

For a long time, my real father was around but emotionally distant, shadowing his pain with can after can of beer. Although I saw him often, we were more far apart than ever. He ran into trouble with the law, lost almost every possession he ever worked for, except his business. But the most painful loss was his two youngest children, my half siblings, who are with their mother in an unknown location. Eventually, his emotions and the law caught up with him. As a young adolescent, I observed his behavior and vowed I did not want to become like him. After losing my two closest family members, the rest of the family somewhat dispersed and eventually lost touch. However, I continued to visit my grandmother, her sister (Hilda), and her husband (George). *Mis Viejos,* as I call them, means "My Elders."

During our lunches *Mis Viejos* tell me about their lives growing up and family values. They argue about religious beliefs (Seventh Day Adventist vs. Catholic), talk about family I have not met in Peru, and discuss social problems they heard on the news. I often think about how it will be one day when these people, who are so close to me, are gone. Aunt Hilda always tells me in Spanish, "I will always care for you until the day I close my eyes and take my last breath." For years she has said this to me, but not until recently have those words meant something to me: no matter what, my family will always love me, and with them, I will give back that same kind of love.

If it was not for my daily lunches with *Mis Viejos,* I would not have found the willpower and patience to become the person I am today, a person who values family more than anything. And with that I hope to pass those same traditions and love on to my descendants. So as I sit at the table, day after day waiting for *Mis Viejos* to finish their meal, I am grateful that after all the tragedy our family has gone through, we have stuck together and remained close.

Essay 3: Cultural Identity and Personal Exploration

Thirty-nine owls sit perched upon my shelf, each one with a unique design and story. I began my collection in sixth grade, and, since then, I have compiled a motley crew made up of Japanese, Chinese, Venezuelan, Peruvian, Vietnamese, Mexican, American, and other international owls. Growing up as a world traveler and an immigrant exposed me to a wide range of people, cultures, and histories. With this, I gained a greater understanding of the diversity surrounding me and an appreciation for the similarities between these seemingly disparate societies.

My colorful Venezuelan owl doubles as a whistle. This quality is significant in that the first words that came from me were in Spanish. My multilingualism began with my birth in Venezuela and continues because my parents reiterate the importance of learning several languages. As a result we only speak Spanish at home. I also spent the summer before last improving my Spanish at a school in Argentina, while living in my Argentinian family's home, immersing myself in the language. This reminds me of the value Hispanic culture places on family. *Mi familia* plays a huge role in my life. I spend every spare moment laughing and playing with them, reveling in their company. Clearly, the gregarious nature of Venezuelans has rubbed off on me.

My grandmother passed on her own owl collection to me, her elegant creatures originating in countries of Eastern Europe. My roots in Europe and my grandfather's history as a Holocaust survivor contribute to my identity. Being Jewish is not only a religion but also a culture. Her owls remind me of the ancient traditions in my family that survived persecution and near annihilation. I live with the burden of finding my place in this world, giving purpose to my life and to my grandfathers'. I find myself conversing with my grandparents about the past, discovering their hometowns and their childhoods through their stories. I gain an appreciation for the similarities between the customs they had in Romania and those, like Friday night *Shabbat* dinner, that I keep alive.

The majority of my owls hail from Asia, because this is where I began my collection, while living in Japan. My friends in Japan were international, just like my owls. With close friends from India, France, Pakistan, Israel, and Korea, not to mention Japan, I learned that we all had commonalities. My two years in Japan included much travel to neighboring countries, but it was also a time for me to adapt to this foreign culture. I quickly accustomed myself to the different language, studying Japanese in school, and customs, making sure to give my seat to the elderly on the subway or bus. In addition to emotionally adapting to a new home, I embraced Japanese idiosyncrasies, such as their punctuality and meticulousness, becoming a detail-oriented worker.

It was difficult to find an authentic "South-Floridian" owl; the ones I came upon were made in China, Peru, even Indonesia. But this makes sense in the context of my home here, because South Florida is a melting pot where all cultures and people mix together—it is an international community in itself. So I chose to buy a Brazilian owl to represent my current home. Living here, I can learn about Brazilian martial arts dance, *Capoeira,* from a friend at volleyball, or understand the Portuguese she speaks with her mother if they slow down the conversation. I know to be true that looks may be deceiving, and I am an example of this. With a "European look" many are surprised to hear me speak to my siblings in my native tongue, but in South Florida everyone is comfortable and expects to hear conversations in various languages.

My owl collection is dear to me because it reminds me of the international immigrant that I am. These inanimate objects have traveled far and wide with me but always remained true to their roots. Despite relocation, I have never lost sight of my family's values and ideals. No move has diluted my being; if anything, moving has strengthened the person I am. Accepting from and assimilating to the cultures I encountered in my travels enriched my life. Furthermore, I learned to start anew in a place where I had no history, but I always made sure to carry my history with me. At Rice, I will pursue my purpose in life, approaching my studies seriously and actively participating in community service. With this new stage in my life, I will find an adopted family and support group while discovering yet one more owl.

Essay 4: Cultural Identity and Personal Exploration

I journeyed to Argentina with one small suitcase, a diagram of my family tree, and an embossed, leather-bound journal. A few years earlier, I had visited the country with my family. But this time I was alone. When my mother was 17, she backpacked Argentina, learning the land of her parents and building relationships with her extended family. When I turned 17, I decided to follow in her footsteps.

My quest began on a ranch in Capitan Sarmiento, a rural town on the outskirts of Buenos Aires. The idyllic campo (ranch) featured gallant, richly-dark racehorses, a medley of farm animals, and lush plains. The natural simplicity and humble beauty of my cousin's ranch was totally foreign and completely intriguing to me. I felt an intuitive satisfaction in being at the campo and observing the freedom to live simply on the self-sustaining ranch. During my stay, I relished in the epic, 3-hour meal times with my cousins, devouring handmade chorizo (sausage) or ravioli caseros (homemade), watching the cebador (server) prepare the mate (tea) for the next lover of the heady, herbal brew.

I began to recognize a vast contrast between Argentine and American culture—namely the role of intimacy. Argentines create an inclusive environment that begins and ends with a kiss and embraces all the passionate chatter in between. I am not usually comfortable with this level of physical affection, but I soon began to find it intoxicating. It promotes incredibly meaningful and sincere social interactions.

I also observed cultural similarities. I discovered a deep commonality inherent within me, the Argentines, and disciples of philosophy. During a car ride with my cousin Paula, she confessed to me her fear of living a life pursuing materialism rather than humble satisfaction. A few days later, I was at the campo helping set the table for dinner when I thought about the inherent differences between Paula's urban life and the world on the ranch, surrounded by close family and the calm of nature. Life on the campo lacks the technology and convenience of big-city life, but it offers an extraordinary world of autonomy and tranquility.

Existentialists would say that life is inherently meaningless, and that human endeavors solely serve to pass the time until death. Everything is subjective. I have often wondered whether humans spend too much time feeling caught up in what the future has without capitalizing on the present moment. First and foremost, Argentina illuminated this for me.

I ventured to Argentina seeking my familial and cultural understanding. What I found was similarity and a unifying quality within humanity. I found that sometimes the best education and insight into human nature transcends the walls of the classroom. I found that I enjoy unearthing the core of the human condition. Exploring these questions binds us together. More important, I found that I enjoy grappling with these human queries from different perspectives.

What do philosophy, politics, and psychology have in common? An Argentine-American girl sipping mate at the kitchen table.

Essay 5: Cultural Identity and Personal Exploration

It is April 1915. All the men in town, including your father, have been executed. Your mother, siblings, and neighbors huddle in the church, praying for divine intervention to save them from certain death. You aren't with them. Your mother sent you running when the soldiers came. Now, you are half way to the border with money to buy a one-way ticket to Greece. Forced away from the land, culture, and people you love to save your life, you make the only choice a 10-year-old boy can: You keep running.

When my great-grandfather Takvor, the sole survivor in his family, and other Armenian refugees fled during the genocide by the Ottoman Turks, they left behind their beloved homeland, never to return. Today, a worldwide Armenian Diaspora outnumbers the population in the Armenian homeland because of this forced dispersion. The refugees couldn't foresee the better quality of life that has graced their descendants outside Armenia; because of the refugees' courage and faith, their descendants can provide aid to a homeland ravaged by earthquakes and political unrest. Shouldn't we, the Diaspora, help the descendants of those left behind? If we don't provide aid to our brothers and sisters, who will?

It is June 2012. I have persuaded my mother to leave her private medical practice and embark with me on the Armenian Missionary Association of America's Medical Missions Trip to set up ambulatory clinics in remote Armenian villages. Traveling with a team of 7 doctors, following a grueling schedule, with limited technology, we treat over a thousand patients in clinics in Stepanavan and Vanadzor. I test urine samples for blood and glucose and help distribute the prescription drugs we purchased through fundraising. We work nonstop, seeing and serving the land and people my ancestors so tearfully fled.

The close of the clinic's eighth day brings a pounding on the monolithic church door in Vanadzor, one of the major centers of destruction during the 1988 Spitak earthquake. The team is running on the fumes of exhaustion, but I open the door. A distraught mother pushes past me with her young son, begging in Armenian, *"Our en Pjishgneruh?"* ("Where are the doctors?") She has traveled hours and begs me to have her son Vahe seen. Each night, with our medical team overcome with fatigue, I crush the hopes of those, like this woman, who arrive too late and send them away. But tonight I'm drawn to this child who shares a name with my father and long brown hair and big brown eyes with me. Save for his weak body, he could pass for my younger brother David. I don't have the heart to turn them away. "Let me find my mother," I reply, knowing she will share my compassion.

In the makeshift examination room, we learn that Vahe has diabetes, and his family spends most of its income on insulin to keep him alive. He sits stoically, never flinching, peering at me with sad determination as I prick his finger. My heart melts as his mother speaks of her hope that we have a cure from America. She is desperate, but no amount of desperation can change the fact that there is no cure for Vahe anywhere in the world. My mother turns to me with tears in her eyes and asks, "How am I supposed to tell her?"

While watching my mother's caring treatment of Vahe and our Armenian brothers and sisters she ministered to on the trip, I was in awe of her ability to meet their needs both physically and spiritually, pushing herself beyond human endurance to serve the countrymen my great-grandparents left behind. It was in these moments that I understood that it is now my turn to study medicine and inherit this gift of healing from my mother. I will return on the mission this summer to end my great-grandfather's journey and begin my own.

Essay 6: Cultural Identity and Personal Exploration

Every summer. Every Sunday. Every sundown. We prepared to sacrifice our body and our spirits to experience perfection. Some simply call it meat. We call it marbled bliss. Some say A-1 Steak Sauce. We swiftly reply Chimichurri. Some call it barbeque. We think tradition. We call it "Asado".

When my Grandpa arrived in this country fifty years ago to complete his psychiatric residency, he brought much more than an Argentine medical license, his wife, and belongings. He brought with him the tradition of the Argentine barbeque: El Asado. My Grandpa, "Nono," compelled me to learn this art not so much for sustenance, but primarily for emotional wellness.

Four hours, many dollars, and three carnecerias ago, the process began. I slowly moved my quivering hand towards the waiting flesh. Using my finger as a tool, I examined the cut. My eyes closed, full attention on the cut, knees trembling, selection made. *Perfection, I know it is—consistency perfect—full marbling—grain fed—oooh it's gonna be amazing.* Of course, for the Asado we had to use charcoal.

I tossed each mesquite charcoal into the aluminum starter basket; I struck a thick wood match and the red-stained tip hissed in pain as it ignited. The black grill sizzled as it reached to touch the cold red chops. My Nono took over 3 hours to cook the meat. All the while we spoke of politics, medicine, philosophy, and diet. My family sat in anticipation of what this week's Asado would bring. Glistening with molten fats, smelling of sweet burnt mesquite wood, the steak marked in a criss-cross pattern, we pulled the chops off the barbeque.

Before serving our masterpiece, I instinctively analyzed the steak for any impurities. My serrated stainless steel blade subtly punctured the outer layer. I carefully inhaled the pungent aroma like a wine connoisseur inspecting his glass. The gleaming yellow sun lowered to a deep mesmerizing swirl of orange and light purple.

This is definitely worth it.

"La carne esta lista," Nono assertively exclaimed.

I miss those Asados with my Nono. Unfortunately, he passed away two years ago. I know now that he solidified, through this rich tradition, his chance for immortality. More important, he imparted to me this spiritual technique for relaxing the soul, refocusing the mind, de-stressing the body. With his departure, I feel a renewed sense of life.

The legacy of my Nono will live on vicariously through my actions and passions. His relentless enthusiasm for the Asado reflects his love of culture. His legacy will be carried on through the morals he gave to me.

Essay 7: Cultural Identity and Personal Exploration

We were told to smile as we posed for a group photo. It had the makings of a perfect shot—a cloudless sky, a picturesque background, and several laughing students in the foreground. I huddled with my classmates for warmth as we joked around like any other rowdy seventh-graders. All would have been wonderful if not for the destroyed building that stood behind us. As we stood in front of what remained of the Atomic-Bomb Dome, Mr. R. counted down. "Three . . ." We made sure everyone was visible, "Two . . ." I held hands with my friends, "One . . ." it was all gone.

This same countdown preceded the atomic bomb's release, instantaneously obliterating an entire city. Here, the gravity of Hiroshima's history seemed heavier than ever. I realized that someone standing in front of this building sixty-seven years ago was wiped off the face of the earth when the bomb exploded.

Later, we sat quietly listening to Miyoko M.'s broken English as she told us her story. Recalling the day she survived the bombing, she mourned the loss of her classmates who were not as fortunate. I noticed the scars on her face, hidden by makeup and treatments. But I saw past this, noticing the torment in her gaze, which was completely unveiled.

Meeting Matsubara S. and traveling to Hiroshima enabled me to see history through the eyes of another. Until then, I always associated World War II with the Holocaust, since I am the granddaughter of 2 survivors. As an American citizen, I understood the losses endured by our soldiers. Living two years in Japan helped me appreciate and recognize that there is more than one side to every story.

Hiroshima, once an empty wasteland and graveyard of a town, is now inhabited by those who live with the reminder of its terrible history. *Hibakushas*, survivors like Matsubara-san, deal with the repercussions of war and hate. I came to this realization because, unlike most teenagers caught up in pop culture, I was gaining a greater understanding of the world around me. I had the power to see past superficial scars, the sensitivity to see beyond the physical world.

After these two years my outlook on life was completely changed. I gained an understanding of how to connect with people on a deeper emotional level, and this affected every aspect of my life. As a biomedical engineer, I will apply this gift to advancing the ways humans interact with technology. I hope to work beyond the insensitive metallic qualities of technology, integrating a necessary human touch into the approach used to make machines, to achieve my ultimate goal of bettering the lives of others.

My diverse life experiences as an immigrant, a Hispanic, a woman, and a global nomad allow me to see from many perspectives. The photograph we took and my experience that day in Hiroshima taught me that there is more than what we see in a picture. Every story is multifaceted, just as the one of a group of kids in front of a crumbling building.

Essay 8: Cultural Identity and Personal Exploration

I jumped up and down to catch a glimpse of what everyone was looking at, but it was useless. I found myself in a mob of people struggling to see the awe-inspiring event. As I squeezed through the throng of people, my body brushed up against the arms and legs of the crowd. Finally, I found myself adjacent to the display that had brought so much attention. Soon I was dragged into the show as 2 dancers pulled me onto the stage. I peered down at my feet and theirs, trying to follow the crossover steps and footwork they performed. I moved in a large line of girls and boys who all performed in unison. We encircled musicians playing unusual instruments. A handsome looking man blew into the skin of a goat. Whoever thought that a dead goat could make such an interesting sound? "Yiasas!" and "Ela!" the dancers shouted. High-pitched whistles, clapping, and cheers from the crowd dictated the beat as the music and rhythm quickened. I glanced at the audience and saw faces of fascination, relaxation, and enthusiasm. All eyes fixed themselves on the stage. Tables of families, couples, friends, and children gathered around the music. Mingling, sipping coffees, talking, and eating, the entire crowd was euphoric. This was my first exposure to Greek dance.

"George, what do you think about joining Greek Dance?"

"Well, I am not exactly a great ballerina, Mom."

"It is not ballet, and even if it was, haven't you heard of the professional football players who dance to help their footwork skills? Your God brothers George and Eli also do Greek dance," she stated.

"Oh, really? I'll think about it."

"Good! I signed you up today," she remarks.

"Are you serious? Even Dad thinks dance is for wussies and girly men."

"Pshhh . . . Your father met me at a Greek festival, and he was mesmerized with the dance."

My first dance practice. I stared at the clock wondering when I could leave. I glanced around the room and saw 13 girls and only 2 other boys, who looked especially weird to me. One was awkwardly tall, and I automatically thought he was here to fix his basketball footwork. The other looked like a skateboard punk. I could not imagine that these boys would eventually become my 2 best friends.

V. was my director. He spoke quietly yet sternly. He began practice by showing me steps from the Greek island of Kalymnos. This type of dancing was light-footed, quick, and elegant compared to the music and dance of the island of Crete where most songs dealt with war and times of hardship. I followed his steps and quickly caught on. What was especially surprising was that on the very first day of practice, V. placed me in the front of the line. I had heard of the consequences of becoming the line leader. Not only did the leader have to maintain a fit circle, but he also was responsible for providing the tricks or intricate footwork that judges critiqued. Each practice I returned to the middle of the line, but each time V. moved me to the honor of the front. Slowly my love for Greek dance grew. No longer a chore, I now look forward to dancing every week. I am only as strong as my weakest link. Although my skills greatly improve, I assist my male and female partners so we can all dance in perfect unison.

Greek dance teaches me camaraderie and teamwork and ignites my passion for my culture. Whether it is performing complex footwork, squats, or even being able to jump the highest, I put forth my best effort. I have learned that if I truly love what I am doing and put in effort, hard work, emotional commitment, and time, my passion translates to the audience who responds with greater enthusiasm. Learning to apply this philosophy has also impacted my work on the golf course, the classroom, and in my volunteering. I try to be passionate and give my full heart to what I pursue and hope that my enthusiasm is contagious. Also I am now less quick to judge new ideas and situations different from the traditions that are familiar to me; Greek dance makes me more open to new ideas and cultures.

Dance is now my passion—a discipline, joy, and skill I will carry with me and continue to perfect throughout my life. Not only has it been contagious in my life, but it has been a communal energy that has evolved in the lives of millions of Greeks throughout the centuries.

And surprisingly, to my mother's delight, Greek dance enhances my social skills and has even helped my soccer skills, too.

Essay 9: Cultural Identity and Personal Exploration

Unlike most English freaks who cling to the words of Shakespeare and Whitman, my life motto has been set since the second grade. "Ready or not, here I come," has always been my personal apothegm, even before I could comprehend poetry, literature, and philosophy.

As a child playing hide-and-seek, I always volunteered to be the hider—never quite having the courage to close my eyes and count to 10 before seizing a challenge. As one who is not afraid of new adventures, I have tasted every flavor of Yoplait yogurt, belted a solo in the spring musical, and built a snowman with orange peppers instead of a carrot nose. But I had never been the seeker of my own destiny.

Most people grow up and leave childhood secrets on the playground, but I kept mine locked away throughout most of high school. At a small, private, and religious school, I strived to uphold the image of a perfect Jewish girl, serving as president of my town's B'nai B'rith Youth Organization chapter and striving to be a role model for my community. However, no amount of Hebrew classes or Jewish youth conventions hindered my secret from surfacing. I was divided into two persons: the Jewish me and the lesbian me.

During my junior year of high school, the seeker within me emerged, fueled with a new sense of confidence and pride that soon catalyzed into action and self-discovery. I spoke up, and a supporting network of family and friends began to surround me. Recently, I embarked on a weekend *Shabbaton* in Connecticut through Keshet, an organization that promotes inclusion for LGBT individuals within the Jewish community. I was struck with an epiphany. Eureka. Suddenly one moment brought all essences of my being into coalition: the reality was that I had always been an observant Jew and a proud lesbian. However, I have never known how to be a proud Jewish lesbian. I had never even considered two diverse defining traits to be used in the same sentence.

With shaking palms and great aspirations, I was elected Regional President of the South Florida hub of BBYO this past March. My success was validated by the idea that my peers recognize me as a leader for both the Jewish and the LGBT communities. As a hider who was once conformed to societal pressures, I now seek to find myself and redefine the misperceived notion that religion and sexuality cannot coincide.

In the process of breaking down the stereotypes and barriers of both communities, I am learning how to be a voice not only for myself but for my peers as well. From founding the Diversity and Identity Club at my Jewish day school, to working as a freelance writer for *Miami Herald*'s Gay South Florida, I have spoken more in the past year than I have in all of my seventeen years of existence.

As an advocate, a dreamer, a fighter, and a storyteller, I have shed my childhood secrets without forgetting what is was like on the playground. I haven't quite yet won a Pulitzer Prize or written a best-seller, but my veins bleed ambition and pump curiosity. So, ready or not, here I come.

Essay 10: Cultural Identity and Personal *Exploration*

"That's so gay." This common, seemingly innocuous teenage phrase that I often hear is something that I used to say—but not anymore. Every time I hear the word "gay" or any other derogatory term to classify a homosexual person, I look down to my left wrist and read the words imprinted on my faded yellow-green bracelet, "Change the Course: AIDS Walk SF" and remember the summer experience I had and how it changed my life forever.

When I arrived at camp last year, I joined 26 other teenagers who had no idea what was going to happen in the seven weeks ahead of us. We were taught about AIDS in every way possible: through programs, articles, movies, and motivational speakers. I learned that before much was known about the AIDS virus, homosexual individuals were blamed for the disease. We watched the movie "Philadelphia," and I was shocked by the prejudice shown in the film. Throughout the movie, intolerance and discrimination were demonstrated again and again. I promised myself that I would become more tolerant, and this exposure marked the beginning of my transformation to becoming a more socially aware person.

A few months later I found myself in an uncomfortable situation. I volunteered in San Francisco for my Jewish youth group. I passed out fliers trying to educate the public about the iniquities that immigrants encounter when seeking U.S. citizenship, and I collected over 100 signatures to lobby for equal rights. My friend Mica and I approached a respectable looking man in a business suit and asked, "Would you please sign our petition to help people seeking citizenship?" Mica is a Chinese-American and, like me, is also Jewish. The businessman glanced at the Jewish Star of David symbol on our t-shirts. He responded coldly, shocking me with his bigoted answer, "Why would I help you? You, stupid Chink-Kyke." Mica miraculously kept it together, but I could see her barely holding back the tears. She somehow managed to squeeze out a very polite, "Thank you." My face burned in shame as I comforted my friend and empathized, "What a jerk! Obviously that guy is anti-Semitic. He could certainly use a lesson in Tikkun Olam (Hebrew for 'making the world a better place')." My friend nodded and we hugged tightly.

Before my transformation, I'm embarrassed to admit that I was probably like many other Caucasian males who are raised in a homogeneous community. I had not come in much contact with diversity or adversity. But now that I have become more aware and educated, I see myself as a budding activist.

Another key opportunity presented itself when I participated in the AIDS Walk San Francisco. The starting pistol went off, and thousands of bodies began moving—the culmination of our six weeks of preparation for the event that included fundraising and a blood drive. The blood drive was the hardest part for me since I'm petrified of needles, but I gritted my teeth and gave my healthy blood for a good cause. The 10K walk raised over $4.2 million, and I was proud to have been a part of that. Completing the AIDS Walk symbolically completed my transformation. During the walk it occurred to me: I no longer cared if someone was gay or straight, black or white, Chinese or Mexican. It didn't really matter.

Recently I found out that a very close friend of mine is homosexual. Although I hate to admit it, before my enlightening experiences these past summers this news would have been a problem for my relationship with him. Now, I don't see Adam as gay; I see Adam as Adam. Tolerance is a virtue that anyone can learn if they choose to be open-minded and educate themselves. I'm happy that I have changed my perceptions and preconceived notions. I didn't realize how sheltered my community was with regard to people who are "different." I look at my faded bracelet on my left wrist often and remind myself of what I have learned. So now, whenever I hear a comment like "that's so gay" from a friend of mine or witness any form of prejudice, I speak up and make sure my voice is heard.

In college, I will bring my open-mindedness to my campus community. I look forward to appreciating others' differences as I continue to learn and grow as a tolerant human being.

Humorous and Miscellaneous

Some essays just don't fall into a clear category. There are those that are simply funny. Others are about topics that are quirky and daring. And other essays take their reader in new directions. Many students also play with their writing style in various creative ways. If you are an outside-the-box kind of person, have a wicked sense of humor, or are a bit daring, these essays might appeal to you.

Essay 1: Humorous and Miscellaneous

"Just a couple hours on the weekend helping with some simple work," is all that my mom said about the job that she had found for me. The real job description was helping an older neighbor woman with work in and around her horse stables, right down the street from my house. My new boss told me what tools I needed before I came, so I went to a supply store to purchase my equipment. The first item, rubber boots, should have been a dead giveaway for what was ahead. This could mean one of two things: she cared about me getting my shoes dirty, or the boots were a necessity for the job.

The first Saturday was a blazing 90 degrees, and not only did the heat affect me but also the work I had to do made it even tougher. I had to level out all of the horses' stalls with sand. My new boots were quickly saturated with urine and manure and other barn crud. Back and forth I trudged the whole morning, with nothing more than a wheelbarrow and a shovel. My arms were ready to fall off, and my shoulders had never burned more in my life. To make matters worse, my gloves had not done their job. I had huge blisters developing on the palms of each of my hands. I thought my boss, Nancy, would have a water fountain or at least offer me a drink. But, unfortunately, she didn't, so I was left to drink warm, rubber-tasting water from a crusty, green hose.

After the first two weeks, I pretty much had established my routine: I'd fill the small trash cans, empty them into the larger cans, and haul those cans to the dumpsters. Then I would grab the most worthless rake from the shed and rake up the small branches from around the stalls. Next, I'd take a hoe and chop at weeds the size of trees. I would also clean up the hay that had been pushed out of the stables by the horses. As I did my work, I would overhear the owners talking to their horses. These conversations were some of oddest I had ever heard. These people were having complete dialogues with their horses, and even singing to them! Even I talk to my dog by saying things like, "Good boy," or "Are you hungry?" knowing that he won't answer except with a wag of his tail. But these people were talking to the horses as if they were expecting a reply. It was hard to work and keep myself from laughing at the same time. By the end of that day I thought to myself, "I'm earning money, getting free entertainment, and making a difference to the stable owner, so why even complain about only making $5 an hour?"

A few weeks into my job there was a turn for the worse. It had rained during the week, so I figured it would be dry by Saturday, my work day. But no, it wasn't dry at all; it was horrible! I couldn't even walk through the mud. I was wearing the rubber boots made for the job, and my feet were cemented in sludge. At every step my boots seemed to sink further and further into the crud. This wasn't the part that was hard to handle. It was the smell. The sickening odor was hard to stomach. The smell of horse urine and manure made me gag. Having to walk and work in this pool of stink and worse, and having it splash on my clothes, pushed me over the edge. I thought I felt bad, but the poor horses had to stand in it all day! They had no place to escape and of course they couldn't lie down. Due to the harsh conditions that day, my priority was to take twenty bags of sawdust and spread them throughout the horse stalls without agitating them even more. I lugged bag after bag to each stall and spread the dust to absorb the excess water. This would hopefully prevent infection in their hooves. The minutes seemed like hours that day, but I knew I had to get the job done. Nancy and the horses were depending on me.

After two years of shoveling and raking every Saturday, enduring the elements for little money and a lot of praise, I would probably still be working for Nancy if her stables hadn't been closed down. It's from all of the time spent toiling, shoveling, sweating, hauling, dumping, scooping, and swearing that I've learned some important life lessons. I have a new respect for manual laborers and the hard, back-breaking work they do for such minimal pay. I also understand how much work is involved in caring for and tending to animals. I was amazed at the affection people feel for their animals. Whenever I look at my rubber boots, which are stored in the shed on the side of my house, the memories of my time spent at Nancy's stables come flooding back, and I chuckle and smile.

Essay 2: Humorous and Miscellaneous

Author's Note: This student references a specific name of a college here. I have made it generic for the purposes of publication. The school he applied to was one that did not use the Common Application. Instead, it had its own independent online application, which was why he could reference the school directly.

My sister Jessie is a junior in college.

I was born into this world approximately two years and eleven months after Jessie; she took the blow exceedingly hard.

Before I was born, Jessie had been on easy street. She had an entire family, a parent, grandparents, aunts, uncles, and cousins, all under her complete and total domination. Basking was what she did best, and the attention she received was always undivided—sharing was a concept totally unconnected to her life. And then, just as it seemed there could be no conceivable obstacle to her continued hegemony, I showed up. Jessie was not happy.

Simply by existing, I shattered her whole way of life; I was cute. Honestly, I was damned cute, and suddenly people were looking at me, complimenting me, focusing on me. My sister was devastated . . . but by no means was she finished. Jessie was smart, and, more than that, she was ruthless—by the age of 3, she could have taught Bismarck a thing or two about real politik and added a few more chapters to Machiavelli's manual. When I was born, I ended Jessie's dictatorship over the adults of our family, but I provided her with a new subject over which to extend her rule.

The manipulation began at once, and, as usually is the case in these situations, enslavement followed soon after. As soon as I could control my hands, I was giving her the things she wanted; as soon as I could walk, I was getting her the things she wanted; as soon as I could speak, I was saying the things she wanted. My mother, peering down from her Olympian heights, had no idea what went on. She saw only what Jessie wanted her to see; she'd observe us take our snacks outside to eat them, but she'd never notice that three and a half of the four mini-doughnuts went into Jessie's mouth; she'd see us playing in the back yard, but she never once glimpsed me eating dirt because my sister said it would taste like nachos.

Oh, the lies. The lies were her specialty. They were like pieces of art to her, each processed and created with the utmost love and care. And I was absolutely defenseless against them. She was three years older than I was; she had three more years of life experience and knowledge to sharpen into arrows, and her aim was flawless. Some of the stories were just plain bizarre; I remember in particular the full week I believed that, next Friday, a real Princess was coming to our house for dinner, but I wouldn't be allowed to come because the Princess hated boys with curly hair. My mother caught me twice during that week trying to cut off my own hair, but I could give no truthful answers to her questions because she might tell the Princess that my hair had been curly before I cut it off, and then I'd be right back where I started.

Mom was gone large parts of the day, and the babysitter was easily dismissed, a mere prop. Jessie was my father, my mother, and my master, and I was indubitably at her command. But there comes a day in every such relationship when the child breaks from the parents, when the slave rises up against the whip. My day came, and it was glorious.

Strange as it seems, this monumental day began quite normally. Nothing happened that morning that would have caused anyone to think a momentous occasion was about to unfold. I was playing with my dinosaurs when Jessie announced I was to help her continue construction on the dollhouse we were creating from cardboard and our mom's carpet samples. I obeyed, of course, as usual—little did I know that something very, very unusual was about to happen.

I don't remember the moment perfectly; it has over time fizzled and expanded into an almost dreamlike recollection. But what I remember is enough. Jessie needed scissors, and she ordered me upstairs to bring them down for her. It was a perfectly normal order, the type that I had fulfilled thousands of times in the past without thinking. But this time, I did think. For the first time in all my 5½ years, it occurred to me that I had gone to get the scissors last time, and the time before that, and the time before that. In fact, it suddenly occurred to me that I went to get the scissors *every* time Jessie needed scissors, which, it suddenly occurred to me, was not good and not fair. And Jessie was repeating, her voice full of power and ice and puppet strings, "Aaron, go get me some scissors."

I looked at her in the eyes, and I stood up, and for an instant, time stood still. Birds stopped chirping, trees stopped rustling, and the Earth was silent. And suddenly a gust of wind blew in through the basement windows and wisped around my small body, and at that moment I was Harriet Tubman and Abraham Lincoln and Moses, and the noise that burst from my mouth was an underground railroad and an Emancipation Proclamation and a parted sea, and the entire world was motionless except for my one word ringing in the air, and I said, "No."

The wind held the word up for an impossibly long time, a fraction of a second, and then blew it away, along with the faint sounds of ice breaking and strings being cut. Jessie's widened eyes went back into her head, and the moment was gone. But both of our lives were irretrievably, irrevocably altered in that second and that word, the first of its kind to have ever left my lips. Not many people knew it; it was not on the news or in the magazines, but that day a thousand monarchs fell and a million slaves were freed, and Jessie sat for several seconds in thought, and then got up and went upstairs to get the scissors herself. She came back down with them, and we continued to play much as before. But everything was different, and when the Princess died three years later, I knew with almost complete certainty that my curly hair had had nothing to do with it.

That's why it's really ok with me that I want to go to your college. It may be her college now, but I'm confident that next year, if I'm careful to bring my own scissors, I can make it mine, as well.

Essay 3: Humorous and Miscellaneous

It is creased, it is dog-eared, and it is extremely important to me. It travels everywhere I go securely tucked into the front right pocket of my pants, and, if I don't have any pockets, it gets folded into my left sock. My *To Do List* and I are rarely apart. At first glance, my *To Do List* may seem unimportant and insignificant. In fact, to the untrained eye, my *To Do List* may appear to be just a piece of trash. To me, however, this ugly, absurd piece of paper is more than sentimental: it is my life!

I understand that this object is not "important" in the way many people's parents, siblings, or best friends are. However, this does not make my list any less valuable. My list and its regular use are disaster-prevention measures. How many moms will be going to college with their offspring to keep lists for them of everything to be done? I know my mom will not be! I anticipate an increase in the number of items on my list in college, and with detailed planning and some luck, my *To Do List* will travel with me working overtime to keep me organized.

Now, what significance could a 3.5 x 5-inch piece of paper have to a teenager? Well, this piece of paper helps me sleep better at night. It accomplishes this by lessening stress. First, there is no better feeling than crossing something off my list, whether it is something big like writing a speech for Spanish class or just a small thing like returning a phone call. The simple act of running a satisfying line through a few words always feels great. Second, everyone, at one time or another, has spent a sleepless night pondering, "What have I forgotten to do?" The lucky ones are the people who have not forgotten anything because they, too, have a system for remembering things. An iPhone or electronic planner may work well for many people, but my old-fashioned paper-and-pencil method suits me just fine. The unlucky ones are those who have lost an entire night of sleep and have still forgotten something important or even just spent a night trying to remember something until sunrise. I, however, just pop up, write my thought down and go back to my *"zzz's."* With a *To Do List* I know I have not forgotten anything, and therefore I sleep comfortably. A *To Do List* is also a "timely" companion. My *To Do List* forces me to make good use of my time and avoid procrastination. The list always seems to be standing over my shoulder (perhaps that's just my conscience), constantly reminding me that I have several important tasks to complete, like buying my friend a birthday present or meeting with a teacher before school. Come to think of it, without my *To Do List*, this essay probably would not have been written for two more weeks!

A *To Do List* keeps me organized, focused, and on-track regarding my responsibilities. Completing jobs in a timely and efficient manner is a habit I have worked to establish. Being responsible is a way in which I would like to be perceived by others. Carrying and following a *To Do List* help me achieve these goals. I wouldn't live without it!

Essay 4: Humorous and Miscellaneous

I like to laugh. I like to have fun. And, sometimes, I like to be ridiculous. Yes, ridiculous! In fact, I think ridiculous is highly underrated. Ridiculous is defined as "deserving or inspiring ridicule, preposterous or silly." But, in order to inspire ridicule, you need to take a chance—a chance to be laughed at or a chance to succeed.

My love of the ridiculous is not to say that I do not take things seriously. I do. I work hard at school, and I try to be the best athlete I can be. I am an intense competitor both in the classroom and on the field. But embracing the ridiculous, the willingness to be ridiculed, can be more personally rewarding.

Like most high schools, fall semester social life centers around the football games. Largely, these games are just an excuse to get together with friends to laugh, have fun, and, yes, be ridiculous. But unlike most high schools, mine does not have cheerleaders. Notably, I think this is ridiculous (defined here as "preposterous or silly"). Along with a few of my friends, we decided to rectify this American travesty. But, because we were "a bunch of dudes," we could not become a cheerleader squad in the traditional sense. What we came up with was the Shockers.

The Shockers are a band of spirited friends each with a different, self-made costume. Green is the school color, so the costumes became a zany collage of mismatched green and white tights, headbands, hats, and other garish accessories. We selected one of the privileged beings to be our designated mascot, Bolt Boy, and created a whole Tolkien-like story around the creation of Bolt Boy and the Shockers. We were able to share our elaborate mythical story at the school assembly before our first game appearance.

When the Shockers appeared at the game, to my amazement, the fans seemed as if they were watching and cheering for us more than the football team. In each subsequent game, both the students and the parents welcomed my ridiculous band of friends in green and white tights as a missing ingredient to the football season. Our game appearances grew more staged, and attendance at the football games grew.

It has been nearly a year since creation of Bolt Boy and the Shockers, and the tradition seems destined to live on; a new Bolt Boy has been selected to continue the legacy after our graduation.

By some accounts, dressing up in a ridiculous costume to cheer my high school football team is completely inconsistent with my personality. In so many other respects, I am intense. I am intense about school; I am intense about soccer and lacrosse; I am intense about coaching soccer; and I am intense (and passionate) about computer programming. I have taught myself HTML, Delphi, Pascal, and C++. The college course I took this summer was in particle physics. Most people probably would not think these are ridiculous endeavors. But to me, ridiculous does not mean stupid or even foolish; it means occasionally taking chances.

I took a chance by dressing up in a garish green costume. I ran the risk of being ridiculed by my peers. Nonetheless, the chance I took forged a fun school tradition. When people learn about my love of computer programming or that I spent part of the summer studying particle physics, similarly, I run the risk of being ridiculed—or at least teased. To some, these subjects may seem boring, or perhaps I may seem boring for liking them. But I can honestly say the passion I feel for programming and science has never been diminished by the possibility of being ridiculed. I enjoy being ridiculous.

Essay 5: Humorous and Miscellaneous

Author's note: Sometimes a stream-of-consciousness or "evening in the life of" essay can offer your reader a glimpse of who you are. While this essay is a bit lengthy, I believe it does provide the reader with a genuine sense of the life of the writer.

I didn't think we could fit a drum set, three amps, a keyboard, a guitar, and a skinny freshman in the back of Ty's Jeep Wagoneer, but somehow they all got from point A to point B—and all of the other spectators from our first performance traveled together in another car. It was Friday night in December, and, earlier that evening, Ty and I had braved the traffic through the canyon to reach the Aliso Viejo Autobahn where Andy B. lived. We couldn't find his house among the tract homes where we parked, so we walked around the block yelling his name . . . and nearly gave up. (I always preached that a cell phone was a restriction on my ability to retain my whereabouts' status as my business and my business only.) Andy had asked Ty and me, also known as "the Love This," to perform in his living room. We didn't expect anyone to be there but Andy and maybe his little brother. After we gave up yelling Andy's name and got in the car to leave, Justin F. came out of a house and stopped the car as we were pulling out of the circle. We looked at him and rolled down the window, probably exchanging malicious grins and grunting, "Hey!" He motioned toward the house, and we parked the car and began the exhausting but always exhilarating task of unloading the musical equipment into the living room.

Inside of the house, Andy's mother was at the refrigerator and was dealing with the infant in her arms. She paid the young hooligans in her house no attention. Inside we found Andy and 3 or 4 of his neighbors who had swung by his house because they heard there was a band playing. One of them, Matt, was in my PE class at school. He had slick black hair and a gold necklace and always called the PE teacher, "Coach." When he saw me he greeted me with a devilish, surprised grin, saying my name probably for the first time ever, and I gave him a passing "what's-up" as I went back out the door to get more of the drum set. Ty and I set up all the equipment, including crude microphones, on the carpet in front of the living room couch, dismantling video game consoles in order to get at the power outlets; after about 10 minutes, we turned up the volume and began to play. Ty played the fast, ferocious, dance-beat drums for "the Love This," and I played the disco synthesizer, funky bass, and detuned guitar with four strings on it. Our original songs had come together over the past few months, and the kids on the couch were simply laughing into their laps out of sheer enjoyment at the thrill of a 2-man band playing atrociously loud in Andy's tiny living room. After a few songs, a neighbor came by because he was afraid the noise would bring the cops. But when we agreed to turn it down, he told us that he was more interested in hearing us than scolding us.

When we had played about five songs, Ty and I looked at our watches and knew that we were cutting close to the wire if we wanted to get to downtown Laguna in time for our tentative show in front of the Golden Spoon frozen yogurt store. It was a big tourist night in Laguna, a night many high school students spent out in town. So Ty and I sloppily loaded our drums and equipment back into his car, figuring the audience of 5 or 6 had seen and heard enough for one night. They insisted, however, on coming with us to see us perform on the sidewalk downtown, and so we managed to fit Justin in the back seat of Ty's car underneath cymbals and thick metal rods, while Matt enthusiastically volunteered to take the rest of the crew, saying, "Yo, Coleman, you work hard doing this man. I'm telling Coach to let you off a piece." Whew!

The most exciting time of the night approached as Ty drove us out of Aliso Viejo to Laguna and we neared the sight of the Golden Spoon.

The 50 kids standing on the sidewalk and in the parking lot behind the ice cream shop saw us pull in and began to finally make up their minds not to leave. Unfortunately, though, our friend Mike, who worked at Golden Spoon, gave us bad news when he let us know his manager was with him so we couldn't plug into the Golden Spoon electrical outlet as he had promised.

Luckily, though, a shady character named Chris, who also went to school with us, worked in the liquor store next door. He argued with his boss and somewhat covertly gave us the plug, and we set up our stuff once again, playing noisy fast beats on the sidewalk, with about 50 young kids surrounding us and dancing. A high school teacher, who everyone knew, was there with her husband. After about 45 minutes, the cops showed up.

There comes a point in everything when you have to realize you've done enough, so as the fuzz directed kids off of the sidewalk (too close to the road, some of them on the road), I quickly began taking the equipment down, thanking Chris. Meanwhile, the cops lectured Ty and threatened to give us a ticket and take away our equipment. A man from city hall was there with his wife, and he stepped up to the cops and began arguing for the kids' right to have a good time on a night that was supposed to be a celebratory night, anyhow. The cops backed off at that, issuing nothing more than a "We're warning you," and so we had spent another typical night entertaining those who were willing to listen.

Essay 6: Humorous and Miscellaneous

Some people squeeze stress balls or contort their bodies into yoga's downward dog in order to unwind. I ride buses. I began riding the bus to visit my grandparents, who had moved to South Miami at the same time I obtained my license. My mother, fearful of my driving inexperience, insisted that the bus would provide the only transportation for me to see them every other weekend.

Initially, I thought the ride would be a tedious venture that would hungrily consume my free time. I soon realized, however, that this "interruption" was an opportunity for me to gain a new perspective from my environment.

Whether I am riding the bus to visit my grandparents or to get home from soccer practice, the convenience definitely has its perks. Notwithstanding the obvious need for transport, I enjoy the bus for unconventional reasons. My seat, although not designated, serves as my personal haven. Sometimes I use it as a place of solitude where I can reflect on my thoughts or study for exams. (Tranquility is often scarce in a home with 7 siblings.) Mostly, I use my bus time to observe and meet the people sitting beside me. I regularly embrace my bus community and listen to the untold stories of other travelers.

Talking has never been my problem. My siblings tease me for being a "Chatty Cathy," saying that I love to hear the sound of my own voice; meanwhile, my mother fears that I will talk to someone dangerous and get abducted. The truth is I like to talk; the thought of awkward silence unnerves me. I find it extraordinary that some of my riding companions can last for hours without muttering a syllable to their neighbor, determined to keep their social vow of silence and ignore others. Not only do I wish to acknowledge the people I encounter, but I also find that engaging conversation with an unfamiliar traveler is raw, honest, and forthright. I have discovered that people are more willing to express their views on various affairs either current or personal to complete strangers. Despite my loquacious personality, on the bus I choose to listen.

So, for $2.35, I can listen to my companions' stories and experience an intriguing perspective beyond my limited home and school environments. Through my bus travels, I have met an elderly man who fled from Cuba on a raft to obtain political asylum, a bright-eyed female teacher for juveniles in detention centers who is committed to showing her students that education is key to success, and a handicapped couple who ride in fear of losing another child in a car accident.

Although I have always been very outgoing and approachable, the bus rides have broadened my horizons and blessed me with numerous opportunities to experience the "real world" through passengers in the nearby seats. These encounters have helped me to appreciate the people that live in my community. We may not attend the same school, shop at the same grocery store, or have the opportunity to scrimmage each other in a soccer game, but on the bus, we have the opportunity to talk and understand each other.

By listening to fellow passengers' stories, I have endured loss and understood hope. Discovering new impactful people, reflecting within myself, and contributing to the lives of passengers riding with me on the route of life, I have learned to talk less and listen more. Indeed, life is one long bus ride with a beginning, an end, and many stops along the way. People come and go, but I have decided it is my duty to hear the stories of others, acknowledge the existence of the riders, and eventually enrich the lives of others with the stories and lessons I have learned on the bus.

Essay 7: Humorous and Miscellaneous

There they went: I watched as the green, red, orange, and white ones disappeared into her mouth. It all began with a solitary pink Starburst jellybean in the second grade. My best friend Molly had won a plastic Easter egg full of jellybeans. I sat on her couch, experiencing immense pain as I watched her indulge in the tangy candies. Never before had a confectionary treat caused me so much inner strife. Finally there was one left—the pink jellybean, my favorite kind. I wanted that last jellybean so badly I could practically taste it. I reluctantly broached the subject and pleaded for that last jellybean; never before have I been so quickly and utterly denied. The exact happenings have escaped my memory, but somehow the battle over who would enjoy the last jellybean escalated into what seemed like a 5-hour brawl of willpower on the living room floor. Panting heavily, foreheads glistening with sweat, and slightly chuckling over the ridiculousness of the situation, we both emerged from the battle with sticky pink hands and a squished pink jellybean. Traumatized, we decided to savor that jellybean and the memory in a small, plastic zip-lock bag that we, to this day, have no idea of its whereabouts.

Two years later, the argument resurfaced. At a family gathering, Molly and I retold the comical tale of the pink jellybean to all of our neighborhood friends. Our storytelling was quickly stymied: I was determined the jellybean was pink, but Molly was adamant that it was red! The battle began again, this time over an entirely new quandary. My stubborn nature and persistence refused to let me back down, just as with regard to many other issues in life. I have always been opinionated and a strong advocate of fighting for what I believe in, and this situation was no different. Fifteen preteen story listeners started taking sides, resulting in a trashed room, laughter, shoe throwing, and a broken lamp.

The final branch of my jellybean saga is this: who thought the jellybean was pink first? As told above, I did; but Molly is still convinced that the red sweater I wore in my preschool picture indicates that red was my favorite color, proving that I thought the jellybean was red! The bold statement of "I thought it was pink first!" has haunted eight years of birthday cards and yearbook signings. Ironically, this seemingly incidental childhood memory has provided me with one of life's greatest lessons: the art of compromise. We could have easily shared the jellybean by cutting it in half, or even gone to the store to buy an entire bag of the delectable Starburst candies. This experience has taught me the value of a simple compromise and to never let my stubbornly determined nature hinder a friendship or important decision. Whenever I am faced with opposing ideas or viewpoints in the future, I will remember with humor that squashed, sticky, desired pink jelly bean and the values it has instilled into my everyday life.

Essay 8: Humorous and Miscellaneous

I am certainly not one to sit in the bleachers, except when on occasion I am forced to sit on the sidelines.

By the age of 10, I had already traded up my man-powered mountain bike to the brute force of a gas-powered motor-bike. After a long day on the track, my brother, sister and I headed back to the car. In my adrenaline-fueled stupor, I decided to throw myself into an epic slide stop, leaving the dust whirling behind me as I whipped off my helmet like some sort of mystical heroine. In reality, the bike quickly slid out from under me, trapping my leg in between the muffler and the tire. I was left with a third degree burn that would take two surgeries, including a skin graph and a shaved head, to heal, but I gained a lifetime street credit and infamy, including rumored stories of how I spared my leg from amputation.

Moving on from motorcycle to horse . . . His petite stature and white mane gave Noah the illusion of being this cute little obedient pony, but oh was I wrong. As we approached our first fence I gave him a secure and encouraging leg as I began to feel his striding to the jump. Just as we were set to depart, he refused the jump—and I didn't. Hurtling off the horse, my body was thrown towards the hard ground, while my arm crashed into jump. After another surgery to repair my broken radius and ulna and two 6-inch incisions to place the two metal plates and screws, it would take me more than a painful fall to keep me off the horse.

This next one is a knock out. While on one of our many photo excursions, my father and I set out into Yosemite with a camera in tow. Bushwhacking through the brush, suddenly I saw the shot. How I got there, I am not sure, but in my craze I hadn't exactly factored how I was going to get back. My father braced himself on the opposite side of the river, and I began my running approach. In a momentous leap, I cleared the river only to plant my foot right into the mud. My father lurched over, setting the camera around his neck in motion all the while pulling me into it. In the end it was well worth the shot, and the story of how I got my black eye.

These events only skim the surface. Yes, I've been burned by a motorcycle, I've broken bones, and I've managed to give myself a black eye, but I've also made an ice skating rink out of a pool, I've skated in ice skating shows with Nancy Kerrigan and Michele Kwan, raised eight kittens, nine dogs and a miniature horse, I've gotten trapped in an elevator, I've been thrown off a horse twenty-nine times, I've gotten back on twenty-eight times, I've jumped off a horse on two legs to land squarely on a fence, I am known as the problem solver, I was the first girl to go to the principal's office in first grade, my biggest wipeout came in the jaws of a 7-foot wave, I've shaved half my head (for a skin graph), I've played on a broken foot to finish a volleyball game, I've worked on photo shoots with Bengal tigers, I've jumped off a chairlift when I was in sixth grade to win a bet, I've jumped off a 30-foot pier, I know how to trap shoot, I found someone's $100,000 wedding ring and returned it, I've been a famous photographer's muse, I used to eat bricks of butter, I'm an expert thrift store shopper, I have an uncanny ability to remember random facts, I have become the resident therapist for countless girls at my school, my former principal from eighth grade still refers to me as a pistol, I always win raffles, and to hear all the rest you will just have to get to know me.

Author's note: The following three essays take one common theme and string together many shorter stories in a creative and unique way. I like to call these "bulletin board" essays, since they allow your reader to take a peek at your personal "bulletin board" (or any randomly collected group of items or themes) and catch many glimpses of who you are by scanning and reading specific nuggets "tacked" to it.

Essay 9: Humorous and Miscellaneous—"Bulletin Board"

Postcards

"Wishing you were here! Love, Kathryn"

I don't know what it is about postcards that attract me to them. Maybe it's the beautiful pictures of white sand beaches on the front or just knowing that the person who sent it ignored everything except me at that particular moment. Whether the postcard is from an old, dingy tourist trap on the way to the Grand Canyon or of a huge castle on the lush, green rolling hills of Europe, each one is priceless.

My threadbare album of postcards sits on the very top shelf of my overfilled closet. I used to put them all in a box that I kept under my bed, but I just felt something so special deserved a more dignified resting place. As I flip through the album, vivid memories of past friends and relationships stream back to me. In a way, the postcards serve as a tangible form of my childhood. Each postcard represents a different stage in my life where new experiences and lessons were learned.

At first my postcards all originated from my grandmother and grandfather, who have a passion for traveling to the most beautiful places in the world. It wasn't until I was 6 or 7 that my friends acquired the proper writing skills to send me postcards. But when they finally did start sending postcards, my collection became even more precious.

They were not eloquently written and did not contain interesting stories, but they were special to me because they were for me and no one else.

At the beginning of my album you find postcards with simple phrases like "It's fun here. How is your dog?" Then as you turn the pages, you begin to find more personal and thoughtful phrases, such as "Hawaii is beautiful, and there are so many places you would enjoy here." Each postcard is unique, so it doesn't matter to me that I have ten from the same location. My friends all know that this is one of my quirky collections, so they send me one from everywhere they go, even if it's from the other side of town. My family has also helped my collection grow at an exponential rate. My mom takes it on as her mission to find the perfect postcard for me whenever she goes on a trip. My dad also contributes to my collection in a huge way because he travels all around the world and stays at the most beautiful place. He always brings me back a postcard of the hotel he stayed at and they help me connect to him because we both know where the other is.

When I was in kindergarten, we had a show-and-tell time every week where everyone would bring their most precious item to show the class to impress them. This would seem like the perfect occasion to show off my postcards, except I didn't want to show anyone my collection. It was so special to me that I felt that nobody was worthy of viewing them. I chose to take a small insignificant teddy bear to class rather than expose my postcards and, with them, myself to all of my classmates. The first time I showed the collection to my best friend I made her pass a rigorous challenge to make sure she deserved to see them. They represented part of me and I felt that revealing them to others was like revealing myself.

The postcards serve as a constant reminder that people care about me. They also represent all the beautiful places I would love to visit someday. They motivate me to be in the position where I can travel the world and learn about the different cultures and destinations. Postcards aren't just pictures to me; they are snapshots of different cultures that stand for all the different stages in my life. They are romantic and capture all the beautiful aspects of nature in one shot.

In today's society, where everything is so fast paced and everyone is obsessed with their cell phones, it is nice that postcards still exist to remind people of the way things used to be. The fact that someone has to find a place to write, ponder up a personal yet not too intimate message that has to fit in a tiny area, has to buy a stamp, and put it in the mailbox is something that makes postcards priceless. People in today's modern societies have forgotten the simple pleasure of handwriting a letter or postcard. It is special for both the writer and the recipient. It is a stark contrast to the impersonal text messaging and e-mails that dominate today.

Essay 10: Humorous and Miscellaneous— "Bulletin Board"

Stuff in My Car

A Spanish dictionary, *The Best Local Hiking Trails* guide book, a calendar stacked full of upcoming charity events, a brand new pair of lacrosse cleats, and photo-copied pages from the *Cooking with Trader Joe's Cookbook* are all random items found in my car that visually demonstrate my strongest traits.

I describe myself as being open to "trying new things." Although there is no perfectly matched word with the meaning of the phrase, my fearlessness to reach out and absorb everything is endless. I discovered a *Cooking with Trader Joe's Cookbook* hidden among other dusty books in the garage the other day. Having never opened a cookbook before, my family took surprise that in the next 30 minutes of my discovery and a quick run to the grocery store, I had already begun cooking a three-course meal. Although the food did not turn out perfectly, I persisted in cooking and didn't give up. Like my cooking experimentation, I picked up a sport that I have never played. After a few persuasive conversations with my friends who played lacrosse, the next week I began throwing and catching with a lacrosse stick, and the week after, I purchased a new pair of cleats. My characteristic of being open to "try new things" will enable me to join many of the clubs your college offers or even start new ones to inspire other people with the same interests.

Organizing a group hike in the local mountains is a common occurrence for me. I prefer action to lounging on the sofa, and drumming up enthusiasm in the people around me is what I love to do. I found the *Best Local Hiking Trails* guide book in a nearby bookstore, and, from then on, I encouraged many of my friends to get away from their computers and text messages and hike with me. I know I could use this quality to share my opinions and inspire my fellow classmates to try and do things they might love. An outgoing personality usually emerges in every group, and I am the one who fills this role.

With over 200 hours of community service over my high school career, a very hard-earned characteristic of mine is my philanthropic side. I participate in every philanthropic activity that my charity league offers, including Loaves and Fishes, a local soup kitchen; Susan G. Komen Race for the Cure; Tustin library; and Working Wardrobes, a program centered around getting people back on their feet. Giving back to the community is of high importance to me, and I will continue giving back in college and join clubs with classmates who enjoy doing the same.

Essay 11: Humorous and Miscellaneous— "Bulletin Board"

Days of the Week

My eclectic passions and tastes attract me to activities that appear to be polar opposites. Although I enjoy the sunny beaches of Orange County, I dream of heli-snowboarding in the colder parts of the world. Even my background is somewhat of a dichotomy. While I value my Jewish heritage, I am eager to embrace my Argentine roots. Maybe there is no better way to describe my unique blend of interests than to experience a week in my life.

- **Monday:** The Dodgeball Tournament that our ASB Board organized has just begun. Mr. M., my IB History teacher, just asked me to share my opinion on the existence, or lack thereof, of an egalitarian approach towards education in America. As I quickly sum up my points, the lunch bell rings. Do I have time to continue this stimulating discussion with my teacher and peers and also fulfill my ASB duty to assist with the tournament?

- **Tuesday:** I have lunch with Dad at his work place on Main Street. I drive through the downtown feeling at home in the Hispanic environment because it bears a sentimental resemblance to Resistencia, a city I visited this summer with my Argentine cousins.

- **Wednesday:** IB Theory of Knowledge class. Mr. H., my teacher, is bringing me *On the Road,* a book that I want to borrow from him because of my interest in Beat Generation literature. If I make it before class starts, I'll have time to chat with him about my theories on *Brave New World* and other dystopian novels.

- **Thursday:** I register at the Community College for the social and political philosophy class taught by the professor I had this summer. Upon my return, Mom and I watch a documentary on New York City in the 1950s, prompting our discussion on Nono's (my grandfather) immigration from Argentina to the United States to study psychoanalysis during the fifties.

- **Friday**: Mom needs my help setting up her new office so she can begin seeing patients. Having a social worker as a mom, I learned to analyze the world with emotional awareness. I am extremely sensitive to friends' interpersonal and intrapersonal dilemmas. To me, problem-solving within the realm of relationships is extremely meaningful because it is raw and real.

As my weekend approaches, I imagine it will be filled with more adventure, academia, family, and books. This is just a small glimpse of where I come from, but what will really define me is what awaits me in my next four years of college.

Chapter Four

The Activity Paragraph

And now, just when you thought the main essay and the bulk of your writing was complete, on to more writing! Some students choose to work on the activity paragraph before the main essay, to use it as a sort of warm-up or preview of what is to come. You can choose to do this or the main essay first, or work on both back and forth at the same time. Sometimes students even begin this activity paragraph and find that it evolves into a much larger story that actually becomes a main essay instead of an activity paragraph.

Think of the activity paragraph as a "mini essay" and another opportunity for your reader to hear your voice and get to know you better. Don't let the short length of this question deceive you into thinking that this (or any piece of writing you are asked for) is a "throw-away question." That would be a big mistake. Spend a significant amount of time on this question and others like it.

Before 2013, the Common Application asked all students to elaborate, in 150 words, on one extracurricular activity of interest. That required prompt has been eliminated, but some schools do use some version of it as one of their supplemental questions.

Please briefly elaborate on one of your extracurricular activities or work experiences that was particularly meaningful to you. (About 150 words)

Other schools that are not using the Common Application often ask activity-related questions. For example, Lafayette College's application offers what I call a "recycle question." This allows you to use the same answer you provided for the Common Application's activity paragraph with a few more words if necessary.

Why Lafayette? (Required and 20–200 words in length)

There's a difference between being busy and being engaged. Lafayette comes alive each day with the energy of students who are deeply engaged in their academic, co-curricular, and extracurricular explorations. In response to the prompt, keep it simple—choose one activity and add depth to our understanding of your involvement.

What do you do? Why do you do it? (Optional and 20–200 words in length)

Activity Paragraph Dos and Don'ts

Review the Dos and Don'ts before reading the samples that follow. After you read the writing samples, you should be inspired to get started!

Dos

- Do approach this paragraph as if you are writing a mini-essay by being visual and anecdotal.
- Do choose an activity that illustrates an aspect of who you are and about which you are passionate.
- Do use the first person when you answer supplemental questions.

- Do choose to write about the activity that best illustrates an aspect of who you are. "Depth and breadth" are terms colleges use to signify your commitment to an activity. If you have participated in an activity and began as a "worker bee" and worked your way up to a leadership position, that is ideal. If you are just a worker bee, that is okay, too. Just show what you have done to be involved.
- Do put yourself into that activity when you write about it.
- Do be selective with each of your words. Since you have a limited space to articulate your thoughts, be sure to make each word count. Do be vivid and concise.
- Do be sincere in what you write. Your truthfulness will show through if your writing is honest.

Don'ts

- Don't make this paragraph a dry repetition or elaboration of your activity that reads like a summary.
- Don't simply describe or define the activity.
- Don't use linking verbs; use active verbs.
- Don't use language directly from your brag sheet or school catalog that describes the activity you are talking about.
- Don't choose to write about an activity that you have just begun in your senior year (unless it is the only thing that you have to write about!).
- Don't use words that you would not use in your ordinary conversation. In other words, don't be "thesaurus happy."
- Don't be predictable. If your activity paragraph is not personal and could have been written by anyone, then you have not done it justice in conveying your voice. Try again.

- Don't be fooled into believing that the admission reader really wants to know more about that activity. They really want to know about *you*.
- Don't be vague. Be specific.
- Don't write about any topic that overlaps with your main essay(s). The activity paragraph is not the place to repeat anything that can be found elsewhere.
- Don't have a big head or a big ego. Yes, you can celebrate your accomplishment(s) within an activity, but be careful about tooting your own horn too much!
- Don't think of the activity paragraph as a "throw-away" answer. It is there for a reason and is important, so treat it as a critical piece of writing that allows your reader one more way to get to know you better.

The best advice is to just write and get the ideas out before worrying about word limits. Words can be cut, trimmed, and consolidated once you are done. The samples that follow offer a wide range of topics and areas that students selected. Again, be sure to treat this assignment as an opportunity to write a "mini essay" that illustrates another piece of who you are.

Activity Paragraph: Academic Experiences

Intensive Seminar—What I Also Learned

"Katie, it looks like we're at war with Iran and Russia."

At 9 a.m., the only response I can think of is, "Good morning to you, too, Mr. Secretary."

Last summer, I spent two weeks in an intensive seminar regarding global grand strategy. The seminar was both grueling and exciting: I did the equivalent of a semester's worth of reading for a two-week course, weathered a weekend-long simulation of a SARS breakout and hostage crisis, and presented a Marshall Brief before a group of instructors known as the "Murder Board." But beyond the formal elements of the seminar, what really stood out was the community. It was exhilarating. We went late into the night sharing ideas, debating arcane points, laughing, and jamming on guitars. In this group of highly diverse people, each of us contributed our own unique perspectives. The seminar was great, but the real lesson of my summer was that community is everything. I found that I had learned just as much, if not more, from the students as from the professors. I learned that I am most energized when I am in a community like this, surrounded by friends who are like-minded in their love of learning and curiosity.

Children's Hospital Internship

I'm always excited to hear the last ring of the school bell . . . particularly on Wednesdays. Every Wednesday, the back seat of my car contains a pair of black dress shoes, socks, a long-sleeve

collared shirt, and crisp black slacks—"uniform" attire for my job at
Children's Hospital. There, Dr. D., a pediatric endocrinologist, waits
for me. He actually began as my own caring physician curing my
Growth Hormone deficiency. As our relationship grew, he became
my mentor. As I rush through the clinic doors, I squeeze alcohol
sanitizer onto my hands. Dr. D. greets me and we continue on with
his list of patients. It goes something like this: "First patient, female,
13 years of age, Type 1 Diabetes, non–English speaking family," Dr. D.
informs me. Luckily, due to my Hispanic heritage and four years of
Spanish, I can understand and speak pretty well. Often I serve as Dr.
D.'s interpreter as he speaks broken "Spanglish." He introduces me,
"Esa es mi colleague, es una estudiante de highschool. Es OK if he sits
in on the appointment?" "Ahh . . . si." The patient's mother usually
smiles. My job is to observe. I stand and study the patient's reaction
while taking careful notice of what Dr. D. advises. After each case,
we discuss the specifics of the disease or ailment and then look into
the biological mechanisms behind the drug used to treat the illness.
I don't interact much with each patient, but I do learn the basics of
patient care and bedside manner. I realize through observation that
there is an art behind building respect between a physician and patient.
Shadowing for six months gave me the opportunity to experience
and emulate those fundamental skills. This experience furthered
my passion for medicine. It combined my love of troubleshooting,
biology, and technology into one field. I even continued my studies
and completed one Emergency Medical Technician (EMT) class, and I
also earned my Health Care Provider Card. I hope to get licensed as an
EMT when I turn 18 and to continue my pursuit of a medical degree
at Brown University. In addition, the exposure I have had to lower
income, oftentimes Hispanic families inspires me to want to study
during my junior year in South America, administering healthcare in
rural Argentina. I want to learn more about how to help people of my
common ancestry.

Mock Trial

There was no jury. Just a small room filled with people wanting to see a performance. But I was still nervous all the same. My brow brimmed with sweat, and the countless hours of preparation that my direct lawyer and I conducted would slowly be forgotten. My breath quickened and I became more and more nervous while all eyes were on me as my direct examination ended. But as the opposing lawyer mentioned my stage name, "Good afternoon, Detective Brown," my anxiety quickly disappeared. I knew where I was, and I remembered the script to follow. I wanted to be a flawless witness on my first cross. Now, with my second year of Mock Trial complete, and my third soon to come, I am prepared and excited to be the lawyer I was once before. Being a witness was much more different than a lawyer. As a witness, I tried hard not to fall into a ditch, trapped on all sides. As a lawyer, my goal was to dupe the cross-witness with impenetrably, inescapably ingenious questions that another lawyer could not counter during a re-direct. But what excited me the most was the re-direct itself! The fact that I always had to pay attention and stay on my feet as the opposing lawyer tried to pin my witness down with questions, trying to make objections here and there, while attentively listening, preparing a strong re-direct, kept my blood pumping. Mock Trial is both stressful and fantastic.

Activity Paragraph: Community Service

Volunteering at Special Camp for Special Kids

For the past five summers, I have volunteered as a counselor at Special Camp for Special Kids, a week-long day-camp for mentally disabled children. Campers arrive early Monday morning anticipating the fun activities planned for the week, while eagerly awaiting their new counselor, an automatic "best friend." As I drove to the first day of camp this summer, I braced myself for a challenging experience. My camper, Spencer, was diagnosed with autism and a seizure disorder. The first day at camp consists of on-campus activities such as carnivals, snacks, crafts, and activity centers. As I ran around with my new friend, another camper boldly approached Spencer. "Spencer, can we be best friends forever?" asked Aaron, a beaming 9-year-old full of spunk. Spencer responded with a giant toothy grin and an all-consuming bear hug. As I hung back observing this exchange of kindness, I was stunned by the instant friendship of these 2 little boys. How often in today's world can 2 people form an immediate amity with no pre-judgment or biased preconceptions? I entered camp rather anxious for the hours to fly by since this annual experience is always trying and exhausting. Unexpectedly, however, I left camp this summer with a new sense of people and relationships. Spencer and Aaron reminded me of the importance of acceptance, regardless of the past, of someone's background, or physical or mental limitations. The untainted innocence I witnessed in these campers will sit in the back of my mind and encourage me to emulate them the next time I am quick to judge another.

Hospital Volunteer

Every Sunday morning, I walk through the emergency room doors wearing a monogrammed Oxford shirt, identification badge, and a smile. I register with my supervisor who informs me where I will be stationed for the next 4 hours. Although I have been assigned to various duties, including checking in visitors, delivering meals to patients, and working with pharmaceutical technicians to prepare prescriptions, as a senior volunteer I request being assigned the inpatient floor where I find that my time is best served with the patients. While tending to their needs, I personally interact with patients in an effort to distract them from their dispiriting daily reality; I entertain them with board games, stories of the good ol' days, or (my favorite) serenading the fine ladies and gentlemen on the geriatric floor with some of their favorites tunes from Sinatra and Jolson to Frankie Valli and the Four Seasons. While medicine does most of the healing for the patient, I feel that a positive outlook really helps them heal mentally. I find my experience meaningful because it allows me brighten someone else's day even if it occurs from 8 a.m. to noon one day every week.

Tutoring Autistic Children

Tutoring autistic children has not only improved my patience, it has made me value the achievements in the people I tutor. Dominic, an autistic sixth-grader, was struggling the most in math, particularly formulas involving the area of circles. Dominic had never seen formulas before, and this new concept frustrated him and created a barrier that he could not overcome. I struggled to find a way to connect the math ideas to his brain. As we began to go over every possible variation of the "area of a circle" problems, I realized that he was more of visual learner. We started to cut out circles together with the correct measurements. We dissected the circle components so that he could visualize how each of them relates to the problem. Through repetition and visualization, he gained confidence. Every time he saw a problem he smiled slightly as if he had already completed it correctly. The next week I received a call from Dominic saying he got his first "A" on a math test this entire year. His newly gained confidence transferred over to help him succeed on his test, making both of us proud of his performance.

My Work with Homeless Children

The family of 5 quickly paced into the camp. They were full of attitude. Their hair was dyed bleach blonde, and their bodies were covered in piercings and tattoos; even the 12-year-old girl had a nose ring. Nate was the most interesting to me. He was close to my age and had a gauged pointed eyebrow ring, with a matching pointed stud under his bottom lip, straight centered. His oldest sister, wearing a midriff revealing tattoos and a belly button ring, carried her own 1-year-old baby into the camp followed by her tattooed mother also carrying her own baby. My 15-year-old mind was too quick to judge this family, and I was 100% wrong on every initial opinion I made.

I passed judgment on Nate and his family the moment they arrived at 360 Student Travel. This program offered me the opportunity to travel to Hawaii for three weeks to work with homeless children in a camp that I helped clean and manage. Nate's family differed from all of the other "typical homeless families" who didn't interact with the volunteers and came only for food. As it turned out, Nate was one of the most kind, polite, and intelligent people I have met. Nate was not a taker. He gave. He worked alongside his family helping to serve food. And only after everyone else was fed did his family eat. Nate was a part of the best example of a family I have ever seen. He never fought or argued with his family; they always remained supportive of each other and stayed close together. From this observation, they have impacted me tremendously. After knowing this amazing family, I now pass judgment so much less. My experience at 360 Student Travel is evidence of the truth in the saying, "you can't judge a book by its cover."

City Planning Department Volunteer

Abruptly interrupted, I heard my supervisor say, "George, a colleague of mine needs your assistance." I glanced at the woman. From her European features and strong accent, I knew exactly what she'd want: decaf, lots of milk, pinch of sugar. "Hi, George. I could use your assistance in editing this letter informing the citizens of Manhattan Beach about the new jogging path." *What? No coffee?* I thought to myself. From that moment on, I was upgraded, promoted, raised from the endless monotony of filing at the Manhattan Beach City Planning Department where I volunteered for the past four years. Coffee, paperwork, file. File, paperwork, coffee. I carefully reviewed the papers in the manila file folder, while my supervisor prattled with another architect. Expecting to see some type of buried treasure, I discovered nothing but old sheets of paper discussing remodeling plans and city limitations about the property. Editing the letter was the trampoline I needed to spring to more sophisticated tasks. Since the quality of my work became recognized, the following week I was assigned a project to submit to the mayor. I gained a promotion to manage, record, and coordinate the Manhattan Beach Senior Health Fair. I noted the number of booths to set up. I recorded ways to improve the medical form each doctor had to complete for his booth. My job went from momentous to fascinating overnight. What I learned from the city became irreplaceable. Being in charge of the Manhattan Beach Senior Health Fair, I have learned about all the behind-the-scenes work that is necessary for a successful event. From creating forms that each medical business needed to fill out to obtain a booth to contacting shuttle services that would help transport South Bay citizens from the parking lot to the fair, I had to make sure the fair ran smoothly. Not only did I learn about how the little guy could rise through the ranks from just persevering through the endless monotony of filing, retrieving coffee, and performing paperwork, but also I learned more about my city and how it functions. As a result I have learned to try new things, and, although I may not start out on top, I will strive to rise through the ranks.

Volunteering at a Homeless Shelter

I live in an environment where who I know and how I look often determines how others perceive me. One particular moment in my over 80 hours spent volunteering at Catholic Worker Homeless Shelter stands out in my mind as life-altering. One day, while I worked in a volunteer assembly line passing out necessities to the poor, a beautiful, nicely kept woman entered the shelter. I immediately characterized her as someone who was arriving to assist me in volunteering. As I motioned for her join me, she asked, "Can I get shampoo and lotion, please?" Stunned and embarrassed, I handed her the items. I realized that I had automatically assumed she was "like" me, from a nice home, loving family, and always with food on the table. Afterwards, observing her from a distance, mingling among the other homeless, a growing pain and sadness developed in me. Coming face to face with this reality was humbling. I previously and naively assumed by looking at a person's physical appearance, if she seemed "the norm" then she was "like me." My encounter proved to me this was not the case. Subsequently, this event has led me to try to dig deeper and learn through conversation the story behind a person before making snap judgments or assumptions.

Activity Paragraph: Extracurricular Activity

Drama

Don't mess up . . . you are the opening, you are the closing, you are their guide. It was my first performance, and I had received the leading role in our One Acts Festival, a series of student-directed and -written plays. As I repeated these words in my mind, waiting for the very minute of my opening, I watched anxiously as the audience filled their seats. The lights came on, and all feelings melted into excitement as my lines unconsciously poured out of my mouth with confidence. With each scene I became more and more comfortable performing, more and more excited to feel the audience watching me as I guided them through this story. Then, before I knew it, the play was over, with each audience member standing to give our cast a thundering ovation. As the performances continued, I began to fall in love with acting and being a part of the production. By the end of the entire process, I realized that my childhood dream of acting was a steadfast burning passion that I knew I wanted to cultivate. I'll never forget my first performance, for it was this part, this production, that developed my love for theater and established my desire to continue participating in drama.

Doing Plays

I love doing plays. Auditioning is fun. Running up to the list and seeing—yes! I got the part—that's fun. Rehearsals are fun, getting to know members of the cast, seeing the play transform. Doing the actual performance is wonderful, sculpting the audience this way and that.

And I won't deny enjoying the after, walking out from backstage into the hugs and handshakes and flowers. But really, there's one reason I do plays. All the time, the work, the commitment: it's all for those 5 minutes right before I walk on stage opening night. For compressed into those 5 minutes, I find more . . . feeling, more power, more raw, unbridled worth than I might otherwise experience in a week, a month, honestly, a year. Sitting offstage, waiting, knowing all these months of work comes down to this, these next 2 hours, these next 15 seconds. Knowing that anything, absolutely anything, can happen—I can nail it, I can mess it up. It's all up in the air. And that is beautiful, like my heart, which is thumping so wonderfully I can hear it, not just in my ears but in my fingers, in my toes. We forget so many of our moments, but this I'll never forget, because this is a *moment*. And that's why I do plays.

High School TV/Video Club

It's amazing what can be done with a little innovation, a 10-by-10-foot drama closet, and some high-definition cameras. Every Thursday, I get a chance to broadcast my ideas to 3,000 people, including parents, administrators, and students. As the only appointed and elected director of 53 students and $190,000 worth of equipment, my responsibilities to Foothill High School are great. Our class films every school event, from the homecoming football game to school performances and minor lunchtime activities, and it is my job to delegate and organize a filming schedule for the year. Being in a managerial position over my peers has been a satisfying challenge. Sometimes if my crew can't make it to a game or event, I take responsibility to capture the event myself. I also organize the annual Foothill Film Festival and participate in the Orange County Film Festival. These leadership responsibilities take anywhere from 5 to 15 hours a week in addition to class time. My responsibility as a teacher is also great. Much of my time is spent educating younger classmates and new members on equipment and, most important, how to use video as an effective method of communication. With a 60-year-old conservative principal to please as well as 2,500 students, creating suitable content can be quite difficult. Given my passion for medicine and biological systems, I implemented a portion of the program known as "Foothill T.V. Health." In a 3-minute weekly short, a few anchors and I conduct a field investigation on a popular health topic. My favorite topic was Wheatgrass. I read various statistics and studies on the plant and then toured the local juice bar with cameras and boom mics in hand to capture the full wheatgrass experience. The findings were then broadcast live to the school and surrounding neighborhood via cable. As director of my student-run video journalism class, I'm proud to contribute to our world, which is moving more and more exclusively towards electronic forms of communication.

Color Guard

I lettered in playing with guns and swords. Yet despite the dispute on gun laws in current times, nothing will stop the color guard world from going around. My greatest release since middle school, guard has been a never-ending process: moving from spinning flags, to tossing sabers, to cartwheeling under rifles. What began as a favor to my sister ended maturing me more than I could have imagined. Color guard is more than a flag in the air: it is pushing your body to new limits. It is never being satisfied, learning a turn, then a toss on top of it, then a higher toss, then adding a partner. It is choosing a supplemental family, one that you connect with on a deeper level. Experiences like rebuilding a program through recruiting and training new members one year, then tasting victory as a first-place program the next year are what color guard is all about for me. From freshman to captain, coach to soloist, I have certainly worn my share of colors on my guard, and I would never exchange my experiences for any others. Indeed, nothing has prevented me from playing with guns and swords, despite rules, hurdles, and even myself. Color guard is not a rifle in the air or a performer on the floor; on the contrary, guard has little to do with the equipment we manipulate, and most to do with the people we become.

Activity Paragraph: Leadership

LeadAmerica Ambassadors

My fellow LeadAmerica ambassadors and I stood on top of Mt. Pilatus in the Swiss Alps. Patches of snow lingered in the green grass around the summit, the hazy clouds cleared, and the view of Lake Lucerne took my breath away. Our journey around Europe neared a close, as I reflected on all the leadership qualities I learned while traveling for two weeks with 70 high school students from around the country. I witnessed different types of leadership. Some ambassadors chose to be observant and silently absorb a situation, while others were the first to stand up and give orders to those around them. I believe in a balance between leadership styles. I plan to lead by example, sharing my work with others, while also being open to listen to others' ideas. The leadership qualities I gained and shaped through LeadAmerica accompany me back to high school where I will apply them as the Captain of my tennis team, President of the National Honor Society, in my job, volunteer work, church youth group, and even at home. Reaching this pinnacle symbolically brought together all that I had learned and achieved through LeadAmerica.

Activity Paragraph: My Job

Working in a Cupcake Store

The line is 40 minutes long and around the block; we are out of our limited edition "Summer Cherry" cupcake; the manager is in the back on a phone call; and there are only 3 employees out front attempting to control the 60 customers who have somehow gotten hold of the order pads and are so impatient that they shove orders at me when they finally arrive at the front of the line. It is just a typical Saturday afternoon at the famous Sprinkles Cupcakes, where I have been an employee for the past three months. Working at Sprinkles is my first real job, and it has been a challenging and fun new experience for me. We daily endure complaints that our cupcakes are too expensive, we are out of forks, or we no longer have someone's favorite flavored cupcake. While exhausting, I am going to miss this job when it is time to go back to school. Most of my favorite memories and stories from this summer have something to do with Sprinkles and the diverse array of people that I have encountered while working. This experience has taught me how to better get along with people, how to nicely and patiently accept criticism, and how to deal with the hungry public. I have come to realize how difficult it is to work at a busy store. Now, whenever I am a customer at a store or restaurant, I make more of an effort to smile, say "thank you," and leave a dollar in the tip jar. I know from experience that those small gestures are truly appreciated.

My Job in an Ice Cream Store

For the past two summers I have worked at Gelato Paradiso, a small, Italian ice cream store located on a secluded lane in my hometown. For many reasons, working at Gelato is one of the most coveted jobs that a local high school student can possess. The most popular reason is that our manager, Buddy M., actually makes working seem fun. Buddy takes his job really seriously: he makes sure all of his employees know the importance of a clean store, high-quality customer service, and the difference between Limoncello and Lemon Sorbetto. While Buddy works hard, he has a good time at work as well. Normally, a teen would hate to work on a Saturday night, but at Gelato it's one of the best shifts available. For a Gelato employee, Saturday night equals Buddy's famous "30-second Dance Party." When the store is packed with customers, we turn off all the lights, crank up our techno music, and dance behind the counter. Thirty seconds later, we résumé working and pretend as if nothing happened. As a bonus, the amused customers tip us generously. When I grow up, I fear becoming someone who hates her job. Along with teaching me lessons in responsibility and customer service, Buddy assures me that it is possible to enjoy a job, too. It's okay to work diligently and have a little fun at the same time, even if it's only for 30 seconds.

Chapter Five

The Academic and "Thinking" Paragraph

M any colleges require you to write a paragraph (or an essay) that demonstrates how you think. They are seeking what I refer to as a "thinking" paragraph or essay, one that shows the reader how your mind works and connects ideas. Admission officers want to try to imagine what you might be like in a classroom setting or how you could contribute in a college seminar class that requires students to speak more and often lead discussions. A prompt seeking to elicit an academic response might be "What intellectual idea excites you?" or "What subject or class has been the most stimulating?" or "Have you pursued any academic interests or research outside of school? Please share one with us." Students applying to Stanford University might find this question: *Stanford students are widely known to possess a sense of intellectual vitality. Tell us about an idea or an experience you've had that you find intellectually engaging.* Sometimes, the "how you think" writing can also be illustrated by sharing an intellectual passion or hobby that you have pursued.

Academic/Thinking Paragraph—Dos and Don'ts

Dos

- Do write about a topic that truly interests you, that you are an "expert" in, or that shows best how your mind works and how you think and connect ideas.
- Do teach your reader why you are interested in this subject, or grab them with your curious question.
- Do include questions or thoughts running through your mind to bring the reader deeper into your head.

Don'ts

- Don't be preachy or so much of an expert that you come across as braggy.
- Don't choose the obvious or cliché topic or topics that are too broad to write about in one or two paragraphs (e.g., chicken and the egg, nature vs. nurture, big bang vs. Adam and Eve).
- Don't skim over this question, think it is unimportant, and provide a generic answer about how much you like to learn and share ideas with classmates. There is a reason why this question is included: to give you the opportunity to show what makes you tick and how you think.

You can choose to answer thinking questions in a variety of ways: discussing an academic subject or concept or a comment or quote from a teacher, coach, classmate, or book that excites or challenges you; questioning any idea; or sharing a philosophical thought that you think is "cool." In the examples that follow, you'll notice that responses to "thinking questions" come in all shapes and sizes. The students who wrote these essays or paragraphs all demonstrated to their readers how their brains work. The samples should make you want to meet that student, have a conversation or debate with her, and want to invite her to be a part of your college student body, classroom, or residence hall.

Sample Paragraphs: Academic Passion

Biology

Ever since I was a little girl, I have loved learning. I sat in my classroom with my hand raised half jumping out of my seat because I wanted to be the one who got to answer the question. As I have grown, so has my excitement for learning. I love the precision of math and the way each problem is like solving a puzzle to which there is only one answer. Science also intrigues me because it is what makes the world go around. My favorite class in high school was AP Biology. I was specifically fascinated by genetics and the many different systems that make up the human body. I went home one day after class and spent hours trying to figure out why all the girls in my family have blue eyes, the recessive gene, and all the boys have brown eyes, the dominant gene. To my disappointment, I was unsuccessful in my search because my parents had no idea what color all my great-grandparent's eyes were. I wanted to come to class each day because my teacher always had a new fact that I found interesting and could not wait to tell my friends and family. For example, every night while my family was eating dinner, my dog, Lacey, would inhale her entire bowl of water. We would all be shocked night after night when she did this. One day in class, we were learning about parasites and the side effect that worms have on animals is that they cause them to drink excessive amounts of water. When I told my parents, they took her to the vet, and it turned out she did have worms. It seems to me that almost everything in life is associated with biology in some way or another because my teacher could answer all of my real life–related questions.

Chemistry

Normally I think of myself as an artist, but there was one year where science was one of the most exciting parts of my life. Chemistry was my favorite subject in my junior year. There's something magical about the explanation of life and how it works. I remember walking into the class on lab days with the thick scent of something awful in the air and feeling excited. Something about the equations and reactions just clicked in my mind.

It was not even the witnessing of the reactions that got me excited, though that was quite fun. I actually enjoyed the math part of chemistry a lot. I felt like for the first time the math I was doing actually served a purpose. There was a reason why I had to discover what 34% of 57 milliliters was. Suddenly I needed to find out what "X" was or else everything was going to fail, and it would be my fault! I loved whenever we had to perform a reaction and then use our prior knowledge to determine what it was that we were watching. Chemistry felt like the total opposite of busy work, and I loved it. I learned a lot in chemistry—and not just about the periodic table. I honed my recognition skills and learned a lot about elimination of the impossible.

Latin

I have taken Latin since the sixth grade, but, up until my junior year, never fully appreciated the language itself and all it has to offer. After finishing my last year of Latin, I wanted to conclude my senior year with a language study, etymology. This was a course I had heard of but knew little about. Etymology is the study of the history of a particular word and the derivation or origin of a word. About 60 percent of all English roots and words come from Latin and Greek, which I knew but rarely appreciated until now. Americans communicate every day through language. Many words we use every day are derived from the very words I memorized, translated, and conjugated through the many years of my Latin education. Oddly enough, a simple "textbook," something we use in class every day, has the derivation from a Latin root. The word "text" comes from the Latin word "textus," which literally means "to weave." How strange that we do not make the connection with the woven binding of a "text" book to relate back to the root of the word itself. Even the bases of a liberal arts education are derived from Latin and Greek: "quadrivium," the studies of arithmetic, astronomy, geometry, and music, and "trivium," the studies of grammar, rhetoric, and dialect. High school students study from the bases of Latin and Greek roots every day without even realizing it. But now, I have gotten the chance to learn and appreciate how Latin plays into every part of my life and education. Through this new knowledge I am excited to see how my classroom studies relate to the world beyond my school walls and the overall importance that etymological roots play in my everyday life, and the English language itself. *Aequus accipe meum!*

Mathematics

Math has always intrigued me ever since I was little. I'm a very methodical, deliberate person; I like everything to be exact. When I was younger, I had to line up my Sesame Street toys in a row every night before I went to bed. When I run, I have to run an even number of laps around the track. Maybe it's O.C.D., maybe it's a fondness for numbers and logic. What I love most about math is that it's objective; the answer is either right or wrong. There are many different ways, however, to get to that right answer. So math allows me to think creatively as well. For me, there is nothing more satisfying than finally solving a math problem that I feel like I've been working on for hours. When I get home from school, I always do my math homework first because I actually enjoy it. I think that my passion for math will force me to stay optimistic and focused whenever I may feel overwhelmed as a student. Math reminds me why I love to learn. I also feel excited about learning when I use something from Trigonometry to finish a Physics problem or when I dig up information from U.S. History to expand my background knowledge on an American novel. I notice that each subject in school shares common ground and understand that everything that I learn has a purpose. Learning seems so much more rewarding when I realize that every subject connects and relates to another. Similarly, I use my passion for dance in as many outlets as possible. I dance to express myself and to distract myself from any stress or problems that I face. In addition, dance helps me become more involved in my community. By teaching dance to young children in an underprivileged town nearby, I use my talent to provide them with a new, positive interest. I think that [name of college] will be a great place to nurture my many diverse interests.

Media

For as long as I can remember, I have grown up with a television. I'm applying to the Ithaca Television and Radio Department or, more specifically, the scripting program. My interest in television is almost as long and exciting as a season of *Lost*. My love for television began at a very young age. Like flies to a bug zapper, I was mysteriously drawn to the glowing light. The Television seemed to have a life of its own. As I grew older so did my television. It became more advanced, bigger, and smarter with the invention of Tivo. There is nothing that has the same quality as television. Unlike most things, television appeals to everyone, and it doesn't judge me if I watch *Ugly Betty* or *Spongebob*. The unique quality I bring to television is my complete knowledge of all things "TV Trivia." For certain seasons of *Survivor* for instance, I can remember every single person voted off in order. I spent seventeen years discovering the wonders of television; it only seems right to spend the rest of my life devoted to it. And by writing for television, I can spawn the next generation of couch potatoes.

Photography

After enrolling in two consecutive years of traditional photography class, the simple process of film and photo development never ceases to amaze me. With the safe lights faintly shining down upon the bin lying in the sink, the picture I had taken a few days before begins to emerge onto the photo paper. My mind spins thinking about how rays of light can reflect off a bundle of roses to capture a small image onto a negative. That image is then blown up to an average-size picture, developed with a couple of different chemicals, and within a few hours is hanging on a wall in my house. What a mind-boggling but incredible process!

When my photo teacher first educated me on the chemical process in the dark room, my eyes barely blinked the entire period, so I wouldn't miss the miraculous transformation. I thought about how manipulating different types of light and assorted chemicals composed the entire process for developing in film. But it did not stop there. For example, in a chemistry class lab project I studied the effects of acetic acid; later, in the dark room, I saw its effects as a weak base to offset the development of my photograph. This keeps the picture from turning purple or black when I bring the print out into fluorescent lighting. I am fascinated that photography class is not only an annex to the fine art genre but also more of an extension to chemistry. Chemicals are not merely substances used within the chemistry lab. They are substances with a greater purpose in everyday life. I never realized their importance or relationship before. How amazing!

Photojournalism and Psychology

I've always been interested in a variety of subjects within the humanitarian sector. I've grown up in a family that loves to travel and have found myself drawn to learning about different cultures—the aspects that define each, how they differ, and what connects all of us. Through my travels, I developed a profound love for food, photography, writing, and people. I recorded many of my experiences in countless journals and have written numerous poems. I have several collections of photography, from daily exchanges to once-in-a-lifetime experiences. I have not decided upon a major, yet I'm interested in pursuing something linked to writing and expression. Photojournalism appeals to me because I desire a career that can be shared by people of all backgrounds and strongly believe in the impact of photography on others.

I am also interested in psychology. I've always naturally connected well with others and am a part of the Peer Counseling Program at my school, where 12 students work alongside the guidance counselor and advise students on subjects ranging from academics to drugs. Studying at NYU's College of Arts and Science would provide me with the opportunity to explore my different interests and solidify an area as my primary concentration.

Physics

I walked into Conceptual Physics on the first day of high school already dreading the class; it had a horrible reputation of being the most difficult freshman-year course. After a few days of physics, however, I realized that I was one of the only students who could not get enough of it. To my surprise, Physics soon became my favorite class. Not only did I have an awesome teacher who made the subject accessible and always had a clear explanation for everything, but I felt myself truly enjoying doing the calculations and word problems. Physics combined my two favorite subjects, math and science, into one connected topic. I can still clearly remember learning about how light moves through water, how it is able to calculate the fastest path through the various substances to get where it is going as quickly as possible. Since in "Conceptual" Physics, I didn't apply the math knowledge used in advanced physics classes, when I learned Calculus as a junior, I was amazed at how much it was connected to my physics knowledge. The optimization and related rates problems I learned showed how to find the fastest path to a destination based on rates of change, just like the light equations from my physics class. I was fascinated to discover that light was basically doing an optimization problem in its effort to break through the water. The natural world was "performing" calculus problems, and physics was able to explain how exactly that worked. This interdisciplinary discovery that the world is connected through calculus and physics has made me excited to venture deeper into these two subjects in the future.

Science

Although I am undecided about my future major, I know that I am interested in the health sciences. Having grown up with a nurse as a mom and a doctor as a dad, I feel like I have been exposed to the amount of work it takes to be successful in medicine. I love to visit patients after surgery with my dad. The interaction with the patients is reassuring that this job truly helps the community. I love the sciences, specifically anatomy, and I love to work with people, which is necessary for this occupation.

The hospital is place of weakness. It doesn't matter whether you are rich or poor, beautiful or ugly, or young or old; everyone gets sick.

The hospital serves as a humbling place where people are put into a situation where they are not in control of what happens. I want to be the one that increases their chances and gives them hope that they will get better. The process of healing has a large mental aspect attached to it. With a positive outlook coming from the people working with the patient, the patient will not give up.

Science Independent Research

"I think the protein structure of this crystal happens to be bicarbonate deoxyribose base with an acid-like tail," said Dr. K., my mentor. Dr. K. and I examined our long data chains that we had spent nearly a week analyzing. Our process began by looking at the orders in which colleges across the nation sent their protein structure samples to Cal State Fullerton for structural analysis. Having the access and opportunity to operate one of the most sophisticated machines in the country, Dr. K., with me at her side, took on the task of creating protein crystal structures. These crystals created were not shiny jewels but were tiny, almost particle-like forms that needed to endure through the heat of the beam and ice that formed on top of them. Data would take weeks to accumulate since the X-ray beams were shot through the crystal at every angle to determine the structure of the protein we tested. As the data gather in the computer, red, yellow, and white dots scatter on the screen. As trivial as these "dots" may seem, they notify us where dense forms of carbon lie, which is crucial in discovering the structure of the protein crystal.

Each and every day, Dr. K. and I would climb down into our cave during the early daylight hours and later would return to the surface in the midst of the evening. By the time I left the cave, the day had been eaten up, but the science and lab work that I experienced was well worth the time and toil. Dedicated and committed, the college students, principal investigator, and research associate were somewhat eccentric. I was almost completely isolated from the real world other than a delivery of a Domino's pizza. I began to pick up some of the attributes and characteristics of being a researcher. Sometimes I found myself assisting college students who attended Dr. K.'s labs and classes. I also learned that not only was it important to understand the science behind our testing but also to have other proficiencies. For example, one day we had to move some heavy nitrogen tanks that help cool the crystal, so I became the main participant thanks to my weight-lifting skills. When mounting the delicate and tiny crystals, my piano and laoti fingers also came in handy. As I found my place, the other collegiate professors and colleagues accepted me into their clan, and I was ecstatic. Being part of the interactive atmosphere of college professors, students, and top-tier science resources, I could not have asked for a more in-depth experience of lab work. I understand more about academic researching and have decided that lab research is definitely a new-found passion. I am willing to put in the long hours and effort that is needed to successfully create and run experiments and plan to do so at [name of college].

Spanish

"Un parangaricutirimicuareño le dijo a Gloria Guzmán que encontró una figura geométrica gigantesca en Parangaricutirimícuaro," translates to "A man from Parangaricutirimícuaro told Gloria Guzman that he found a giant geometric figure in Parangaricutirimícuaro." This Spanish sentence, lacking in any literary or analytic substance, was used as a pronunciation assessment in my freshman-year Spanish II Honors class. To this day, the second word of the sentence, parangaricutirimicuareño, undoubtedly stands as my favorite word because of what we have been through together (the word and me).

On the first day of school, Señor L., who refused to utter a single word in English and would not permit any of his students to do so either, intimidated my clueless freshman self. My Spanish skills at that point were weak, and my confidence in speaking the language was even weaker. I decided, however, that I would master the Spanish language before graduating high school, starting with the pronunciation assessment. At first, I stumbled over each word like a kid with her shoelaces tied together. But after a while, I found myself chattering off each sentence quickly and easily: almost second nature.

"Paran-gari-cuti-rimi-cuareño." I found myself saying, over and over. In the car, in the shower, at practice, during rehearsals. Something about the way it encapsulated all my favorite sounds in the Spanish language—each strong vowel, the quick tempo, the rolling "ñ"—made the word infectious. To this day, I find myself repeating this word, strategically working it in to Spanish essays and presentations solely for my personal enjoyment. But more important, I think parangaricutirimicuareño symbolizes my growth in the Spanish language. It has been a constant fixture in my Spanish career: from a blundering freshman to a confident senior. I would never say that I have mastered the language, but I have certainly become proficient and quasi-fluent. I can carry on full conversations with native speakers: a feat that makes me proud.

Sample Paragraphs: Intellectual Passion

Politics and Elections

Campaigns, debates, and a massive field of candidates whittled down to a couple to create a perfect storm every fourth year. Thus, looking back on my study of United States history, I reflect upon over two centuries of the past as a series of elections and various goings-on between each one. A few stick out for me. The election of 1800, for example, produced an earth-shattering outcome: the peaceful transition of power from Adams' Federalists to Jefferson's Democratic Republicans, later known as the "Bloodless Revolution" introduced the idea that a transition of power could take place without bloodshed, almost unheard-of at the time. Or, in 1824, when John Quincy Adams corruptly bargained his way into office by appointing Henry Clay to the Secretary of State post, thereby symbolically christening him as the next President. From Franklin Delano Roosevelt's demolition of Alf Landon in 1936 to Nixon's 1968 win in the wake of Robert Kennedy's assassination, each election has its own story, playing on a reel like movies in my brain. I find modern elections equally, if not more, fascinating. When watching this year's string of Republican primary debates, sometimes I wanted to jump inside the TV and slap the candidates across the face. That may sound rash, and I do respect and identify with many Republican ideals, but I had a hard time swallowing the strategy behind the "anybody-but-Romney" period that lasted for months on end. To me, and surely most Americans, it was clear from the start that Romney would be the Republican nominee in 2012. So why then did the party seem so determined to highlight the other candidates, hopeless in the general election, and thereby tatter Romney's national reputation? Last year, I joined both my Texas high school's Young Liberals club (membership: 29) and Young Republicans club (membership, unsurprisingly: 145) to understand all the political views inside my school's microcosm. I have found, through this process, that some political tactics are complicated. They cannot be explained in a few sentences. Campaigns are fascinating, but they are fickle. American politics, however, are everlasting and ever-changing.

Love of Learning

My father has always claimed that my intellectual and culinary appetites mirror each other. A buffet line is heaven for me—I want to put a little bit of everything on my plate. What can sometimes be a problem, however, is that if something interests me, I want more than just a little bit. I want to know everything there is to know about it and how it relates to everything else. One of the main reasons I am greatly looking forward to college is to finally be able to delve deeper into subjects I am already interested in and to discover new interests in areas I have not yet had the opportunity to explore. Looking over the list of possible majors and courses available at different institutions actually overwhelms me. So much appeals to me—art history, Spanish, international relations, comparative literature, linguistics, film studies, philosophy, psychology, and women's studies, to name only a few. My only concern is that I will not have the time to fully explore these subjects. As I progress with my education I cannot guess whether my interests will become narrower and more focused, or if they will become more eclectic.

Though many different areas of study excite me, the common linking factor between them is that they all relate to people. Anything involving an aspect of humanity, such as human nature, emotion, culture, or accomplishment, fascinates me. This is why I think that I may want to major in cultural anthropology. It seems like that discipline would most broadly cover my interests and passion for learning about the people of the world. Though I am uncertain as to what I will pursue as a career, I am certain that I want to spend my life not only learning about other cultures, but also experiencing them firsthand. I wish to travel and observe and participate in the lives of people around the world. In my search for a profession worth making my life's work, I will look for a way to combine my passions for travel, culture, and writing and my desire to make a positive impact on the situations of people around the globe. I would love to work as a journalist for a magazine like *National Geographic*. I would be excited to travel to Africa and witness and write about tribal wedding rituals, or to go to Spain and research the history of the gypsies.

Sometimes I worry that the world is too big, and that there is so much out there that I wouldn't possibly be able to experience all of it. However, this feeling of apprehension always quickly passes as I remind myself that this means I won't ever need to worry about becoming bored. I am looking forward to life and all it has to offer.

Sample Paragraphs: Philosophical Ideas

Chance

I met my best friend during the first period of my first day of high school. His last name is Morgan, and mine is Mills. So when our teacher assigned seats alphabetically, he ended up sitting directly behind me. We started to talk and soon discovered we shared identical senses of humor and kindred perspectives on the world. We laughed hysterically every time we were together. Over the course of a full year of sitting near each other we became very close friends, and I know that he is the person I will remember most from high school. I often wonder what would have happened had we not had freshman English together, or if Mr. E. hadn't arranged the class alphabetically by last name, or if our names had started with a different letter. Would we never have connected, or would we somehow have gravitated towards each other, being such similar people?

The question of fate is intellectually intriguing to me. Are our lives a random sequence of events, and do we meet the people who are most important to us by coincidence? Or are there some things that are supposed to happen, that would occur no matter what? While I do think that chance, choice, and luck are major components in our lives, I also believe in a kind of fate. Not a written-in-stone-by-the-gods kind of fate, but rather a mysterious, mutable kind. The third law of thermodynamics is entropy, or the theory that all natural processes tend to proceed in such a direction that the disorder or randomness of the system increases. While I accept this as law in all things scientific, I do not believe that life is a science. Instead, I subscribe to a "reverse entropy" theory, based on the belief that the actions and events of our lives are more often than not pieces of the puzzle being fitted together, not broken apart. To take away the presence of fate in life and leave only the roll of the dice would reduce the meaning of our existence.

But I still wonder what would have happened had the seating chart not been in alphabetical order.

Silence

As you are reading my essay, you are probably sitting in a silent room filled with a group of people who are also evaluating admission compositions. But as you are sitting there, I invite you to answer this question: is it really silent in the room that you are seated in? I admit I was entirely confused when I was confronted with the same question. Suddenly, in the midst of reading a Music Appreciation book, my mind began to wander and ten pages later, I realized I couldn't remember anything that I had just read, and all I could focus on was my deep thought: "Is there such a thing as silence?" Upon further reflection, I realized maybe my question was inexplicable, maybe my question had no answer, and maybe there is no such thing.

While I read my Music Appreciation book, I stumbled across a man by the name of John Cage. John developed a musical style called Indeterminacy, where he let chance determine his music after an experience in 1951 when he locked himself in an absolutely silent chamber and came to the conclusion that silence did not exist. Although there were no external sounds to disrupt the silence around John, he could still hear sounds from inside his body. He could perceive the sounds of his blood circulating and the operation of his nervous system. Before reading about this, I had the same thought, but I never realized it had been expressed before. I often would stay up until the early hours of the morning pondering the question, while I would lie in my bed staring at the ceiling. I would go under the covers and listen, expecting to hear nothing, but some sound would always emerge. Whether it was a passing car on the street or the faint sound of a plane passing above in the starry early morning sky, the quiet that I could sense around me would always be disrupted.

I am sure right now, although seemingly silent in your room, you can hear something. Someone is shuffling papers or sniffling. Maybe it is not that obvious. Maybe the only sound you hear is the soft, slight sound of a clock ticking or something even less noticeable like the sound of your breathing. My point is that some sound will always be made. When I hear the question "If a tree falls in a forest and there's no one there to hear it, does it make a sound?" I say it doesn't really matter because even if the true answer to this seemingly baffling philosophical inquiry is no, I figure something will be making a sound.

Time Travel

Time travel fascinates me on many different levels—some of which have been explored by scientists and fiction writers and some which have not. Moreover, I think that time travel represents both the possibilities and limitations of science.

To be clear, when I speak of time travel, I am talking about the concept of moving between different moments in time the same way we move between different points in space. Beyond fiction, there are various ways that a person could travel into the future—at least in a sense. For example, in theory, a person could travel from the Earth and back at the speed of light, with the trip lasting only a few years according to his clock, but return to find that many years have passed on Earth.

Conceptually, engineering and science could allow a person to move at, or faster than, the speed of light. But that is all they could do. Did the person really "travel through time?" Did the trip last only a few years or did it last many? As such, science's limitations have been exposed. What has actually occurred must be interpreted—and not necessarily by scientists.

Further, what are the consequences of such travel? In biology class, I learned that bacteria and viruses have been getting stronger over the years; this is why drugs to combat diseases and viruses have had to become stronger. How does this factor into so-called time travel? It would seem that if one were to return to Earth after the passing of many years, perhaps thousands of years, his body would not have sufficient immunity to the diseases, bacteria, and viruses that exist on Earth at that moment. His ability to survive may be curtailed. Accordingly, for every action there is a reaction; for every accomplishment there is a new challenge.

Chapter Six

The "Why This School?" Question

I used to think this question was such a waste of time for my students. Why would colleges want to hear things that they already know about themselves reflected back to them in the application? What could that possibly teach admission officers about an applicant other than the fact that they could regurgitate facts about a school that the school already knows?

As the years wore on and this type of question appeared in various permutations, I started to better understand the value of it in the college application. My view was quite short-sighted and naïve. This question offers the perfect opportunity for a student to demonstrate interest in a school. How much homework have you really done to learn the idiosyncrasies about the school? Do you know anything beyond what is written on a website? Have you visited the campus? Talked to students? Read the school newspaper? Researched classes and professors of interest to you?

> *"Demonstrated interest" is a term coined by admission offices to help determine how really interested you are in their school. Many offices keep detailed data on any outreach or connection you have initiated to the school. Have you attended college fairs and completed a card? Have you e-mailed the admission office a question? Have you ever called in a question? Have you completed the online registration on the college website?*
>
> *It's important to note, however, that many competitive colleges place little or no value on demonstrated interested, so don't make yourself crazy visiting, e-mailing, or connecting with those schools. In the long run, demonstrated interest won't have a major impact on your admission decision at those institutions.*

There are many key components to include when answering this type of question. Your response should not be generic. In other words, what you write should not be so general that you could be talking about just any or many schools. The "Why This School?" response needs to be personally tailored to each school that asks the question.

Some prompts are just "why this school?" while others add "what do you plan to study or pursue academically at our school?" You can answer the first question by also including what you plan to study, even if it is not asked in the prompt. Remember, though, to still be specific to each school and not general about your academic interests. While most colleges are full service and accommodate all majors, not all campuses have a true Great Books curriculum, a block course program, a national arboretum, or a linear particle accelerator on campus. It is best to know which campuses do and don't have these special features so that you don't accidentally highlight or refer to a feature not offered or list an incorrect "uniqueness" of a campus.

If you mention a campus service, department, or program, be sure you have the correct name. For example, don't assume that all colleges have a department called "Career Services." Some schools may call that office Career Counseling and Support; another campus may have named it to honor an alumni, such as the Joe Smith Career Services Office, and so on. It's the same when it comes to specific programs. For example, one school may call its Overseas Studies Program just that, while others may call it the International Experience Office or the Semester-Abroad Department. Again, this may seem like no big deal, but you don't want to mislabel a school's program or assume it has a program when it very well may not. Your mistakes might imply laziness on your application or a lack of interest in the school. Demonstrate how you spent time digging in deeper and researching that school's specific program and name it correctly in your writing.

The following are some suggested ways to find answers that you can weave into your responses to the "Why This School?" question. Then you can read several samples to see how various students tackled this question in their college application.

Dos and Don'ts for Learning About a School

Dos

- **Do tour the campus and take it all in.** If you are able to visit the actual campus, be mindful of all you see, hear, and even taste! You will learn by reading signs, eavesdropping on conversations, and asking lots of questions. Take note of what you observe—in a notebook or on your tablet or phone device—since after you visit many schools they tend to blur together.
- **Do talk to students when you visit.** Ask as many students as you can the questions that most interest you. Academic, social, housing, food—any topic. Since they are the current customers on campus, learn what they think of their school. Ask about their favorite class, professor, and tradition. And ask what they do on the weekends, even this past weekend, for fun. Take notes

so you can refer back to what you learned from these "interviews."

- **Do peruse the school newspaper and any other student publication.** You can often find it online. Most school papers are uncensored and run by students, so you get the "real" views of kids who are living life there now. You can also gain information about current campus events and happenings, read opinions of students in the op-ed areas, and learn what issues are being supported or debated on campus by students as well as the faculty and administration.

- **Do check out the campus Facebook page, message boards, and other online spaces that offer student voices.** These forums offer great pearls of wisdom and also frank thoughts from students and other campus members.

- **Do visit the school's website and admission section of the website.** But remember that websites are built as public relations tools and rarely show sad or gloomy students—or bad weather for that matter! Websites are the perfect place to get your Frequently Asked Questions (FAQs) answered and other factual information. You can also research faculty members, classes, student organizations, etc., via the website, so spend some time not just poking but digging around.

- **Do visit the school's alumni pages online or in a magazine.** There you can read about what graduates have gone on to do or accomplish and see how tightly-knit the network of alumni really is. How closely do alumni interface with students for summer internships or jobs after college? This is useful information to know.

- **Do research the school lore, traditions, and history.** Oftentimes, the roots of a school grow into a reputation or are reflected in the campus culture.

Don'ts

- **Don't rely on the first answer you receive from a student.** Ask MANY students the same question and you will find your answers somewhere amongst them!

- **Don't let one bad tour or tour guide taint your image of a school.** Be more open minded, especially if you are admitted and can revisit or review a school with fresh eyes.

- **Don't trust that every day will be a sunny day on campus.** If you are lucky enough to tour a school or two in good weather, remember that it snows on the East Coast and gets blazing hot or humid in the South!

- **Don't solely rely on the admissions office's marketing materials and publications.** While they are very helpful, their job is to "sell" the school to you. Students tend to be your best resources. (Have your parents talk to other parents on campus if you are open or willing to let them participate in your research process. Sometimes, they can also obtain useful nuggets.)

- **Don't assume that if you see a dorm room on campus that they all look like that one.** Some rooms are singles, doubles, triples, and even quads. Some dorms are co-ed or single sex. Some have bathrooms on a hallway, while others are on another floor. Some students live in apartments or fraternity/sorority houses, and so on. Again, do your homework, and learn as much as you can once you hone in on your school.

- **Don't beat yourself up about schools that seem out of your reach or too competitive for you to get into.** Remember the numbers that schools publish regarding applicants' admitted test scores and GPAs are just *averages*. That means that there are students who apply who score above those numbers and others who score below.

Sample "Why This School?" Essay Responses

The following are some sample short essay responses to the "Why this school?" question and/or some version of that question PLUS the "What do you want to study at our school?" question. Pay close attention to the wide range of replies, but note the importance of providing specific details about each school and not generalizing. Also, you might want to compare and contrast the answers to the "Why this school?" question that are written by different students about the same school. These multiple answers to the same question provide a unique opportunity to see how different students reflected on their perceptions of the same place.

Why Boston University?

She wasn't looking for a new whale call. But on Boston's shores, a marine science major discovered vocalizations never-before sensed by humans. They were cetacean secrets exposed to inquisitive mammals. And she followed them. It is this spirit of discovery that drives the students of Boston University—and me. I love to perform both medical research *and* musical theatre. BU's environment fosters the inquiry and pro-activity that motivate me and also provides the stage for my creativity. I admire and embody BU students' willingness not only to answer questions but also to *find* the questions. A university that so strongly promotes exploration is the optimum venue for me to pursue my scientific curiosities, especially with UROP. In research and performance, I will search for ways to heal people physically and bring more laughter to their lives. I look forward to feeding my intellectual interests through the comprehensive Specialization in Cell Biology, Molecular Biology, and Genetics major, supplemented by courses in medical anthropology. BU's Accelerated Program in Medicine will provide me immediate clinical training, preparing me for my career as a pediatric specialist. With the opportunity to become a medical doctor in less time than typically required, I will contribute to humankind sooner and for longer. Performing with BU on Broadway presents my ideal theatrical experience to accompany my education. Wearing character shoes at the BU Theatre with the Huntington Theatre Company or scrubs at the Boston Medical Center, I will lead BU as I rehearse for my dream roles.

Why Colby College?

Colby is a college particularly set apart from the rest. The small size, ideal location in rural Maine, and comforting atmosphere first attracted me to the campus. Colby's strong English programs and new art facility also caught my attention because of my genuine interest in these subjects. But the one experience that really made Colby my top choice for college was my overnight on campus spent with the soccer team. Although many Southern California natives may have been discouraged by the weather, I thoroughly enjoyed the cold and rainy October weekend, which gave me the chance to stay in a comfortable, welcoming environment with my peers to feel the genuine encouragement the school offers each of its students. Meeting the Colby Soccer girls and running around during the Oktoberfest made a memorable impression, and I discovered Colby's vibrant campus life and quickly felt connected to the school. The residence hall system greatly appeals to me and the tight community created in each dorm suits me. Ideally, I picture myself up late into the night discussing a literary passage or debating a political idea. Maine is so different from where I live, and my overwhelmingly positive response to the crisp weather, distinct fall colors, beautiful location, and stimulating liberal arts environment led me to the conclusion that Colby College is the place I want to be.

Why Duke University?

The opportunities offered at Duke through the Trinity College of Arts and Sciences to do research and help others—ranging from stem-cell research to helping at Duke's Children's Hospital—seem endless to me. What intrigues me most is the Focus Program. Challenging freshmen from the start on varying topics in free discussion tailored to expand knowledge and awareness provides an exceptional opportunity! I also found Program II of interest because it would allow me to synthesize two interests into one interdisciplinary function. The Villa Corsi-Salviati of Duke's study-abroad program seems fascinating. I would be excited to experience Italian Renaissance art, music, philosophy, science, and technology.

With over 300 clubs and organizations at Duke, I would immerse myself in new organizations and also continue my interest in Greek culture, weightlifting, and debate. The fraternity system raises Duke into yet another realm of renowned schools. In addition, I see myself working and volunteering at Duke's Children's Hospital, helping kids like my younger brother. I have spent a great deal of time in that hospital for my brother's bone marrow transplant, and I believe I owe something to those who helped my brother survive and persevere.

The Trinity College of Arts and Sciences' Winter Forum, a three-day intensive and interactive learning experience where faculty and students come together to problem-solve a global simulation in real time, sounds fascinating. "Learning without Limits," whether Study Abroad, DukeEngage, or taking part in community service in Durham as part of a first-year writing class, whets my appetite for being engaged—not only in the classroom but also outside the classroom. Most important, I believe Trinity College of Arts and Sciences will challenge me both mentally and spiritually by taking me out of my comfort zone. By researching, working, and learning from world-class faculty, I know I will be challenged and pushed to unknown limits.

Why Duke University?

This is what I dream of: waking up one day and putting on a sharply tailored suit and walking to my office on Capitol Hill. But more immediately, I dream of waking up on East Campus and putting on my blue and white sweatshirt. I think that if given the opportunity to wear the sweatshirt, it could one day morph into the suit. During my time in that sweatshirt (I imagine a barely worn-out crewneck), I want to be exposed to new things and new people, to become a change agent within my university, and later, my world. I want to wander through Duke forest as I did on my visit last February, feeling like part of the Duke community. But my visit to Duke showed me that more than anything else, I want to pursue my passions alongside passionate people. My interests are broad, and I want to find crossover, whether through multiple majors or Program II. From history to politics to Shakespeare and from gymnastics to dance to theatre, curiosity and enthusiasm drive me to learn. Fortunately, I am assured by Duke's strategic plan that "Duke is a particularly conducive place . . . for interdisciplinary collaboration to address problems." With this in mind, at Duke I plan to study politics, hopefully studying during a semester in Washington, D.C.; and I plan to continue pursuing the performing arts, on stage and beyond.

This year, I organized a community-service initiative for the Kinkaid Dance Company to bring clean water to Africa. I hope to continue service through art by promoting arts education in Zhuhai as a part of DukeEngage.

When I finally don the suit (a navy pinstripe skirt and matching jacket, the worn-out sweatshirt in the tiny closet of my D.C. studio apartment), with a Duke degree in hand, I plan to join an elite group of women looking to break in to the arena of political hardball traditionally dominated by men. I find the idea of women unequal to men in the political world disconcerting, and I dread facing gender-based adversity. But Duke gives me opportunities to fight this fear by taking courses such as "Women/Political System" or running for student government. From where I sit today, I hope that many more Hillary Clintons exist in my generation than in those past and that, with a Duke education, I can be one of them.

Why Emory University?

Memories and tradition are very important to me. Visiting Emory and looking all around the campus, littered with skeleton decorations during the middle of March, I knew right away this would be my number one college. As I learned about Dooley's history and how he became Emory's unofficial mascot, all I could do was smile and laugh. During my tour, my aunt pointed out which libraries my uncle, father, and aunt would study in, and how they had to move in the middle of the night because one stayed open later than the other. As much as I realize my life does not need to perfectly reflect theirs, once I looked into Emory, I understood why they had enjoyed their experience so much.

I liked what I read about Dr. Keith Easterling and his research on addictive drugs. Biology has always fascinated me, yet a specific focus on drug addiction and how neurotransmitter receptors can be seen as targets in order to treat addictions is understandably interesting. Also, as a personal fan of Andy Warhol, I was pleased to read about his Polaroid portrait exhibit on display at the Michael C. Carlos Museum. Also, the upcoming King Tut exhibit, which is a rare occasion in itself, appeals to me. As someone who tries to be as environmentally friendly as possible, I would like to be housed in the Few and Evans residence, Emory's new "green" buildings. Getting to know more about school life on my tour and understanding what the school has to offer confirmed that Emory is my first-choice college.

Why Emory University?

I was first attracted to Emory University because of its reputation and location. As I started to research more, I discovered the tradition of Dooley. If given the opportunity, I would love to attend Dooley's Ball on McDonough Field in celebration of the university. I enjoy getting involved in clubs, and by joining the Student Programming Council I would contribute my creative ideas to making events on campus more fun. I love the charity group Volunteer Emory. I have many service hours, and I know it would be something I would like to continue into the future. My particular favorite charity organization is similar to Atlanta Community Food Bank where I spend many hours serving food to the homeless.

Why Knox College?

Since sophomore year, I have been deluged with college mail. Green or autumn campuses (never winter), with small groups of happy, diverse students graced postcards and view books, along with a school's wonderful statistics. Among these were some from Knox College in a place called Galesburg, Illinois, with the cheesy slogan of "Opportunity Knox!"

As time wore on and the endless mailings continued, my family happened to drive through Galesburg over Thanksgiving break. While there, we noticed banners for Knox College. Then I remembered: Opportunity Knox! We drove around the city and from then on, I remembered when other items from Knox came in the mail.

About six months ago, I became aware, through my mom, of the book *Colleges That Change Lives*. I found it interesting, especially because in my initial searching I found myself drawn to these smaller, liberal arts schools. Looking through the book, I noticed a familiar name was included: Knox. I attended a CTCL fair in Chicago. There, I talked with a Knox admissions representative and really grew interested.

I visited Knox soon after, and, though I didn't get to stay the whole day, I was able to get a feel for the campus. People there are driven. They choose to go to Knox for a reason and are thus challenged and encouraged to think critically. These are skills I have learned as an International Baccalaureate Full Diploma Candidate. I have challenged myself, especially in my final two years of high school. An environment that encourages thinking differently and critically is therefore a natural progression, and it's what I want as I pursue higher education. I feel confident that Knox will be able to meet these needs.

Why Lake Forest College?

I first learned about Lake Forest College through my college adviser. I had told her that I loved Chicago and wanted to go to school in or near it. She suggested Lake Forest because it was close to the city, which is a big factor for me when deciding where to apply to college. I am interested in Lake Forest because it isn't so large that it would be overwhelming, but there are still many opportunities available. I like that the college is relatively small in size, which means that there are small classes and a chance to get to know many of my fellow students. The "First Year Studies" program is also interesting to me because it seems to create an easier transition to college.

I am particularly interested in the availability of internships and the strong ties Lake Forest College has to the city. Many Lake Forest students get internships in the city, which is something that I am definitely interested in doing. I think that since the college is so close to Chicago I will have ample opportunities to be exposed to the business world when it comes time to get a job after college. I am also interested in the Chicago-related courses that are offered because they provide a taste of the "real world." One professor talked about taking his students into the city to see a play, and another went in the pouring rain just to go searching for birds. These are experiences that I would get no other place than Lake Forest College, a small, intimate college located near the great city of Chicago.

Why Northwestern University?

This summer I had the unique pleasure of attending the National High School Institute at Northwestern University. After spending five intense and amazing weeks on campus, I am totally convinced that Northwestern is the right college for me. The city of Evanston provides a suburban feel in which I am comfortable. Its proximity to Chicago allows me to be in touch with a friendly city, only an "L" train away. Evanston and Chicago also offer great restaurants when Hinman Cafeteria starts to get a little old.

One of the most unique qualities about Northwestern is the Lakefill. During the film program, we were given the task of creating a documentary on this amazing site. It's like a forest, island, and park all in one. The graffiti-covered rocks never came across as vandalism to me but as more of a resident's way to express how they really feel about Northwestern or Evanston in a special way. The ever-changing "rock" on campus was also neat; even during the summer months, when fewer students are on campus, the rock is still painted over again and again.

Northwestern's beauty is only matched by the education it offers. As an aspiring screenwriter, I was greatly impressed that Northwestern offers not only the best instruction but also intimate class sizes with as few as 11 students. This small classroom allows me to connect to my teachers as well as peers who I believe are crucial to my writing process. Having the ability to graduate with not only a degree in creative writing in media but also a portfolio will prepare me better for my career.

With all Northwestern has to offer, how could I possibly go wrong? I hope to take advantage of this prestigious school by taking the beauty and allowing it to inspire my writing. For years I have heard of Northwestern's amazing journalism and writing program, and now I understand why. I am excited to become a Wildcat.

Why Northwestern University?

The color purple screams. It's royalty. It's plums. It's my favorite and the immediate reason I took an interest in Northwestern. The website depicted the "finest band in the land," summoning my color guard–captain name. I was bursting with excitement to visit Evanston, babbling over the trip for weeks, and I wasn't disappointed. Walking into Evanston was like walking into a football game—the entire campus draped in purple-clad students, and their faces: *every* student smiled. It seemed all knew one another personally; I have never seen anything like it.

Northwestern's School of Education and Social Policy (SESP) is a home for fostering my dream of ending human trafficking. Few universities offer an undergraduate school for social policy, and fewer offer the small, tight-knit family of SESP. In addition, the ease with which I could integrate my work with survivors of trafficking and Northwestern is inspiring. Through opportunities like LIFT-Chicago, it would be refreshing to serve in an urban area versus my suburbia. Moreover, researching a self-created topic abroad would be fulfilling, as it is a goal of mine to study how tradition and education have affected culture related to trafficking in Mumbai, India.

It's eerie that simply the color purple led me to Northwestern. However that is how opportunity knocks: unexpectedly, suddenly, and unstoppably. The Wildcat Pride of Evanston is unbelievable: from the posters pasted onto walkways to the integration of Division I sports and award-winning arts, it's no wonder that the student body smiles.

Why NYU?

I've always been interested in a variety of subjects within the humanitarian sector. I've grown up in a family that loves to travel and have found myself drawn to learning about different cultures—the aspects that define each and what connects all of us. Through my travels I developed a profound love for food, photography, writing, and people. I recorded many of my experiences in countless journals and have written numerous poems. I have several collections of photography, from daily exchanges to once-in-a-lifetime experiences. I have not decided upon a major, yet I'm interested in pursuing something linked to writing and expression. Photojournalism appeals to me because I desire a career that can be shared by people of all backgrounds and strongly believe in the impact of photography on others.

I am also interested in psychology. I've always naturally connected well with others and am part of the Peer Counseling Program at Sage, where 12 students work with the guidance counselor and advise students on subjects ranging from academics to drugs. Studying in NYU's College of Arts and Science would provide me with the opportunity to explore my different interests and solidify an area as my primary concentration.

Why Pitzer College?

I have grown up in a world of different cultures. As one with a mixed cultural background, Malaysian and Iranian, I have always loved learning about different countries, cities, and people. Ever since I can recall, I have been traveling the world discovering and learning about the different cultures I was being exposed to. Traveling through a small airport in Kota Kinabalu, Malaysia, I saw a woman of a well-respected class, devouring curry with her hand. I was bewildered as to why she didn't use utensils but then learned it was customary to eat this food with one's left hand. My parents have instilled in me a longing for discovery and a broad sense of acceptance for all that is different. My exposure to different lifestyles in addition to a diverse cultural upbringing has influenced my values and passions. Pitzer's emphasis on intercultural understanding will allow my interests to thrive and provide an environment for further growth.

Through my travels, I have developed a profound love for food, photography, writing, and, most of all, people. I have always been someone people turn to and deem as trustworthy and have always had a natural inclination to reach out. I am a part of my high school's Peer Counseling program, and I regard it as one of my priorities. I believe everyone possesses the power to accomplish, to help, and to succeed. Throughout my life, I have always believed in my responsibility and ability to help those I can. Social responsibility is a characteristic that can be conveyed through art, action, or counsel. I believe Pitzer's community offers an environment that coincides with my values.

The first thing I look at in a school is the course selection and the flexibility within the different colleges (if the school has more than one). I see myself pursuing a career with interdisciplinary emphasis, and I place heavy importance upon the ability to study more than one subject. A learning environment that encourages the expansion of knowledge on all fronts suits what I am interested in pursuing—a career that links or educates people from everywhere and anywhere.

Why Rice University?

While visiting my family in Houston, I toured the campus and fell in love with Rice. The university exuded a sense of community, especially within the Residential College System. It reminded me of my close-knit high school where we have a strong support group. In addition, Rice's friendly atmosphere caught my attention, because the students all seemed to greet familiar faces on their way across campus. The engineering building left me speechless; the unique design conveyed the creativity that originates within its walls. A small school like Rice facilitates the collaboration between undergraduates and professors in research. The campus' central location especially appeals to me because of Houston's renowned hospitals and overall medical atmosphere, encouraging access to research centers and programs through Rice. For example, the BioScience Research Collaborative with the Texas Medical Center provides a valuable connection for undergraduate bioengineering research. As a student interested in international opportunities, I appreciate the study-abroad programs that are available to students—especially those opportunities for students studying engineering. An experience studying bioengineering at India's Institute of Technology excites me, while the prestige associated with Rice gives me confidence for my future endeavors and occupation.

Why The Scripps Research Institute?

I heard about Scripps from my counselor, and my visit to Scripps confirmed why I'm applying. I wandered through the gorgeous gardens around campus and could imagine myself sitting on a bench, drinking some coffee, and working on my laptop. I've seen that the dorm rooms at Scripps are very clean, which is a plus for a neat freak like me. I also immediately fell in love with the Wednesday Tea tradition because it sounds like a great way to get to know my professors and fellow students. I know that if I attend Scripps I will challenge the way that I think through exploring the Core Curriculum of Interdisciplinary Humanities. After I visited Scripps, I strolled along the town nearby and immediately fell in love with it. Even though it's small, there were a lot of shops and restaurants that looked like great places to hang out with friends on the weekends. Scripps is a great place for me to enjoy my college experience, grow as a student, and explore many facets of learning.

Why Southern Methodist University?

SMU's hands-on learning will help me develop into a strong journalist. At an info night, I met enthusiastic alum Marlon Meikle. He was so friendly and explained how the Belo Foundation provided SMU with an entire newsroom! He advised, "On your first day, visit the SMU newsroom, indicate you wish to help, and you will be put to work!" Rick Diaz also influenced me. I interviewed with him in San Diego. He shared amazing student-life stories and SMU traditions, and his passion for SMU was contagious.

Why Stanford University?

I am passionate about computer science. To the surprise of some, last summer I took a course in particle physics at Stanford rather than a course in programming. However, those familiar with computer science know that math and physics are related subjects. While at Stanford, I learned of various experiments being performed at the university and around the world, and I was able to gain a deeper understanding of modern physics theories. I especially enjoyed working in a collaborative group to present our final research paper on BaBar (an experiment at Stanford designed to quantify the disparity between matter and anti-matter).

During my short time at Stanford, as well as from my tours of other colleges, I came to a few realizations about my ideal college experience:

- I don't want to be odd-man-out; I want to be in a school where science is a priority.
- I want the flexibility to choose my own destiny. I want to learn about computer science, math, and physics, but want to choose as much as possible what direction to take with them. I have a strong interest in theory-based programming but want to explore robotics and artificial intelligence.
- I don't just want to learn about great projects, I want to be part of them. The availability of undergraduate research is important to me.
- Sports matter. My passions are not limited to academia. I love college sports, especially football, basketball, and soccer.

While many schools satisfy certain aspects of my criteria, Stanford clearly hits them all. Stanford's science, especially its CS department, is second to none. There is no question that I will not be odd-man-out; as I saw in my summer course, I will be challenged by really smart people who share my interest in computers. Further, flexibility seems to permeate the Stanford CS curriculum as well as its research opportunities. There are many courses I can take and directions I could go, and I look forward to the journey. Even more, I look forward to participating in the research projects. (I intend to join one or more of the research groups to identify which project is right for me.) Lastly, Stanford football needs one more fan, and club soccer needs one more player. I am their man.

Why University of Michigan?

As I open the manila folder, I barely glance at the name—Lisa something—before going straight to the numbers. I plug them into my calculator: find the back-end ratio, document the IRR, and analyze the overall performance. A few years ago, I never could have pictured working at a sub-prime auto lender, an industry partially blamed for the economic crisis. But as I stacked that last file on to my boss's desk for approval, I realized that this car, a 1994 Honda, will provide Lisa with the means to drive to work, a necessity in Southern California, and, with that, the ability to provide for her family.

As I power off my calculator, I think back to my fourth-period Calculus class, where only a few months ago, I learned the mathematics behind the formulas I just used to compute Lisa's growth rate. It seems as if the fundamental question of my education to date has been: "When am I ever going to use this?" It was when fractions became statistics, rates of change showed market trends, and when memorized terms described behavior patterns that my education ceased to be a chore.

Right now I'm particularly interested in studying economics and psychology at Michigan. The relationship between the disciplines is compelling: when focusing on what people do, it is imperative to know how they think. I can see through my studies of psychology that we are creative and complicated beings but, in some ways, quite predictable. I laugh at my dad when he asks me to "analyze him," but know that it would be possible to describe his learning style, parenting type, or even characterize his personality. I look forward to combining these tools with my studies in economics.

I have chosen Michigan's College of Arts and Sciences because I am interested in double majoring in psychology and economics, taking classes like "Economics and Gender" and "Empowering Families and Communities." The community-based learning opportunities, with courses such as "Methods for Economic Development," will feed my interest in connecting volunteerism with economics and psychology.

From testing hypotheses with the Institute for Social Research, to predicting trends with the Research Seminar in Quantitative Economics, to perhaps interning through the Economics 299 program, I am excited to use Michigan's partnerships to get connected. I want to use these tools to bring new ideas to social entrepreneurism, a passion of mine for which I have found both psychology and economics directly relevant. Finally, I am excited to experience the Ann Arbor student life that I have been hearing about from our Wolverine family friends for years.

In short, Michigan's interdisciplinary programs and learning opportunities outside of the classroom are the perfect fit for my educational aspirations. For those reasons, I hope to attend.

Why University of Notre Dame?

Riding in that car on Saturday to Notre Dame, I had no real expectations. The visit was merely a promise to our ND friends. For years, my dad and I rooted for USC as it fought against the Irish in football! And we heard of the great and proud history of the dominance of the Irish. But standing at the doorway of Golden Dome, I *felt* that proud history. Every inch of the entire campus was drenched in "Notre Dame Pride," from my tour guide to Touchdown Jesus to that football stadium that I have seen so many times on television. Even so, my passion is for film, and, before visiting Notre Dame, I had never heard anything about its film program. But now I know a great one exists. Entering DeBartolo Center, I saw that Notre Dame shared my passion for film. Whether it is the "Australian Cinema" course with Professor Pamela Wojcik or production courses with Professor William Donaruma, I am excited to be a ND Film student. So, though my father will probably disown me, I want to be a Fighting Irish.

Why University of Pennsylvania?

When I visited Penn during the spring of my junior year, I knew it was the perfect place for me. As I strolled down Locust Walk, the students were buzzing around in excitement as they prepared for their Spring Fling, one of the many Penn traditions that I wish to participate in someday. Penn has a lot to offer academically. Students are allowed to take some classes in each college, which is a great opportunity for someone like me who has many different interests. As a freshman, I hope to partake in the infamous Econ Scream. I would also love to cheer on my fellow Quakers during sporting events and throw toast onto the field. Living in a big city like Philadelphia would be an exciting and new adventure for me. Since I'm a native California girl, I could actually experience a real winter for the first time! I belong at the University of Pennsylvania because I'm eager to explore new ideas and take part in the Penn traditions with pride.

Why Yale University?

I love to perform—both musical theatre and medical research. Yale's environment fosters the inquiry, pro-activity, and creativity that drive me. I admire and embody Yalies' willingness to not only answer questions but also to *find* the questions. Opportunities to improvise comedic musicals with Just Add Water present my ideal extracurricular experience. I look forward to taking the "From Microbes to Molecules" course, supplemented by seminars at the Peabody Museum—*and* leisurely visits there, too. Wearing character shoes at the Calhoun Cabaret or scrubs at the Yale-New Haven Hospital, I will lead Yale communities, rehearsing for my dream roles.

Chapter Seven

Supplemental Questions: Short Answers & Fill-in-the-Blanks

S hort-answer questions usually appear in the form of a supplement for those schools that accept the Common Application schools, but these questions are also asked by schools that use independent applications. Some schools change these questions year to year; others keep them for a few years and weed some out as time goes on.

Word limits can be tricky. Note the character or word count limits imposed by each question and be sure to stay within that amount—or your work will be essentially cut off and not fully seen or reviewed by your readers. In the Common Application, you are allowed to copy and paste in up to 650 words (no uploads at this time). For other schools not on the Common Application and that offer Supplemental short-answer questions, check their word limits or see if they permit you to upload a PDF or other file. And, always check in the print preview area to see that what you input reads clearly.

Just as is recommended for all of your other application writing, it is best to first compose these answers in a Word document so that you can write as much as you want and then cut down word by word or letter by letter to be sure your response will fit into the space provided in your supplements. Once you have "shaved" your work down to the limit, copy and paste it into the space provided. It's easier to catch errors when you create your response and then copy and paste it into the answer space rather than typing directly into the space provided. Again, sometimes the browser you are using may prevent you from using the copy-and-paste feature, so try logging in with Safari, then Firefox, and so on until it works!

As noted before, these questions are meant to allow and encourage you to show your personality, quirks, and sense of humor (or seriousness). Some are more thinking questions while others are just get-to-know-you prompts. Be true, have some fun, and allow your real voice to come through so that your responses offer a genuine feel for your character and personality. And remember, admission officers can tell when you have spent just a few hours on your essay or much more time being thoughtful and careful. So take your time with these questions, too.

Here are some examples from past years' applications:

Brandeis University:

You are required to spend the next year of your life in either the past or the future. What year would you travel to and why?

Bucknell University

Imagine that you are backpacking through a country you have never been to before. You are interested in engaging with the local population and your backpack includes three items that will help them learn about your family and culture. What are those three items and how do they represent your background?

Tufts University

The ancient Romans started it when they coined the phrase "Carpe diem." Jonathan Larson proclaimed "No day but today!" and most recently, Drake explained, "You Only Live Once (YOLO)." Have you ever seized the day? Lived like there was no tomorrow? Or perhaps you plan to shout YOLO while jumping into something in the future. What does #YOLO mean to you?

University of Virginia

- *What's your favorite word and why?*

- *In 2006, graduate student Robert Stilling discovered an unpublished poem by Robert Frost while doing research in U.Va.'s Small Collections Library. Where will your Stilling moment be in college?*

- *"To tweet or not to tweet."*

Wake Forest University

Give us your top ten list.

Here are some quick questions that Stanford University uses to get to know its student applicants better. Other schools also use similar short questions to add to the snap-shot image of their applicants.

Name your favorite books, authors, films, and/or musical artists.

What newspapers, magazines, and/or websites do you enjoy?

What is the most significant challenge that society faces today?

How did you spend your last 2 summers?

What were your favorite events (performances, exhibits, sporting events, etc.) this past year?

What historical moment or event do you wish you could have witnessed?

What five words best describe you?

[Longer paragraph reply] Stanford students possess an intellectual vitality. Reflect on an idea or experience that has been important to your intellectual development.

[Longer paragraph reply] Virtually all of Stanford's undergraduates live on campus. Write a note to your future roommate that reveals something about you, or will help your roommate—and us—know you better.

[Longer paragraph reply] What matters to you, and why?

Sample Supplemental Essays

What Kind of Roommate Will You Be?

I have an image of my college experience that transcends the classroom. Certainly, I intend to study hard to learn math and science, but also I intend to get much more than book knowledge from my time in college. In short, I intend to enjoy college with my fellow classmates. I look forward to participating in scientific research projects. I want to create something with others, about which we can all be proud. I intend to play club soccer while at college. I only hope that my team will be as tight as my high school team. Being part of such a team makes the academic pressures so much more endurable. Most of all, I look forward to late-night discussions (as I am a night owl) with my roommates on subjects that have nothing to do with my major. What happens after we are dead? Is the world we perceive really reality, or is it just one dimension of reality? Are dogs superior to cats? How did Al Gore create the Internet? Finally, while I love science, sports, camping, and the beach, I do not expect my roommates to have the same interests. I want to learn about their different cultures and/or experiences. I want to experience new things with them—whether it is a new food, film, or sport. Above all else, I want to have fun with them. When I graduate from college, I will not just have a great degree from a great university; I will have good friends.

To My Future Roommate:

Please forgive me for being a closet tomboy. Don't get me wrong; I love reality TV and cosmetics as much as the next girl, but the things that bring me the most joy are typically those associated with boys. Be forewarned: ESPN is my favorite channel, I almost exclusively listen to country music, and if I don't sweat by the end of every day, I feel like a failure. I am competitive and stubborn, and I don't take life too seriously. So I really hope you don't mind, but I will be hard at work on my March Madness bracket this fall; I will always have a window open on my computer tracking my favorite Houston sports teams: the Texans, the Rockets, and the Astros; and sometimes I might frantically yell at the TV during the fourth quarter of a football game. If you aren't from the South, you may find my country music preference objectionable, but I think I can turn you in to a Toby Keith–singing, Zac Brown Band–loving girl by the end of the year. I am also slightly hyperactive. I have to run around at least once a day, or I get stir-crazy. As far as being competitive goes, I, like most if not all humans, have always felt an inexplicable, inherent desire to be right. But I don't see these qualities as negative ones: I think they make me a balanced individual. I also cannot wait to meet you!

Love, L.

What would you want your future roommate to know about you? Tell us something about you that will help your future roommate—and us—know you better.

Dear Future Friend,

If you want to talk about the validity of Freudian psychology, go snowboarding in Lake Tahoe, or make your own journey like Herman Hesse's *Siddhartha*, you've got a roommate in me. You may find me bantering with my classmates, reading a classic in a nineteenth-century armchair within a secret study chamber, traversing the forests and nearby mountains, meeting a friend at Philz Coffee, or discussing what it means to be mindful with my brothers via Skype. You can expect that I will remain eclectic in my actions yet dependable in my values. It is likely that you will find a self-made, blown-glass vase; photographs of my grandparents during the 1950s; and vibrant, Bohemian trinkets decorating my wall. I assume you enjoy delectable meals. If this is true, then I will prepare some traditional Argentinean plates for you, drawing from my grandma's recipes and my mom's memories. I may even whip out my Boca (one of Argentina's club teams) jersey, and we can watch a soccer game or two!

As a forewarning, the scent of paint will permeate our room on game days. With three brothers, I have grown to love football with intensity, so please join me in decked-out, head-to-toe red and white for the Pac-12 football games at Stanford Stadium! I imagine us frequenting *Stanford Live* and the *Cantor Center* to complement our studies with some arts and culture! Also, I think it will be fun and valuable if we get involved in the Emerging Leaders Retreat and the Stanford College Prep program to forge our way into our public service path at Stanford and beyond.

I think, therefore I am a philosophy fiend. To fuel that interest, I would love for you to accompany me to some of *Philosophy Talk*'s shows; we could even discuss the blog's material by lamplight in our dorm! It is reasonable for you to expect me to maintain a peaceful and tidy atmosphere, but, in return, I ask that you share with me your culture, your humor, and your experiences. I can't wait to meet you!

What Is the Most Significant Challenge That Society Faces Today?

I've seen firsthand the obstacles faced by people with disabilities. Politics, loopholes in systems, and bureaucracy of healthcare make tasks such as false bill payments, inadequate nursing aides, and sidewalk ramps impossible to deal with. The most "unheard" are those who can't fend for themselves. [300 characters]

What Historical Moment or Event Do You Wish You Could Have Witnessed?

I wish I could have watched the Boston Tea Party. It must have been amazing to see Samuel Adams and the Sons of Liberty, with Native American disguises, board the ships in Boston Harbor and dump the heavy casks of tea overboard. Witnessing such a rebellious protest would have been so interesting. [300 characters]

What Historical Moment or Event Do You Wish You Could Have Witnessed?

The 1856 brawling of Sen. Sumner and Rep. Brooks, who used his cane as a weapon, on the floor of the Senate both captures antebellum culture and makes me laugh. I would love to have seen Brooks defend his Southern honor. [300 characters]

What Historical Moment or Event Do You Wish You Could Have Witnessed or Participated In?

With the rise of new fashion and music, who could resist rocking away to brand new Doo Wop music while dancing in a poodle skirt in the 1950s? This era also helped create lifetime toys for each generation such as Barbies and Frisbees. Many don't realize the impact that decade has on today's culture. [300 characters]

If You Could Design Your Own Course Today, What Would It Be?

The class I would design would be called "Not-So-Ancient History: Forces Shaping Our World Today." In my years of history classes, we've barely gotten past Watergate. Yes, we've focused on big things that a history class is supposed to focus on, such as the French Revolution and the World Wars, but whether due to time constraints or the nature of the class stopping at a certain point, I have not had the opportunity to take a class that deals with more recent events. I would love to take a class in recent history, maybe just the past twenty to thirty years or even the seventeen years I've been alive. I want to closely examine things that have happened within my lifetime that are shaping my future. Yes, I was alive when 9/11 happened. But I was in first grade. I didn't understand the implications of it or even the cause. In the time I've been alive, there have been three different presidents in the White House. Yet I really only know about the third. There's more to consider than just historic events—the scientific basis for global warming and its pending implications on our world; the sociological impact of the technological revolution; the ethical issues we face as human rights violations around the world come to light—these are just a few potential topics. Living in an era when so much is happening, I want to understand what happened when I wasn't really paying attention (but what 3-year old really would?). With this, I feel I would be able to understand current events and my world more fully and be better prepared to play a part in the future.

How Are You and St. Olaf College a Good Fit for Each Other?

I am a student who has a wide variety of interests and never really shuts her brain off. I love to read and make connections between things I've learned. I believe knowledge is more than just what you learn in class but rather something to apply to life whenever you can. When I visited St. Olaf, it felt like a place that encourages what I already do. It wants students to use life experiences and everything they've learned to think creatively and solve problems. I want an environment that fosters growth through learning, but also one of camaraderie and openness.

Fill in the blanks:

Everyone knows that I _____:

> *am short.*
>
> *get good grades.*
>
> *like to read.*
>
> *love cats.*
>
> *am inquisitive.*

No one knows that I _____:

> *am a Nerdfighter.*
>
> *can't whistle.*
>
> *hate pep assemblies!*
>
> *hate it when people don't use the resources available to them.*

St. Olaf should know that I _____:

> *really like their food.*
>
> *think their campus is cool.*
>
> *am really grateful their campus safety department rescued us (from our dead battery).*
>
> *could be an awesome Ole, even though I'm Swiss.*
>
> *have a lot of potential in a small package.*

We are a community with quirks—in our language and traditions. Describe one of your quirks and why it is part of who you are.

Imagine a quite faded, seriously stretched-out piece of green cloth with exactly thirteen holes of various sizes as well as a few mascara stains, draped over my left shoulder as I write this. My quirk is my continued possession of my baby blanket. I even still like to have it when I sleep at night. I know that might sound a bit ridiculous coming from someone my age. Nevertheless, this tattered little blanket has been my piece of comfort and security throughout most of my life. It is physical evidence of my past, and intertwined around each thread are zillions of memories, beginning with the time I received it at the age of three. Although I currently could not bear to part with this old, faded piece of cloth, when my blanket and I were first acquainted, I loathed the sight of it. It was not my original, but rather a replacement after losing the first one. So naturally in my young mind, it was the most awful thing on the face of the earth. Eventually, however, I warmed up to my new blanket, and in time it became something I could not comfortably live without. It has traveled with me on numerous adventures, seen countless sleepovers, and still keeps me somewhat warm at night. So here I am, fifteen years later, ready to take my blanket with me on my upcoming journey, weaving fresh memories around these cherished threads all the while.

How Do You Think the World Sees You?

Author's note: This supplemental essay is very creative and clever. It also could be used as a "main" essay, as it is similar those that appeared in Chapter Three, in the "Bulletin Board" section (see pages 150–154).

I am red. Red in the morning when my eyes burn and itch from the dryness of a difficult night's sleep. Red at noon sitting in the warmth of the sun on the green grass of a small park at the end of a long run. Red in the afternoon cold when my cheeks, hands, and feet ache from the chill of the blistering wind of a mountain range. Red in the night from the steam of the pot on the red-hot stove.

I am blue. Cool blue walking through the halls of a high school waving with a smile. Deep blue when that one boy looks at my eyes, glistening. Blue when the water from a paddle splashes me in that playful manner. Blue in the lips sitting on the chair traveling so apparently toward the blue of the sky.

I am orange. Orange on my hands from the food coloring of the birthday cake for my sister. Orange on my clothes from the dirt of the trail kicked up, tripped on. Orange on the tops of my toes from the squishy orange mud of the meandering river. Orange on my shirt from the fur of the orange dog crawling on my stomach.

I am green. Green in the winter when the gripe is catching. Green in the spring when the grass is smearing, mixing its pigments with my tones. Green in the summer when the green fuzz from the green blanket coats my coat with lent while the stars are pointed and named. Green in the fall when I press the last of the color into some large volume of something or another. Green in the eyes from the green winter summer spring fall.

I am yellow. Yellow-belly-sap-sucker when my sister yells my names into oblivion for the things that I may or may not have done. Yellow tinted when the sun reflects the sound of parchment or the glare of a plastic boat back to my skin. Yellow of a banana while eating a banana during the awkward it's-not-breakfast-but-it's-not-lunch time.

I am purple. Purple and mushy after that fall from that great height last Sunday, landing on the ice. Purple in the tiny car sitting too close but in control. Purple in the hand and the music pours out into something, then into me. Purple on the hand as the ink misses the paper, misses the point, before recovering to a new understanding.

I am pink. Pink, soft pink, with the bows in the hair and the dress to the knees, and the basket of muffins for the new neighbor. Pink coating my feet in the form of seven-dollar shoes treading carefully, forcefully, meaningfully, sweetly, happily. Pink on the inside from the un-tinted water spewing from the pink-tinted water bottle.

And these colors are me.

Chapter Eight

Additional Information Sections

M ost schools, including Common Application schools, have a place for you to include any additional information that you feel the admission office should know about you. This is a great place for you to include any issues in grade discrepancies; personal, learning, or health issues you feel the school should know about; or anything else that you feel would better round out your application. On the Common Application, up to 650 words are allowed. Here are the instructions: *Please provide an answer below if you wish to provide details of circumstances or qualifications not reflected in the application.*

Keep in mind that when you note something negative in your additional information section, you should also try to address what you've done (hopefully) to remedy those concerns. If applicable, it may also be appropriate for your guidance counselor to confirm these kinds of comments in their counselor letter to the college on your behalf. Be honest with your counselor about what you intend to put in this section so that he or she can also "back you up" if necessary or if called upon to do so.

Additional Information Writing Samples

Author's note: The students who wrote these paragraphs have chosen to remain anonymous.

Personal Issues—Academic

You will note that in the spring semester of my junior year many of my grades dropped significantly. This decline was due unfortunately to some difficult personal problems occurring in my home: my parents were going through a divorce. As you see, also, I took summer school classes to make up for some of those lower grades.

Personal Issues—Academic

My entire sophomore year consisted of many elements that hindered my academic performance. First, I was diagnosed with mononucleosis my fall semester and had to miss many days of school due to fatigue and doctor appointments. Although I tried to work from home and was tutored on occasion, clearly this was not enough to boost my grades. In addition, my father also lost his job during that time, which added to my family's stress—and mine, too. However, once junior year hit, as you can see, I was back to my old self and successful in the classroom, and that has continued through the fall of my senior year. Please do not judge my entire high school experience based on this unfortunate situation.

Academic Test-Taking Concerns

I am not a fill-in-the-bubble kind of girl. Multiple-choice tests taken under time constraints are certainly not my forte. And no matter how much test prep or strategy I try to employ, my test scores were just not what I had hoped they would be for my college applications. Please consider many of my other pluses, such as my strong transcript, community involvement, and leadership. Standardized testing is just not who I am at all; I promise to contribute greatly to your college, though, if you can look past my depressing scores!

A Gap in Education

As you can see, I took a breather between my freshman and sophomore year. To be quite frank, I had burnt out after a hard year of adjusting to an academic setting that was far too challenging for me. I felt stressed out in a tiny classroom, feeling judged by both my teachers and peers. I needed some space to breathe, focus on myself outside of the classroom, and get myself together. Taking a semester off gave me a chance to clear my head; it also helped me realize that I had made the wrong choice in attending a small private high school with a huge academic reputation. To be honest, I was so excited that I had been admitted to this prestigious high school that I didn't really weigh all of my pros and cons fully. Once I was there, it was just too much. I moved to my local public high school for the second semester of my sophomore year, attended summer school, and pushed through to catch up. I am happy with my performance and life at my new school, as you can hopefully see from my grades and teacher recommendations. Thank you for considering what a difficult decision this was for me to leave, and how by taking that risk, I learned more about myself and found a better fit for my high school experience.

Attending a New School

Starting off at my local public high school, I felt like a small fish in a huge ocean. The classes were just too big for me, and I was quickly lost in the shuffle, falling between the cracks. There wasn't the opportunity for one-on-one help from the teachers; there were 33 students in my class. I talked to my parents, and we decided that, with financial assistance, I could apply to a private school near my home. We did not consider this originally because my older brother successfully attended our public school, and the private school just seemed too costly for my parents. I was lucky to gain admittance to St. Catherine's and have worked hard to keep up at best as possible with the academics there. My grades are not exactly what I had hoped they would be, but I do feel I've received the personal attention that I was craving and have learned so much more in the process. I really like school and being a student, and I know I will bring that same positive attitude, strong commitment, and top work ethic to your college.

A Move and Job Loss

It's been incredibly hard moving away from my high school and friends in my senior year! Adjusting to a new high school as a senior in a new city and state far from where I grew up has been a huge challenge for me. This past semester, it may appear that I have given up. Really, though, I have just struggled to figure this new place out on so many levels. Not only am I in a new school, but I'm also no longer a big fish in a small pond. I am lost in this huge new world and trying desperately to find my way. Please judge my academic performance most closely on my first three years of high school and know that I am trying to turn a corner here. Hopefully my second semester will better reflect my true scholastic abilities.

Cheating or Stealing

I am not proud of what I did and know at the time I was not considering the consequences of my actions. I have learned from my mistakes and academic probation. Cheating is a serious crime, and I was guilty and caught doing it. What made me do it? There is not enough space here to write, really, but it was a terrible panic and feeling of fright that caused me to make this mistake. I have learned my lesson and respectfully ask that you not view me as "once a cheater, always a cheater." The public humiliation I have suffered and the pain and embarrassment that I have caused my family and myself are enough punishment to last a lifetime—and to make me think twice before I ever do something that stupid and brainless again. I am truly remorseful. I hope that you forgive me, too.

Alcohol or Drugs

Rehab has taught me that drugs and alcohol are not the right way to bury my problems. I have gone to counseling and will continue to do so as I struggle through my teen years. I do use music as my escape and have taken up running as a healthier alternative to "drown my sorrows" and clear my head. I also really regret that my use affected my grades so much during my junior year. Now I am back on track and have found a new network of friends, as well as the support of a great therapist. Please contact my high school counselor should you have any additional concerns.

Including Positive Additional Information

As mentioned, the Additional Information section is a place to add more details about something you could not discuss elsewhere in your application. These items can also be positives about you, such as a special award you were selected for, a research project you have been working on, or even something positive related to a an academic issue you had—things that you were not able to discuss elsewhere in the application.

Some students choose to copy and paste a more detailed student résumé into this section (as long as it does not exceed the space permitted). If you feel you would like to do this—and your school does not specifically state that you cannot or should not— then by all means, if you have nothing else to put here, go ahead and submit a more detailed résumé instead. Just don't leave this section blank. This section is included for a reason, so be sure to share something new about yourself since the admission office is willing to read it!

And remember, in the Common Application, you are allowed to copy and paste in up to 650 words (no uploads at this time). For other schools not on the Common Application and that offer Additional Information sections, check their word limits or see if they permit you to upload a PDF or other file. And, always check in the print preview area to see that what you input reads clearly.

Chapter Nine

How to "Recycle" Your Writing

Many schools have questions that overlap or could elicit similar responses from you. Try not to rewrite and reinvent new responses when you don't have to. Sometimes, simply swapping out the name of a school and personalizing smaller parts of your essay while keeping the bulk of it the same is just enough to reuse a supplement you have done before. The goal of applying to college is not to have a large quantity of writing that requires you to write something new and fresh for every question you answer. Rather, be creative and try to recycle when you can to save yourself time and tedium. For, example, in the wonderful essay that follows, the name of any college could be substituted for "USC" and also personalized a bit to be used for each individual school.

Sample Essay That Could Be Personalized for Other Schools

When my family and I went on college tours over spring break last year, we visited over twelve different campuses in a five-day period. While other students collected pencils or sweatshirts at the various student gift shops, I made sure to find a copy of each school's daily newspaper to take home and analyze. Once back in the seclusion of my room, I read each one over, with the intent of gaining insight into the student life on each campus. But soon my "Editing Instinct" kicked in, and I found myself with a red pen, circling typos and highlighting journalistic flaws. The papers with the fewest red slashes, such as **USC's** [CHANGE TO NAME OF ANY COLLEGE], moved to the top of my college order of preference.

The Editing Instinct is a habit developed after long hours of chipping away at yearbook copy and helping friends refine theses for English essays. While in base form it may seem an obtrusive obsession with detail, at its core it is a simple desire to communicate effectively. Growing up I have pursed communication through a variety of forums—telling stories collaboratively through theater, making emotion audible through music, interpreting with American Sign Language, and reverting to the original mode of human expression: words.

My pursuit of the written word began when I was very young: while other kids would doodle monsters and unattractive caricatures of the teachers, I filled the corners of my math notes with poetry. I spent my time listening rather than speaking, conveying my ideas not through blabber but rather in the form of hidden journal entries and Word documents. My writing first came to a public forum when I began Yearbook in my sophomore year. My silent spell was naturally shattered as I found myself nosing my way into every school event I could, calling peers and strangers alike to get new perspectives on my stories. No story was too big or too small when it came to immortalizing a year of high school in a single publication. While I gained invaluable technical skills, ranging from interviewing to editing to Photoshopping, my biggest journalistic pursuit was yet to come.

That pursuit came in the form of Open Orchard Productions, a company that 4 students, 1 teacher, and I have built from the ground up. I am Co-Producer of the Core, a podcast that seeks to share teenage voices with the world. We interview students one-on-one and then edit up to 120 minutes of interview material into a 7- to 15-minute clip that will be posted on our website. Stories have ranged from dealing with bulimia to escaping gang life—they are open, honest, and, most important, relatable for a teen or adult listener. Between hours of meetings discussing target audiences, pitching to possible funders, researching marketing opportunities, and redesigning logo after logo, I have found a passion for the radio world and the art of storytelling. Barely six months into production, our little podcast has quadrupled our staff size and has received recognition from professionals such as Jones Franzel at PRX, Alex Shaffert at KPCC, and Peter Clowney from APM. When it came time for me to focus on a career path, radio journalism seemed the obvious field. And when it came to pursuing an education in that field, **the Annenberg School at USC** [CHANGE NAME OF SCHOOL PROGRAM DEPENDING ON SCHOOL LISTED ABOVE], with its readily available internships and plethora of teachers still working in the field, was the obvious choice. [THIS FINAL SENTENCE CAN BE TWEAKED OR PERSONALIZED TO EACH INDIVIDUAL SCHOOL.]

Tweaking Your "Why This College?" Essay

The following six essays/paragraphs demonstrate how you can tweak your "Why This College?" essay so that it will work for multiple institutions' applications. All were written by the same student to respond to some version of the "Why This College?" question. Some had word limits; others asked not only why this school but what do you plan to study at the school, too. Each, however, is a modification of the same reply with as much recycling as is humanly possible to save time while minimizing extra effort. As you know by now, there is a lot to write for college applications, so there is no need to reinvent the wheel every single time if not entirely necessary.

You'll notice several similarities throughout each essay, along with specific details the writer researched about each school, that demonstrate the overlap among the essays while simultaneously personalizing each one. In a few, the first line of the essay is the same. Each essay mentions that the student loves to run and hopes to continue that activity while in college. Each essay mentions her background in French language and how she plans to pursue that in each individual school. Each essay mentions the name of a professor the student plans to meet and/or a class that the student plans to take, as well as a campus tradition or two the student plans to participate in at the school. Sometimes the school mascot or a building or campus location is also mentioned. You'll see examples of this highlighted in bold in the essays that follow.

The applicant treated this question as a "mini-research project," plugging in specific details about each school where applicable or possible within the word limits or constraints of the question. All of these examples show the school that this student took the time to "do her homework" and that she knows specifics about their school. So the response does not appear to be generic in any way.

Why University of Pennsylvania?

I fell in love with Penn the minute I stepped on campus. I felt right at home walking down **Locust Walk** [CAMPUS LOCATION] and hearing about everything Penn has to offer, from the deep-rooted culture and history to the **college house cup competition** [TRADITION]. It would be an honor to attend a college founded by Benjamin Franklin, one of the most innovative and influential Americans in our country's history. I am specifically interested in studying Economics at the

College of Arts and Sciences. It would be amazing to study under a Nobel Prize–winning professor like **Professor Lawrence Klein** [NAME OF PROFESSOR]. I want to attend a university that will educate me in the best way possible for my planned future, and I feel that Penn can do that. Penn's resourceful **Career Center** [CAMPUS LOCATION WITH SPECIFIC/CORRECT NAME] and reputation for preparing students to enter the working world directly following graduation appeal to me because I plan to do just that. The strong background in liberal arts that I would receive at Penn would give me a wider variety of job opportunities upon graduation. Also, Penn's central location in Philadelphia allows for great internships to build my résumé. I **have studied French since first grade and just completed AP French,** so I hope to study at the **Columbia/Penn Reid Hall Program in Paris (BRD)** [NAME OF SCHOOL'S STUDY-ABROAD PROGRAM AND LOCATION]. I would enjoy immersing myself in French culture and practicing my language skills with my French host family while studying in an international environment and expanding my horizons.

Penn has great school spirit, which is one thing I am looking for in a college. I want to attend all of the football games and **throw toast** [CAMPUS TRADITION] on the field while screaming for the **Quakers** [CAMPUS TEAM/MASCOT]! **I plan to run in college, and Coach T. introduced me to Penn's amazing Division I Cross-Country and Track program and the great balance between academics and varsity running. It would be so exciting to watch and possibly even compete in the Penn Relays hosted by Penn's Track team** [SAME SENTENCE USED IN ALL]. I like the **College House system** [SPECIFIC SCHOOL PROGRAM] because then I would have my own smaller community with all of the amenities like a dining hall and study rooms, as well as advisers, deans, and masters inside the larger community at Penn. I would like to experience sorority life and participate in the philanthropic and social events held regularly at Penn. **I am ready to leave Newport Beach, California, and see more of the "real world" and real seasons. I want an East Coast college experience** [SAME SENTENCE USED IN ALL].

Why Duke University?

The strong freshman community is what really attracted me to Duke. The fact that all of the freshmen live on **East Campus** [CAMPUS LOCATION] makes the school feel smaller, serving as my own little community and making it easier to connect with other freshmen and access all the necessary amenities inside the larger community at Duke. I like the tradition of **Midnight Breakfast** [CAMPUS TRADITION]. I could always use a break from studying, especially during finals, so it would be fun to take a break with all of my friends while eating pizza and pancakes. The **Bryan Center** [CAMPUS LOCATION] seems full of resources and just a great place to hang out with the food court and stores. Duke's campus is beautiful, so it would be nice to sit outside and study. I want a college experience with a lot of school spirit, and Duke definitely has that. I want to be a screaming **Blue Devil** [CAMPUS TEAM/ MASCOT] fan at the football and basketball games. **I am planning to run in college, and Duke has an excellent Division I Track and Cross-Country program with all of the latest facilities like the Wallace Wade Stadium and the Michael W. Krzyzewski Center** [SAME START OF SENTENCE USED IN ALL, PLUS CAMPUS-SPECIFIC LOCATION].

Academically, Duke has much to offer. I am specifically interested in studying economics at the **Trinity College of Arts and Sciences** [CAMPUS PROGRAM]. I hope to study under **Professor Tracy R. Lewis** [PROFESSOR] because he also teaches at the business school and has substantial experience in business, the area of my interest. He has written countless articles and books on economics and business management and also has hands-on experience. Professor Lewis has a wealth of knowledge, and I would like to take full advantage of it. I plan to start my career as soon as I graduate from college. **Duke's Career Center and the DukeConnect** program [CAMPUS PROGRAMS] would be very helpful resources. They would give me insight into the careers I am considering. Also, the Career Center would assist me with obtaining internships in order to build my résumé. **I have studied French since first grade and just completed AP French,** so I hope to study abroad at the **Duke in France/EDUCO program** where I would have the opportunity to study with French students [SAME SENTENCE BEGINNING USED IN ALL, PLUS NAME OF SCHOOL'S SPECIFIC STUDY-ABROAD PROGRAM]. **I would love to move beyond Newport Beach, California, and experience more of the "real world" and real seasons** [SAME CLOSING SENTENCE, USED IN SOME WHEN APPLICABLE].

Why Columbia University?

I will grow as a leader in an environment where I am surrounded by other brilliant minds [SAME FIRST SENTENCE USED IN SOME]. Columbia's small class sizes and individualized attention appeal to me. I am specifically interested in studying economics at Columbia College. It would be amazing to study under a Nobel Prize winner like **Professor Joseph Stiglitz** [NAME OF PROFESSOR]. The core curriculum, with a strong background in liberal arts, and the fact that Columbia is located in the heart of New York City will give me a wider variety of job options upon graduation [USED SAME SENTENCE IN OTHERS, BUT CHANGED NAME OF CITY]. I like that the freshmen live together because it would make the campus feel smaller and give me my own little community to be loyal to within the larger Columbia community. I want to attend the presentations by influential people in our society, such as the ones by John McCain and Barack Obama. Because **I plan to run in college,** Coach Wood's emphasis on the great balance between academics and varsity running appeals to me [SAME SENTENCE ABOUT RUNNING WITH SPECIFIC COACH]. **I just completed AP French,** so I hope to study abroad at the **Columbia/Penn Reid Hall Program in Paris** [SAME START OF SENTENCE USED IN ALL, PLUS STUDY-ABROAD SPECIFIC LOCATION]. It would be a valuable experience to study internationally while practicing my language skills with my French host family.

Why Yale University?

I will grow as a leader in an environment where I am surrounded by other brilliant minds [SAME FIRST SENTENCE USED IN OTHER ESSAY]. I hope to study under **Professor Robert Shiller** [NAME OF PROFESSOR], who is conducting innovative research in economics. I plan to attend a **Master's Tea** [CAMPUS TRADITION] and learn from influential people. When I met **Coach Mark Young** on campus, he emphasized the balance between academics and varsity **running** [SENTENCE ABOUT RUNNING WITH NAME OF COACH]. I liked Yale's "Oxford/Cambridge feel." Yale's smaller classes, focus on undergraduate education, and accessibility of professors appeal to me. I was happy to learn that deans, especially during finals, personally call students in their residential college out for breaks from late-night studying. The **Shopping Period** [SCHOOL ACADEMIC TRADITION] allows me to "taste" Yale classes. **I want an East Coast college experience** [SAME CLOSING SENTENCE, USED IN SOME WHEN APPLICABLE].

Why Cornell University?

I plan to pursue my college education with the same dedication and enthusiasm for learning that I have had my whole life [SAME OPENING SENTENCE USED IN A FEW]. I am interested in studying economics, specifically marketing, in the **College of Arts and Sciences** at Cornell [NAME OF COLLEGE PROGRAM/DEPARTMENT] because I enjoy working with numbers and solving problems and am very interested in learning about managing and satisfying the demand for products. I hope to study under **Professor Assaf Razin** [NAME OF PROFESSOR] because of his expertise in international affairs. It is one of my dreams to travel internationally for the company I someday work for. Professor Razin has written numerous books about international economy, so I want to take full advantage of his wealth of knowledge to help me in my future pursuits. All Cornell classes being taught by professors (rather than teacher's aides) would really benefit my learning [CAMPUS SPECIFIC INFORMATION]. I want to study abroad and the many programs available in France appeal to me. **I have studied French since first grade and just completed AP French** [SAME SENTENCE USED IN ALL], so I would love the opportunity to practice my language skills while studying economics in an international environment. The **Cornell Economics Society** [CAMPUS PROGRAM] sounds like an amazing program and one in which I would definitely form valuable relationships with people who could give me expert advice. **Cornell's Career Services** [CAMPUS SUPPORT SERVICE] would be an excellent resource to help me prepare my résumé and conduct my job search.

Why Southern Methodist University (SMU)?

I would like to study at SMU's **Cox School of Business** [CAMPUS PROGRAM]. The Business Associates Program would help me form valuable connections through a Dallas business mentor. I would attend football games and **boulevard** while screaming for the **Mustangs** [CAMPUS MASCOT]! I plan to run in college, and **Coach Casey** introduced me to SMU's amazing **Track and Cross-Country** program [NAME OF COACH AND SAME START OF SENTENCE]. I hope to experience sorority life and participate in philanthropic and social events. **I just completed AP French**, so I plan to study at **SMU-in-Paris** [NAME OF STUDY-ABROAD PROGRAM AND SAME START OF SENTENCE IN ALL].

Another Novel Approach to "Why This School?"

If you are struggling with the "Why This School?" question over and over again, you can always try something along the lines of this student's lighter—but nonetheless "personalized"—route. He created his own "Mad Lib" that he tweaked and adapted for each school to which he applied.

Sample Essay

When I was around 8 years old, my mom asked me where I wanted to go to college and I said I wanted to be a(n) ____(mascot). I never knew much about the college; I just knew that I had to be a(n) ____(mascot). As I got older, I met many graduates who loved their school and some that hated theirs. In all the statements, I rarely heard any complaints about ____(college name). As I approached junior and senior year, I visited colleges and did a lot of research to know that I still wanted to be a ____(mascot) one day. I learned that not only could I say I went to such a highly regarded institution as ____(college name), but I hoped I could have the opportunity to study under such professors as ____ (highly regarded professors and contributions). I want the chance to live in a city like ____ (city name) where I could get involved in ____(city events). From my research, I found that ____ (school name) has many traditions that I would like to get involved with. Some traditions that especially interest me are ____ (traditions/annual events). At ____(college), I would be interested in the sporting events like the ____(sports) and seeing the ____ (teams) in action. Today, if my mom were to ask me where I wanted to go again, I would still tell her that I want to be a ____(mascot).

Finally, if possible, before sending any file or attachment, convert it to a PDF to preserve your font and eliminate the unsightly "colored squiggles" that can appear under words for grammar or spelling.

Chapter Ten

The Brag Sheet—Advice for Writing Your Résumé

I n addition to all of your college essay writing, some other writing needs to be created to outline everything that you have done in your high school career outside of the classroom. Most colleges have a chart or drop-down menu inputs that you complete to list your activities since the summer after eighth grade. (Remember, high school begins when you graduate from eighth grade, so the summer after eighth grade "counts" for college.)

This list is a chart that has four columns:

1) Name of activity—extracurricular, club, athletics, etc.

2) Years/grades you have participated in the activity

3) Hours per week/weeks per year of involvement

4) Description of activity—details about it, leadership roles you may have had, honors/awards within activity

The brag sheet sample you make for yourself can work as a template for a reference piece and may also help you come up with ideas for possible essay topics. In addition, you may be able to use your brag sheet as a supplement for schools that are not on the Common Application, especially if those other applications allow you to upload or include an activity sheet. But for the Common App schools, you should create a "Top 10 List" of the most significant activities you want to share IN ORDER OF IMPORTANCE TO YOU—those with the most hours or years dedicated or those that you rank as most essential in your life. You don't need to list a club you only did in ninth grade, for example, or a one-day community service project, unless you have little else to post. Also, there is no need to panic if you do not complete all ten spaces so don't try to just fluff or fill in to stretch your experience.

It is a good idea to begin a notebook or computer document, such as Word Tables or an Excel spreadsheet, to keep track of all of your involvement as you go along, so you don't forget things when it comes time to fill out this chart. Be sure to include the following sections:

- Extracurricular Activities—Organizations/Clubs/Athletics
  - » You can have a subsection for sports or include them in order by most involvement (in school years and hours) to least involvement or most recent to farthest back in time (reverse chronological order).
- Community Service
- Employment
- Awards and Honors
- Summer Activities
- Hobbies and Interests

When you fill in your brag sheet, you will need to become a good abbreviator since you have very little space to elaborate on your activity (one line that allows 150 characters to describe your activity and 50 characters to label or name your activity and list the title or position you had). At the time of this book's printing, the Common App offers 10 spaces for activities, and there is a separate section to include up to 10 honors and awards. Get good at creating and using a shorthand—symbols such as "&" instead of "and," numbers in numerical form (8) rather than written out (eight), or "Pres." for "President."

Use the following brag sheet samples as a reference guide to show you the various types of items that could be included on yours. Do know, however, that most brag sheets you encounter will be much shorter than these examples.

Sample "Brag Sheets"

Brag Sheet: Sample 1

Activity	School Years	Hours per Week/Weeks per Year	Positions/Honors/Description
Organizations/Clubs			
Student Ambassadors	12	15/36	VP (12): 25 seniors chosen to be school role models helping at school events and reaching out to the community through service.
NHS: National Honor Society	10–12	6/36	Pres. (12). Worked as Teacher Assistant; helped raise money for Lily of the Valley Orphanage.
HS Impact Mentoring	9–12	2/36	Mentor (10), Team Leader (11–12). Mentored freshmen and helped with adjustment to high school.
HS Journal—School Newspaper	11	10 hrs/month 18 weeks/year	Features Editor. Created inaugural issue of newspaper.
Soul Sisters	9, 10	1/36	Girls religious/social club to enhance Catholic faith. Activities included school sleepovers, social outings, etc.
Teams/Athletics			
HS Tennis	9–12	12/18	Captain (9–12); Varsity (10–12); Coach's Award (9); MVP (10); Lion Award (11); Tennis Inaugural Season (9).
Junior USTA Tennis	9–12	6/52	Participated in various S. CA tournaments; Junior Team Tennis representing Laguna Niguel and finished in 2nd place in S. CA (11).
Softball	9	15/18	Varsity Letter; 1st Place in Estancia Tournament.

Activity	School Years	Hours per Week/Weeks per Year	Positions/Honors/Description
Community Service			
S.U.R.F. Team— Serving Under our Righteous Father	11–12	5/36	Church group. Organized and led youth group "Insight" nights, youth masses, and retreats.
American Cancer Society Discovery Shop	9–11	25 hours per year	Worked in thrift shop to sell donated items to raise money for ACS.
Champs	9	2/12	Helped team of special needs kids practice and play softball.
Employment			
Uniforms 4 U	10–12	6 hours/18+ weeks (summers)	Worked in store to sell uniforms to 6 different private high schools; organized store rooms; cashiered.
Awards and Honors			
Scholar-Athlete	9–12		Achieved a 4.0 GPA or greater during all seasons of sports.
Principal's Honor Roll	9–12		Received all semesters at HS for earning a GPA greater than 4.0.
CSF: California Scholarship Federation	10–12		An honor program for high scholarship, service, and citizenship.
National Society of High School Scholars	11, 12		Recognition for academic excellence and character.
Faculty Award	11		Each year, 1 male and 1 female student selected by faculty, based on academics, character, and citizenship.
Kairos Leader	11, 12		One of 6 juniors to attend a senior retreat, "Kairos," to lead senior class the following year.

Activity	School Years	Hours per Week/Weeks per Year	Positions/Honors/Description
Penn State Gatorade Award	11		Selected by Penn State summer tennis coaches as best all-around player.
MVP	10		Most Valuable Player for HS tennis.
Summer Experiences			
LeadAmerica	11, 12	6 days (11) 15 days (12)	Attended Leadership Conference in D.C., by invitation, based on academics and character (11); Leadership Conference abroad with Ambassadors Abroad, earning 2 college credits (12).
Impact Mentoring	10–12	4 days	Training Program to prepare mentors to connect with freshmen.
USTA Tennis	9–12	6/12	Participated in California tournaments and matches.
Penn State Tennis Camp	9–12	5 days	Attended tennis camp at Penn State. Practiced drills and match play.

Hobbies/Interests: Photography, movies, HGTV enthusiast, family road trips, and exploring.

Brag Sheet: Sample 2

	School Years	Hours per Week/Weeks per Year	Positions/Honors/Descriptions
Organizations/Clubs			
California Scholarship Federation	9–12	4 hours per semester 1 day per semester	Cleaned up state beach; picked up trash after HS sporting events; set up for cancer benefit walk; and fundraisers. Need 3.5 min GPA.
Hilltoppers Community Service Club	9–11	2 hours per week throughout school year	CHOC Walk; car washes; holiday gifts for children; all earnings benefit CHOC Hospital.
JW Basketball	9–12	6+ hours per week year round	Coach and teach children the basics and fundamentals of basketball.

	School Years	Hours per Week/Weeks per Year	Positions/Honors/Descriptions
FHS Boys Basketball	9–12	12+ hours per week year round	Member of boys' basketball team.
Community Service			
CHOC Walk	9–11	4–6 hours per event	Walk to benefit cancer research and CHOC Hospital.
Beach/ Stadium Clean-ups	9–10	2 hours per event	Picked up trash at state beaches and high school sports venues.
Car wash	9–11	5 hours per event	Washed cars to raise money for CHOC Hospital.
Santa Sacks	9–10	4–6 hours per event	Made holiday sacks and filled them with presents. Delivered to cancer patients at CHOC hospital.
Awards and Honors			
Scholar Athlete	9–12		4.0/3.83/3.67 GPA while a member of the FHS basketball program.
Principal's Honor Roll	9–10		For earning 4.0/3.83/3.67 GPA.
Summer Experience/Employment			
Roller Hockey Club	12	10/10	Pick-up games with local recreation league.
JW Basketball	9–12	12/12	Coach children at summer basketball day camp.
Newport Physical Therapy	12	4/12	Internship. Record exercises; prepare heating pads and ice packs for patients; greet patients.
FHS Basketball	9–12	20 hours per week	Tournaments and travel.

Hobbies/Interests: Zippo lighter collector, travel, roller hockey, Dane Cook fan

Brag Sheet: Sample 3

	School Years	Hours per Week/Weeks per Year	Positions/Honors/Description
Organizations/Clubs			
LBHS's Central Asia Institute	11, 12	1/36 + events	Treasurer in current and inaugural years; plan bake sales to raise money; manage money donated each year.
LBHS's Dance Council	10–12	1/36 + events	President (12), Secretary (10, 11). Took notes at mtgs., helped choose themes for & advertised concerts & other events; coordinated Car Wash fundraiser.
Dance			
Student Choreography Show	9–12	5/5	Choreographer (9–11), performer (9–12); select dancers, choose choreography and music, and design lighting and costumes.
Kinetic Dance Project	11	5/40	Preprofessional dance company; audition required for admission; rehearse 2x weekly to build repertoire; perform in various dance concerts in S. CA and in company's show.
LBHS Winter and Spring Dance Shows	9–11	6/18	Played leading role in spring concert, "Alice" (10).
Theater			
West Side Story	11	12/16	LBHS Spring Musical; Jet girl dance ensemble.
Meet Me in St. Louis	10	5/8	Community Theater; dance ensemble.
Once on This Island	10	2/8	Produced by Generation Gap; fundraised and organized bake sales.
Oklahoma!	9	6/14	LBHS Spring Musical; dance ensemble.
The Diary of Anne Frank	9	6/14	Produced by Generation Gap; played leading role; designed costumes.

	School Years	Hours per Week/Weeks per Year	Positions/Honors/Description
Awards and Honors			
ROP Distinguished Student Awards	11		Award Finalist for Arts and Design in Dance Production/Classical.
LBHS's Superintendent's Award	9–11		For maintaining a 3.8 GPA or higher.
Special Recognition MACY Award	11		For playing Jet Girl dancing role in *West Side Story*.
LBHS Excellence Awards	9–11		9–Human Ecology (Helpful and Friendly); 10–Dance Performance; 11–Physics (Upbeat Attitude and Hard Work), Classical Dance Production, Honors Pre-Calculus (Hard Work and Effort).
LBHS Dance Gala Awards	9–11		9–Most Improved 2nd Semester Classical Dance; 10–Most Dedicated, Best Dancer in Spring Show "Alice"; 11–Dancer of the Year of the Junior Class.
Community Service			
El Sol Academy Summer Camp	12	8/4	Teach jazz and hip-hop classes to children grades 2–8
Pink Ribbon Club	10–12	1/36	Volunteer at "I Am the Cure" event; annual Parker Games fundraiser: sell raffle tickets, decorate, dance at half-time show, work bake sale; make holiday care packages for breast cancer patients.
National Honor Society	10–12	1/36	Tutor 4th and 5th graders in math; participate in beach clean-ups; collect recyclables for Recycling Committee; work at bake sales to raise money for charities.
Vacation Bible School	9, 10	8 hours/5 days	Day camp counselor for children ages 6 to 12.

	School Years	Hours per Week/Weeks per Year	Positions/Honors/Description
Summer Experiences/ Employment			
Gelato Paradiso	11, 12	30 hours/10 weeks summer	Scoop ice cream and make waffle cones.
Laguna Beach Dance Company's Summer Intensive	9–11	8/4	Attend class and rehearse for a showcase 5 days a week for a month.

Hobbies/Interests: kickboxing, baking, Rummikub addict, piano, travel, camping

Brag Sheet: Sample 4

Organization	School Years	Hours per Week/Weeks per Year	Positions/Honors/Description
Foreign Exchange Student	11	5 months	Traveled to Argentina with AFS as exchange student for 1 semester. Lived with family and immersed into the culture.
Extracurricular/Clubs/Organizations			
National Charity League	9–12	175 hours total 50–74 hours/ year 10 hours/year required	Charity organization that provides labor for local charities as a team. Corresponding Secretary (9); Social Chair (10); Historian (11); VP of Programs (12). Received multiple awards. See below.
California Scholarship Federation	9–11	1/36	Organization established for students with good GPA. Participated in peer tutoring 2x/week.
Basketball	9–11	6/36	JV (9), Varsity (10, 11 summer).
Tutoring	11	4/12	Tutor autistic sixth-grader in math.
Working Wardrobes Club	10, 11	4/36	President (10), Secretary (11). Solicited and provided prom dresses for disadvantaged girls. Provided counseling.

Organization	School Years	Hours per Week/Weeks per Year	Positions/Honors/Description
Supportabil- ity Club at FHS	12	2 hours	President (12). Raised money for disabled students to attend college.
Basketball/ Volleyball	11	6/12	Played basketball and volleyball on local team in Argentina.
Summer Experiences			
Basketball	9, 10, 11	20/12	Basketball camp for FHS players; practice and games; 3 away tournaments.
Summer school	11, 12	20/12	Course work completed to allow for Foreign Exchange experience spring semester junior year.
Tutoring	12	4/12	Paid position tutoring autistic sixth-grader in math.
Awards			
National Charity League	9–11		Yellow Rosebud award for 50 hrs over requirement (9–11); Mission Bell award (11); Mother-Daughter award (10, 11).
Basketball	9–11		Honor roll, scholar athlete (9, 10); most valuable player (9).

Hobbies/Interests: snowboarding, swimming, steak lover, Scrabble, hanging out with friends, the beach

Brag Sheet: Sample 5

Extracurricular Activities	School Years	Hours per Week/Weeks per Year	Description
Laguna Canyon College of Art and Design: Art Portfolio Program	11	4/12	Learned figure painting and various other techniques to broaden my approach. Learned to assemble proper portfolio for college and career.
Laguna Beach Frosh/Soph Soccer and JV	9–11	10/18 + games	Tried out and selected for the Frosh/Soph girls soccer team (9); JV (10, 11).
West Coast Soccer Club	10, 11	6/12	Selective club. Improved skills; learned plays and strategy.
AYSO Soccer	9, 10	5/10 + games	Played on AYSO 16 and under team.
AYSO Spring Select	9	5/10 + games	Played spring select.
Honors and Awards			
Laguna Art Institute	11		Selected for Scholarship Program.
AP Art Studio class	11		"Excellence in Professional Work Ethic" award.
Color It Orange	9, 10		Art recognized and displayed at local show.
Imagination Celebration	10		2 pieces of my art entered and selected to be placed on display for event.
Art in French Magazine	10		My art was selected to be published in a French magazine. Financial award as well.
ROP Fashion Design Award	9	3/18	My dress design dress won first place in the final contest.
Community Service and Clubs			
360 Degree Community Service	10	23/3.5	Went to Hilo, HI and worked with homeless families. Assisted with 80+ children in summer daycare program for homeless children. Served meals, played games, packed backpacks for school children.

Extracurricular Activities	School Years	Hours per Week/Weeks per Year	Description
LBHS Theater Backdrops and Homecoming Floats	9, 10	2 weeks	Backdrop for Hurley "Walk The Walk" Fashion Show (9), Homecoming Float (10).
Employment/Summer Experiences			
UCLA Painting Program	11	2 weeks	Full-time residential program. Course in oil painting for college credit.
Eastern Washington University Photo Course	11	2 hours/10 days & final essay	Made photo diary and itinerary along with overall retrospective of Holland people and culture.
People 2 People Sports Ambassador Program	11	8 full days of soccer practice and games	Applied and selected to travel to Holland with the P2P program to play for the U.S. team and learn leadership and philanthropy.
Lala Boutique	9, 10	4 hours/day 2 days/week	Gopher: Answer phones, help customers, organize and inventory merchandise, pick up lunch. Learned about manufacturing and ordering, forecasting trends, and customer service.
All Star AYSO Team	9	10/8	Went to Chicago and played in the all-star tournament.

Hobbies/Interests: crocheting, knitting, sewing, and creating my own clothing; surfing; meeting new people; and travel

Chapter Eleven

Interviews with Deans of Admission: Insights, Tips, and Wisdom

D eans of Admission possess wisdom, insights, and perspective from their roles in working with students on both sides of the college application process, from their on-the-road recruiting and presentations to their keen eyes that have read and evaluated thousands of personal statements and college applications. I asked dozens of deans for their input on the following questions. This chapter shares some of their thoughts with you. I hope their words will help enlighten your process and add to your success in your college application writing. Some chose to answer all of the questions below; others selected a few.

Leigh Weisenburger, Dean of Admission and Financial Aid
Bates College
Lewiston, Maine

What are your suggestions on how to tackle the college application process in general—when to start and how to best approach it?

Students and families who begin the college search process during the junior year of high school are in a great position. Even starting during second semester of the junior year gives you ample time to conduct a thoughtful and thorough college search process.

As for how to best approach it, I offer these key pieces of advice for students:

- *Keep an open mind. You may never know what surprises will excite you. You might like a smaller college, you may not want to play a sport in college after all, or you may want to be near a city. There is a wide array of institutions out there, so don't "go by the book," follow your friends, nor do precisely what's expected of you. Cast a wide net at the start of your college search process, and do your research. You may find some exciting offerings and surprising truths about yourself.*

- *Stay true to yourself. The college or university that is/was a great fit for your family members or friends isn't necessarily what's best for YOU. If it doesn't feel right—the community, the curriculum, the location— don't force it.*

What is your advice for essay writers: How do you know when you are done? How much time should you spend on the essay? When is enough, enough?

The summer before senior year is a great time to begin the college essay writing process. Start by jotting down some essay topic ideas. Nothing needs to be completely thought through—simply brainstorm some of these ideas. Occasionally go back to those ideas and test what feels comfortable, motivates you, and is genuine.

From there, take one to three topics and begin outlining the essay. If it comes together easily, I suggest that should become the subject you choose as your college essay. If thoughts flow fluidly and you're engaged, chances are the reader will be engaged as well.

So when do you know you're done? I suggest you ask a few people to read your essay—after you've read it aloud yourself. Share it with a close friend, a teacher you trust, your college counselor, and/or a family member. Share it with people you trust and who know you well. They will tell you honestly if your writing sounds like you and if it fully illustrates you and your character. You are not asking them to completely overhaul your writing. Rather, you are asking them to simply provide a few suggestions and an overall sense of how effective your essay is in conveying what a college/university must know about you and won't get in another portion of the application.

What are some basic dos and don'ts about college essay writing?

- *Write like you speak. Read your essay drafts aloud, and if you trip up on words, phrases, and/or ideas, chances are the application reader will as well.*

- *Don't use a great deal of thesaurus words and lengthy sentences with a mixture of commas, colons, and semi-colons. Keep the language and the sentence structure simple.*

- *Know your audience. Now I realize it's impossible to know precisely who is reading your application, but be mindful that the admission professionals reading your essay(s) have varied backgrounds. What you might find amusing as a subject, they may not understand fully or may even find offensive. So while taking a bit of a risk with your topic(s) is worth exploring, and sharing your true ideas is always important, you need to ask yourself the following questions: "Are they going to understand what I'm trying to say? Are they going to laugh or be perplexed?" If you hesitate at all when asking yourself these questions, it may be time to go back to the drawing board and ponder some new topics.*

Would you share a memory or highlight of some stand-out (or poor) essays you've read through the years, if you are comfortable sharing some of those thoughts?

Some of the most effective and revealing college essays I've read over the years keep things simple and, in doing so, ultimately tell us a great deal about the applicant. More often than not, the most mundane elements or occurrences in your life can be the most revealing. For example: Your morning drive to school may shed light on how you think and approach all that you do. Or, rather than telling us about your entire summer job experience, share the details of one pivotal day where you learned a valuable life lesson. It's impossible to share your entire life story in 650 words or less, so zero in on one moment or key instance rather than trying to share everything.

What suggestions do you have on the shorter writing pieces (activity paragraph, academic paragraph, why this school? etc.) and the role and importance they play in the application process?

It's very important that students recognize that there may be multiple opportunities within the college application to showcase their writing skills. For many selective colleges and universities, there may be two or three areas within the application in which students are asked to respond to questions. Oftentimes, these shorter essays are forgotten or left until the very last minute. As a result, the shorter responses or supplemental essays are where we tend to see the most mistakes or a real lack of complete thoughts and construction of ideas.

What I always advise students to do is to use these multiple spaces and opportunities wisely. Highlight your array of interests. Don't write about biology, biology, biology or baseball, baseball, baseball in all of these writing spaces. Tell us how dynamic you are by sharing your range of passions. In addition, you may wish to showcase your different writing styles by writing analytically for one essay and then more creatively for another.

Do you have any other advice—words of wisdom—that you have cultivated through the years?

Admission professionals are educators and are curious about you. Colleges and universities are looking for ways to admit you and celebrate your array of talents and interests. Use the admission professionals as a resource if/when available, and take them up on their offers to assist you in the process.

The college process can be effective and it can be successfully accomplished by spending only 1 hour a week discussing it with your family. It does not need to be the discussion on every drive to and from school, nor does it need to take over every family dinner conversation. Schedule 1 hour a week with your parents to discuss how your college search process is unfolding. Check in with what you may be working on, such as researching a particular college's academic programs, while your parents are making travel arrangements for your campus visits. You each need to respect your roles in the process and share all that you're learning, but it does not need to take over your lives for months on end, nor should it dictate all family conversations.

Be open and honest about what your family can afford for your college costs. Do your research and know what each institution's financial aid policy and offerings are. What is merit aid? What does need-based mean? Is a college/ university need-blind or need-aware? There is a lot of jargon and policies surrounding financial aid. It can be overwhelming and scary as money is often an emotional topic, but you will be best served and informed if you ask these key questions up front while simultaneously discussing what your family can afford.

HAVE FUN!! College is an exceptional opportunity, and the college search process is a thrilling and reflective developmental period for high school students. While there certainly will be many highs and lows, enjoy all that you're learning about yourself and the number of institutions you're researching.

Are there any additional comments you would like to share about your university and the kinds of applicants you seek in terms of finding the right fit or match?

Bates is a selective liberal arts college located in Maine's second-largest city, Lewiston. Founded by abolitionists with egalitarian values, Bates has been co-ed since day one, has never had any fraternities or sororities, and has always openly recruited and admitted students from all racial, ethnic, and religious backgrounds. Our history is alive and well today as we are a community that values diversity and inclusion. We have thirty-one varsity sports, over 60 percent of our students study abroad, all students complete a senior research thesis, we have a robust community-engaged learning program where students participate in over 50,000 hours of community-based learning, and, finally, we have a unique calendar with a five-week short term in May where students can take an array of interdisciplinary courses, practitioner-taught courses, study abroad with Bates faculty, and/or have an internship. Most recently, our renowned debate team won the national championships, and, in 2013, Bates was named a Fulbright Top Producer. Students who are intellectually curious, value learning for the pursuit of knowledge, are engaged community members, are collaborative in all that they do, and are curious about the world around them will be challenged and will thrive at Bates.

Robert G. Springall, Dean of Admissions
Bucknell University
Lewisburg, Pennsylvania

What are your suggestions on how to tackle the college application process in general—when to start and how to best approach it?

The application process starts immediately after a student's junior year is finished. The summer is a great time to collect one's list of activities, think about all of the teachers and other adults to seek recommendations from, and to start jotting down potential topics for essays. The Common Application usually has locked in essay topics for the upcoming year by the end of the previous school year. By starting early, a student can start compiling an application as a set of small steps that can be tackled a little bit at a time instead of tackling it all closer to the actual deadlines.

A generation ago, it was more typical to be submitting the bulk of college applications after the Thanksgiving or even winter holiday break of one's senior year. I talk to so many students now who have early decision, early action, or rolling admission applications to do in the fall. Those students have to spend a lot time in their first half of their senior year to prepare thoughtful college applications. If you can knock work out in the summer, do so!

What is your advice for essay writers: How do you know when you are done? How much time should you spend on the essay? When is enough, enough?

My go-to piece of advice for essay writers resonates better with those who understand the game of baseball. I always tell students that the essay should be a solid base hit and not a home run. (Play it safe. Just look to get on base.) In other words, the chosen topic should be interesting for 250–500 words, but it does not have to be so risky or unique where that might not resonate with the reader at all. (Home run hitters often strike out.)

Often the best essays that I read are the ones where students talk about a day in their life, or a teacher they admire, something unusual that happened to them, a friend, a personal cause that they have championed, and so on. Those topics can become some of the best essays. When a student takes a very controversial stand or tries to make an achievement sound more spectacular than it is, there is a great risk that the essay is going to come off as boring or disingenuous, or even offensive.

How do you know when you are done? There is no perfect answer to that question. My advice is to look at your college essay as an example of a very polished writing assignment that you would turn in for a history or language class. How long does a piece of writing of 500 words take you when you are writing it for a grade? It's important to keep in mind that when you're writing for class assignments, you are often asked to express your reaction to something that has already been written or happened. There is less thinking about telling the story since you are reacting to one that already transpired. A college essay often asks for self-reflection or telling a story from personal experience, so it is going to take you a little more time.

What are some basic dos and don'ts about college essay writing?

You *don't need to stay away from controversial topics, but remember that you don't know about the personal proclivities of your readers. You don't know their politics or their religious or other personal views, and so on. So it's best to write for an anonymous audience. If you take a firm stand and only state your opinion, you run the risk of offending your reader. It might be a stance that might be in opposition to his or her views on that subject. On the other hand, if you are stating a firm belief and you clearly explain to your reader how you came to believe what you do, you are treading on firmer ground. But, again, be very careful because you don't know the proclivities and interests of your audience.*

Don't *dramatize any illegal activity, no matter how petty or serious. Just explain yourself to your reader. Be honest and straightforward. If you've learned something from the episode, say so.*

If the school asks on its application why you want to go there or why you want to attend a particular program, do your research on the school specifically and what makes it distinctive. Don't *make that response generic. Each school has its own traditions, campus culture, and areas in which it thinks it excels. Take the time to understand the college, and tell your reader how your interests fit its unique characteristics. Be careful to speak to the school. For example,* don't *write about what it would mean to attend a Catholic university on an application for a non-religious institution. (It's happened.) If you're using the Common Application, remember that the pieces that all of your schools share must be generic. So,* don't *name a particular college in your main or general essay.* Do, *however, use the school supplement to talk specifically about that college or university.*

Would you share a memory or highlight of some stand-out (or poor) essays you've read through the years, if you are comfortable sharing some of those thoughts?

One of the most memorable essays I ever read was during my very first year in college admissions. I was reading applications for my university's engineering program. There was an essay by a young woman who was number one in her class. She very clearly wanted to be the type of engineer who was not just book smart but one who could apply the science—the best part of engineering! Her high school did not allow honors students to take vocational-technology courses. In her essay, she wrote about appearing in front of the school board to argue for a seat in a tech course she wanted to take simply because it was interesting to her. Her passion moved me. I was so compelled by her essay that when I finished reading it, I called the Chair of the Mechanical Engineering department and said, "Once this student is admitted, I want you to personally call her and convince her to come here." And thankfully she did!

What suggestions do you have on the shorter writing pieces (activity paragraph, academic paragraph, why this school? etc.) and the role and importance they play in the application process?

I find students sometimes don't take as much care in writing shorter essays as they do in their main essay, and this is a mistake. Be sure these shorter essays are proofread and spellchecked! Take some time to draft and edit those essays before you place them in the box on the application.

What are your thoughts on letters of recommendation and interviews?

There are no interviews at Bucknell. We prefer that the campus visit experience be about the student and family investigating the school and enjoying their visit instead of a student being nervous about an interview and the impression he or she will make in a 20-minute meeting. We ask for writing and recommendations and will see a student's whole record, so we do get to know them enough through their work. We would rather our visitors enjoy their day on campus and not stress.

With regard to recommendation letters, I love to see a student choose to get a recommendation from someone who can tell us about the student in a classroom setting without focusing on that student's grades. I prefer to hear from a recommender who has had some personal interaction with the student and who perhaps is being asked for a recommendation since it is a subject that the student might want to pursue in college. I hope the recommender can address how that student has interacted with his or her peers and how the student has demonstrated an understanding of the material taught in that particular class.

Do you have any other advice—words of wisdom—that you have cultivated through the years?

Remember that the college application process and the process to search for a college is one that culminates in one question: where are you going to go in the fall? But in order to get there, a hundred questions need to be answered and pieces of research need to be done about the options to determine what you want in your college experience. And no one person or resource can answer all of those questions for you.

Are there any additional comments you would like to share about your university and the kinds of applicants you seek in terms of finding the right fit or match?

Bucknell is a unique liberal arts institution. It is a place that believes in people who have open minds and a high amount of curiosity in combination with an interest in thinking about the world that they are going to affect after graduation. Bucknell students are thinkers and—absolutely—are doers. And that is great source of pride for us. The students we look for are those who have been active in their community and school, have already started to develop good habits of mind (they like to read, think, debate, discuss), and who see college as both an opportunity to explore the world around them and prepare for a successful life after college.

Christoph Guttentag, Dean of Undergraduate Admissions
Duke University
Durham, North Carolina

What are your suggestions on how to tackle the college application process in general—when to start and how to best approach it?

It is a really interesting question because the answer is different for different people. In general, if I were to give one piece of advice, it is to read what we say [the deans, author, and student essays in this book] the same way a person reads a self-help book. Read with a thought about the following: Does this fit the way I work? Can I implement these kinds of suggestions? If there were only one way to run a life, then there would only be one self-help book, but the bookstores are full of them. A lot of people find they need advice from all kind of quarters. Take advice keeping in mind the idea: will this work for me?

For example, when I speak every spring to the student recipients of the TIP grand recognition award (students who took the SAT in seventh grade and have done very well), some of them come from schools or communities where there isn't very much support for going on to college, or they attend a school without many resources. These students are outliers because of their abilities and interests. For this select group, seventh or eighth grade is not too early to start thinking about college. Conversely, other students who attend schools where 85–100 percent go on to four-year colleges—where the topic of college is part of their regular conversations and a normal expectation—those students can relax more since they have the institutional and personal support systems in place to help them stay on track. Typically, students start talking seriously about their college list in their junior year, and that is right for most students. At that point they have enough of an academic record to know the range of schools that they are competitive for.

What is your advice for essay writers: How do you know when you are done? How much time should you spend on the essay? When is enough, enough?

I think honestly that writing the application essay is in some ways the hardest part of applying to college. Not to minimize all of the work, researching, planning, and traveling that can be involved in the admission process, but this essay seems to be the hardest part. Writing a good essay is very challenging for lots of reasons. Students have not had the opportunity to do this kind of writing before, and this type of writing has to fulfill many purposes. It is not a kind of writing or process that is easily taught and learned. If it were, we'd have even more applicants!

I think writing college essays is particularly difficult because of what is expected, the personal nature, and because the stakes are so high. The best piece of advice I have when a student writes an essay addresses the issue of personal style. I believe an essay is good when the writer can stand in front of somebody and read it out loud and have the listener say both "this makes sense" and "this sounds like you."

When we are reading an application, we are creating in our minds an image of the person whose application we are reading. We try to piece together a person from that idea. You know the movie, Admission, with Tina Fey? When she is reading the application and the candidate magically appears in front of her, this image is so evocative of my own process of reading an application—sometimes I can almost picture the student in front of me.

I think I may be in the minority in giving the following essay advice. Some feel that an essay has to include an opening hook and a scene painted for the reader. I take a somewhat different view in thinking that the essay is not so much a piece of writing as it is a part of a conversation. When I am reading the essay, I am reading it as if it is being spoken to me. I find that some students end up with beautifully crafted and evocative pieces, but then I often don't hear their voice. Since their pieces are so carefully written, I don't always get a sense of the person standing in front of me. It's like trying to get a sense of a person from a piece of art that they have created rather than looking at the person themselves. If an essay is too carefully crafted, it almost gets in the way of my understanding of who a student is. If the essay can be read out loud and treated as a conversation between an adult and a high school student, I think it's successful. Not all of my colleagues may agree.

How do know when you are done? Two things need to happen: 1) when you feel like you have said what you wanted to say within the word limits. And 2) when you can put down your essay for a few weeks and not think about it, and then come back and it still feels right, then it's done.

What are some basic dos and don'ts about college essay writing?

Do: *Have your essay express the style and personality that is really a part of you. Things don't go well when writers try to represent a different version of themselves in their essay. Someone who has always been glib, cerebral, or edgy may be able to pull that off in an essay, but someone who isn't naturally that way, but tries to be, often fails. It just feels false if you write in a style that is not the way you normally communicate. As much as possible, be who you are in the essay and write about something that matters to you, not what you think will matter to the admissions office. At its core it is going to be better and more thoughtful and evocative if your essay reflects you honestly.*

Don't: *Never write about your girlfriend or boyfriend. Just don't do it! In my thirty years in admissions, I have read one or two good "girlfriend/ boyfriend" essays. I was in shock when I read it—I was so surprised to read a good one. I have read between 50,000 and 100,000 essays in my time. That particular topic demands distance and excellent writing tools to pull it off. And most students don't have the experience or ability to make that the subject of a compelling essay.*

Would you share a memory or highlight of some stand-out (or poor) essays you've read through the years, if you are comfortable sharing some of those thoughts?

One of the essays I remember reading that did not help the student was a poem in a standard meter and rhyme scheme about a topic that was important to the person but didn't really tell us much about the sort of person she would be in our university community. My rule of thumb about poetry is that unless more than one adult who is neither a family member nor a friend tells you that you are really a great poet, don't submit poetry. Some poems do stand out, but in my experience, none of them seems to be about a topic that allows me to really get to know the student.

There are so many terrific essays I have read through the years that it is impossible to select just a few. The essays that I remember well reflect what a student does well. When I read a good essay, I get to know the student and gain insight into how the student thinks, what is important to them, and how they view and react to the world in a manner that is consistent with what others say about them. I wish there were a style or manner or subject that unlocked "the great mystery of the college essay." I know I haven't found it. I know that when I read a good essay I feel as if I know this student better and have new insight about that student as a person in a way that is consistent with what I see elsewhere in the application.

What suggestions do you have on the shorter writing pieces (activity paragraph, academic paragraph, why this school? etc.) and the role and importance they play in the application process?

I like the shorter essays. They are a great way for students to tell us what they think in a straightforward manner without having to labor over it too terribly long. Being direct and conversational is the way to go on those answers.

What are your thoughts on letters of recommendation and interviews?

At Duke, we only offer alumni interviews for students who have applied. Letters of recommendation should come from a teacher the student has had within the last eighteen months (namely their junior and senior year) and for whom they have done excellent work. It is not so much the grade received in the class that is important as it is the quality of the work that they have done for the teacher. We want students to show themselves at their best. A good recommendation will be from a teacher who could talk about how a student functions and contributes in the classroom as a thinker and contributor beyond the grade on the transcript.

Do you have any other advice—words of wisdom—that you have cultivated through the years?

My advice is this: be thoughtful in choosing colleges that are a good match for you. Every college that you apply to absolutely must be a college that you would be delighted to attend. Do not apply to a college that you don't want to attend. There is such a wide range of colleges out there. If you go through the process intelligently, you are capable of ending up with college that is wonderful match. It's both a parent's and student's responsibility to research these schools. That does not mean you can't have a first-choice or two, but be sure that you love your list from top to bottom.

Second, while in high school, do things that matter to you and you love the most, not things that you think are going to "look good" on an application. A person who is motivated to do things, to make commitments and sacrifices because these things are important to them, is better served in the admission process because he or she is excited and tends to come across as more authentic to their reader.

Are there any additional comments you would like to share about your university and the kinds of applicants you seek in terms of finding the right fit or match?

I tell people if there is one attribute of students at Duke that I would mention first it is that they are doers. They do things. They like to be involved, engaged, and make a difference. They don't like to sit still much, so we have a vibrant campus that is full of students who are energetic, motivated, ambitious, friendly, spirited, and supportive—all at the same time. It is a terrifically exciting place to be for students, for faculty, and for administrators like me.

Vince Cuseo, Vice President for Admission and Financial Aid
Occidental College
Los Angeles, California

What are your suggestions on how to tackle the college application process in general—when to start and how to best approach it?

If you have a good sense of the colleges you're interested in, review their websites to get a sense of their application process and the application itself, even if it's last year's. It's valuable to understand in advance what an application asks of you.

Don't underestimate the amount of time and attention necessary to complete college applications, at least if you're planning to apply to multiple colleges. While much of the biographic and demographic information has been normalized in "standard" applications, colleges often ask you to respond to an auxiliary set of questions that are uniquely their own. And these are as important—or even more important—than the common prompts.

No matter where any college sits in your pecking order, treat its application with the same care and attention as the others. Don't bother applying if you're not going to offer your best effort in every application. Remember, each application is a reflection of you.

What is your advice for essay writers: How do you know when you are done? How much time should you spend on the essay? When is enough, enough?

Think of essays as hardwood floors. You want them varnished only to the extent of remaining warm and inviting. It's time to call it done when any more tinkering would render the essay inauthentic. Some essays are polished to such a sheen that the personal connection to the reader gets buried under the perfectionism. We ask ourselves whether the "voice" is genuine; that may matter more than the flawless syntax and diction.

What are some basic dos and don'ts about college essay writing?

- *Be specific and descriptive. Use the active voice and use detail. Tell a story about yourself to provide detail.*
- *Be patient. Good writing requires multiple drafts. Well-crafted pieces aren't effortless.*
- *Make sure it passes your personal test. Does it reflect something that is deeply meaningful to you?*

What suggestions do you have on the shorter writing pieces (activity paragraph, academic paragraph, why this school? etc.) and the role and importance they play in the application process?

Most selective colleges, though not all, ask you to respond to an additional set of prompts. Since these are specific to the college, they often are considered as critical as—or more critical than—the longer essay in the evaluation process. The proliferation of a "standard" application for virtually all the colleges to which you may be applying is a relatively recent phenomenon.

The effort you dedicate to answering the supplemental queries is an indication of your level of interest in that college in the eyes of an admission officer. How well you know the school—even if that understanding is in the form of research over lived experience—offers reassurance that your application submission is thoughtful and well-reasoned.

The questions range from the familiar to the quirky. Consider them carefully and have fun with them. Think of them as opportunities, not annoying impediments. Admission officers want to gain a sense of you beyond the numbers and the listings. The supplemental responses are grand opportunities to display your personality and distinctive self. Take advantage of them.

Do you have any other advice—words of wisdom—that you have cultivated through the years?

To paraphrase the late, iconic musician James Brown, you don't want your application to be "like a dull knife that just ain't cuttin', talkin' loud and saying nothing."

Make all your responses thoughtful, meaningful, pithy, and personal. Introspection doesn't come easily to everyone, but the process of applying to college requires a degree of self-assessment and self-reflection. Such understanding allows for not only a more compelling and convincing application but also a more discerning set of potential college destinations.

Are there any additional comments you would like to share about your university and the kinds of applicants you seek in terms of finding the right fit or match?

Occidental prizes what most other liberal arts colleges do—intellectual and social engagement in an intimate, residential campus experience. But at Occidental, it's the liberal arts experience with an unusual twist, since we're located in one of the most influential and diverse cities of the world. Our students access the LA Basin's urbanity and biodiversity in educationally formal and informal ways. And the student body itself is more diverse than most colleges of our ilk.

We seek students who prefer to interact with the world outside our campus borders, whether it's with field work at a local community organization or a semester in Jordan. But we do this without sacrificing community-mindedness on campus; students are open to sharing what makes them both similar to and different from their peers.

Theodore (Ted) Spencer, Associate Vice Provost and Executive Director of Undergraduate Admissions
University of Michigan
Ann Arbor, Michigan

What are your suggestions on how to tackle the college application process in general—when to start and how to best approach it?

The first thing that you should consider is why you want to attend college and then what you are looking for when choosing a college. The first requires a certain degree of self-assessment—which means a reality look at your GPA (including your grades in challenging and rigorous courses), test scores, outside of the classroom activities, and critical writing and thinking skills.

In the process of choosing a college, there are generally five factors you should consider:

1) *What is the academic reputation of your top schools? This includes the availability of faculty, as well as their academic credentials. You should also consider the number of courses offered in your academic area of interest. Perhaps most important to consider is the college's freshman return rates, as well as the overall six-year graduation rate.*

2) *The admission process. Can you get into your first-choice college? Find the GPA and mid-fifty percentile test score ranges of students that school has admitted, and the percent of applicants it admits each year, and weigh your chances of getting in. Be sure to note all deadlines and any other special instructions about the application process. Most of this information can be found on the college's website.*

3) *The cost to attend is often a family decision. The availability of loans, grants, work-study, and affordability plans will help you and your parents decide if the value is worth the cost.*

4) *Social life is an important part of student life. For most, it means, "what is there to do when I'm not in class"! Look for organizations, clubs, sports, fraternities and sororities, and other activities on campus or in the nearby town. The location of the institution is really important—you don't want to be in a fast-paced city if you want to have a campus-based college experience in a small town or suburban community. Also remember to investigate any study-abroad opportunities.*

5) *Finally, will the degree that you worked so hard for work equally hard for you after you graduate? Find out placement rates for people with your major, as well as how many students are accepted for graduate and professional schools.*

What is your advice for essay writers: How do you know when you are done? How much time should you spend on the essay? When is enough, enough?

Keep in mind that the essay can make you shine, or, in some cases, be less competitive.

What are some basic dos and don'ts about college essay writing?

Be honest: write about something small in scale—a story only you can tell in your own words. Let your voice be heard. If there is something strange about your record, you should explain it (e.g., academic trends primarily). Don't try to guess about which topic we want to read. Don't use language with which you are unfamiliar. At the end of the day, we want to get the sense of you as a person.

Would you share a memory or highlight of some stand-out (or poor) essays you've read through the years, if you are comfortable sharing some of those thoughts?

One bad example was a student who didn't use spell-check properly. The student wrote proudly about the amount of time spent "torturing" young inner-city students—but he intended to say he was "tutoring" students.

One of the best essays was from a student from the upper peninsula of Michigan, who, when writing about diversity, stated that in her environment she didn't really know what diversity was. However, she just knew that she needed a lot of it. But she went on to explain that perhaps her experience— when shared—could help people to better understand why there was such a lack of diversity in her life. What you heard in her essay was a story in her own voice.

What suggestions do you have on the shorter writing pieces (activity paragraph, academic paragraph, why this school? etc.) and the role and importance they play in the application process?

The essay should show your character and personality—not just bragging about your list of accomplishments. One of the short essay questions we ask is about activities: of all the activities you listed, which one is the most important and why? We look for essays, on any topic, that will enlighten us about you as you relate to the chosen topic.

What are your thoughts on letters of recommendation and interviews?

In a letter of recommendation, interview, or essay, we look for the following:

- *Depth in one or more academic areas of interest*
- *Evidence of academic passion*
- *Grasp of world events*
- *Intellectual curiosity*
- *Special talent*
- *Writing quality: content, style, originality, risk-taking.*

Brian T. Lohr, Director of Admissions Operations and Management, Office of Undergraduate Admissions University of Notre Dame South Bend, Indiana

What are your suggestions on how to tackle the college application process in general—when to start and how to best approach it?

It is never too early to start that process. I encourage students to begin the process of evaluating schools and the application processes as early as their freshmen year of high school. The earlier students start to think about potential schools, the easier it is to take a more discerning approach to the process. I use the word "discerning" because researching and applying to colleges and universities is an opportunity to reflect on who you are as a person and what you want to do going forward with your life. It should be an exciting process of discovery.

What is your advice for essay writers: How do you know when you are done? How much time should you spend on the essay? When is enough, enough?

At the University of Notre Dame, we receive approximately 18,000 applications a year. We utilize the Common Application, so every applicant must submit the common application essay, plus we require applicants to submit three of five supplemental essays specific to Notre Dame. And, applications go through several comprehensive reviews. That gets to be a large number very quickly. I think there are three simple but important points for applicants to remember. First, follow the directions outlined by each school as it relates to the essay prompts. Secondly, if there is a word limit, be sensitive to that constraint. Lastly, be creative and write from your heart!

What are some basic dos and don'ts about college essay writing?

I think this goes without saying, but the essays submitted need to be the applicant's original work. Once the applicant has completed the writing process, it is a good idea to have an independent person read over the essays. You never want to have grammatical or spelling errors. The writing of the essays is both an academic and non-academic process that gives us a look into the applicant's heart.

What suggestions do you have on the shorter writing pieces (activity paragraph, academic paragraph, why this school? etc.) and the role and importance they play in the application process?

Short answer writing pieces are a great opportunity for applicants to tell the Admission Committee about their interests—why they want to attend our school, why they want to pursue a specific major, etc. It is a great opportunity to show desire. Shorter writing pieces offer applicants a chance to be crisp and concise in their thoughts. Applicants can be deliberate and direct in their communication with the Admission Committee. Again, any essay is an opportunity for the applicant to show his or her uniqueness.

What are your thoughts on letters of recommendation and interviews?

At the University of Notre Dame, we require a letter of recommendation from one of the applicant's teachers and from the guidance counselor. The bottom line with any recommender is that the recommenders need to know the applicant well and that they can communicate this effectively through the letter. The recommenders need to give a fair and accurate reflection of you and your accomplishments.

At the University of Notre Dame, we do not offer application interviews at the undergraduate level.

Do you have any other advice—words of wisdom—that you have cultivated through the years?

First, writing is a process and there are going to be multiple drafts and revisions as applicants work toward a final product. If you enter the writing process with the mindset of "this is a first draft and it will be a process that will allow me to get to a point where I am extremely comfortable with my submission," that is an excellent place to begin. Second, one of my college professors told me to "challenge every word that you use." Be sure each word you use is necessary and appropriate. Finally, I encourage students to "sleep on it." This old adage really works! Your mind will continue to process information and solutions to potential problems. It is a good practice to give yourself distance from your work and revisit it later with a fresh perspective.

Are there any additional comments you would like to share about your university and the kinds of applicants you seek in terms of finding the right fit or match?

At the University of Notre Dame, we look for students who are committed to academic excellence. We also look for students who are going to be leaders in their own style and who will be supportive and positive teammates. One could argue that every college and university is looking for this type of student. I feel our students are unique in their consideration of and concern for others. Students seek to utilize this great educational opportunity at the University of Notre Dame to truly be a "force for good in the world" as our founder intended.

Jonathan Burdick, Vice Provost and Dean of College Admission
University of Rochester
Rochester, New York

What are your suggestions on how to tackle the college application process in general—when to start and how to best approach it?

The college application process includes the following:

- *Long-term: taking courses that prepare you for academic success in college, and engaging with your school and community in at least a couple of in-depth ways that help you prepare for life success during and beyond college. In this sense, the time to start thinking is pretty early. By the time you were in sixth grade, hopefully, your parents began evaluating the school and non-school experiences that were likely to help you develop intellectually and socially in a college-centric direction.*

- *Medium-term: gaining some direct familiarity with the college environment. The foundation for this probably best sits in tenth grade. That's a time to take a first look at college entrance examinations and to take advantage of experiences that are available for high school students on college campuses, including the most robust, "precollege" course experiences during summer. But sports camps, explicit precollege workshops, and even going on a college campus for a talk or entertainment are all valid.*

- *Short-term: by February of your junior year in high school, you should be looking at information from specific colleges—publications and web sites—giving your address to college admission offices you find interesting, registering for college entrance and achievement exams, and making any plans you can for visiting a few college campuses, near or far. Your aim is to cast a pretty wide net at first (I don't think reading online admission pages for up to fifty colleges is too much), and then establish a strategy for narrowing that list a lot between February of your junior year and mid-October of your senior year. The number you feel comfortable applying to will vary from one (early decision or early action) to maybe as many as twelve. Considering selectivity, it still works to apply to two "reaches," two "matches," and "two safeties." And you might want to repeat that same logic with financial information in mind—two "reach" schools that appear guaranteed to be significantly less costly, and so on.*

What is your advice for essay writers: How do you know when you are done? How much time should you spend on the essay? When is enough, enough?

I'm a big fan of multiple rewrites. I would advise you to write the first draft during that first day in July before your senior year when the beach fun and the novelty of the part-time job has begun to wear off, and before the family vacation. Write it in a hurry, and then put it in a safe place. Pick it up again for a re-edit after waiting at least two weeks. Repeat that as many times as you need until you have an essay you like—five, six times is not too many. What I think students do waaaay too much of is consulting with everyone else. Your parents and probably a lot of your teachers love you. They're not great, objective editors of your personal essay. Great writing isn't "writing by committee." It's personal rewriting. Ask anyone who's made a lifelong study of any famous author's scribbled, crossed-out manuscripts.

What are some basic dos and don'ts about college essay writing?

See my previous suggestions! Also, don't write about any topic that you've heard/read/been told somebody else wrote about. Think of it as picking a name for your first child. The last thing you're going to want to do is pick the same name that your cousin or neighbor just picked for her child. Hearing about someone else's essay subject should be your clue to run as fast as you can away from that same topic.

Would you share a memory or highlight of some stand-out (or poor) essays you've read through the years, if you are comfortable sharing some of those thoughts?

The best essays break the rules, and they usually come from students who are enthusiastic, lifelong readers. If you're not a lifelong reader, get out of your own head when it comes to writing. The process of writing can seem overwhelming if it's not your favorite thing to do. But you know how to talk. So face dad or your friend or your dog in the opposite chair and, instead of writing anything at first, get a recording device and just talk about yourself— everything you can think of that's worth saying and half the things that probably aren't worth saying. Then re-start the recorder while you're sitting at the computer, and put yourself through the painful process of listening to your own voice and transcribing what you said. It won't be great prose, but it will have the most important quality of a college application essay—authenticity. It will become your first rough draft, which you will then rewrite multiple times during the next few months. Your essay will be great in the end, I promise.

What suggestions do you have on the shorter writing pieces (activity paragraph, academic paragraph, why this school? etc.) and the role and importance they play in the application process?

For a selective college using the Common App, the other stuff you are asked to write is way more important than your standard essay. I know that doesn't seem fair, but that's the way it is. Each college to which you're applying is putting a lot of emphasis on how much effort you make. So for those schools that are your top choices, spend just about as much time and the same process of writing and rewriting on their short-answer questions as you invested in writing your main personal statement.

What are your thoughts on letters of recommendation and interviews?

Letters of recommendation: Ask a teacher or counselor who has known you long enough to watch you evolve from a grubby ninth- or tenth-grader into the accomplished sophisticate you are now. They will tell that story, and that's the story you want the college to hear, especially if it's a teacher who gave you a generous B– a couple of years ago.

Interviews: I love them, swear by them, and think that colleges that don't offer them or use them are missing out on most of the fun in college admissions as a profession, as well as risking unnecessary mistakes in the review and admission process. So if a college does offer them (even if they say they're "non-evaluative"), take advantage of that. As for how to prepare, I'd say keep a light touch on your preparation. It's okay to walk in with three general goals of things you'd like the interviewer to hear and understand. For example:

1) Your main academic interest(s)

2) Your main non-academic interest(s)

3) The reason you think this college would be a good place to pursue both

In addition, walk in with at least one interesting question that wasn't already answered in 72-point font on the college's website. If you walk in with

2 hours of well-rehearsed answers and lovely phrases, most interviewers—and certainly all of the smart ones who interview several students per year—are going to see right through that. They may accept your canned answers without challenge, which means they're being lazy and you're both wasting time, or they may have a particular delight in probing with a question that's designed to get right under your skin and throw you off your well-rehearsed game. You can avoid that antagonism by not being too rehearsed.

Do you have any other advice—words of wisdom—that you have cultivated through the years?

Parents and students should talk about the college process for no more than 1 hour per week, probably between 7 and 8 p.m. on a Sunday. The rest of the week, don't talk about it. Don't. Don't text about it. Don't leave notes on the refrigerator about it. Keep that "One College Hour" as a sacred trust so that you keep making steady progress on the applications and deadlines without driving each other crazy.

Are there any additional comments you would like to share about your university and the kinds of applicants you seek in terms of finding the right fit or match?

Honestly, there is great fun to be had in making this First Big Decision in Life. Look for the fun. If you're having zero fun, you're doing something wrong. So take a couple of steps backward to figure out where the extreme pain or anxiety is coming from, and tackle that directly before you move on. For example, you may be diligently planning your applications to several colleges that offer the kind of medical preparation that your father always wanted to do but couldn't because his family was poor, all the while harboring a deep secret that you'd really rather be designing the packaging covers for video games. If this is your situation, I will warn you that every minute of this college process is going to hurt—including your first full year of college nearly flunking out of chemistry and biology classes—until you work up the courage to tell dad that "My Daughter the Doctor" isn't going to happen after all. Get it over with now. Same goes for My Son the Legacy. My informal studies in thirty years of doing this tell me that most students actually don't want to attend the college that mom or dad attended, and an extremely large percentage don't want to attend the college that both mom and dad attended. This is cringe-worthy, tears-of-rage-inducing stuff in the best of families. Get it over with now.

University of Rochester is looking for students with a high degree of confident self-direction. We offer a prolific research environment, an astonishingly diverse but half-sized residential undergraduate student body, no general education requirements or guidelines, and no required subjects. We have professors and advisers who will give you plenty of advice, but it always starts with a question to which only you have the answer: "What do you want to do?" You don't have to have an answer like "raise the first chinchillas on Mars," but you do have to be able to walk yourself through some introspective swerves and pick your first four classes here for yourself. That's challenging but so worthwhile. Once you've started on a path of utter freedom to choose what you want to learn, go in the direction that your thousands (maybe millions) of genetic variations and almost unlimited number of variable sensory experiences are leading you. Rochester thrives on identifying students who believe that "there's a destiny for me alright, and it wasn't chosen for me fifteen years ago by a faculty committee, and definitely not fifteen centuries ago by Martianus Cappella." Sometimes the best Rochester students are those who didn't color between the lines throughout high school; they get a lot of good grades and scores because they're smart, not because someone else thought they should. More than anything, I like applicants who couldn't care less what I think of them and don't try too hard to impress me. Instead, they put their exact selves "out there" as an applicant, and if I like them, great, if not, "c'est la vie."

Timothy Brunold, Dean of Admission
University of Southern California (USC)
Los Angeles, California

What are your suggestions on how to tackle the college application process in general—when to start and how to best approach it?

There can be times that are too early to give colleges a lot of attention. You can think about it early, but it makes the most sense to begin thinking about the application process and actual schools you want to identify on your list toward the end of sophomore year and into the junior year. In making your list, ask yourself: What kind of experience do I wish to have in college? That is the first step. This is also a process that can go on throughout the summer and the school year. If you pace yourself, it is better than saving it all for the summer before senior year.

What is your advice for essay writers: How do you know when you are done? How much time should you spend on the essay? When is enough, enough?

One of the most important things to consider is why colleges ask these questions. Colleges are going to use your answers as an opportunity to hear your voice. So before you begin writing, think about what you want colleges to hear from you and how you want to present yourself. Basic tips: use your voice, your writing style, and write a piece you are satisfied with. Don't be preoccupied with what someone you don't know will think of it. It is fine to get reactions from adults and have someone else read your essay. But your work does need to be your own and a reflection of how you want to represent yourself to the college. A common pitfall is trying to second-guess what an admission committee wants to see and pursuing that approach rather than being genuine and yourself. It may be hard for you to imagine that, as a 17- or 18-year-old, you know yourself so well that you can produce a piece of work that you think would be impressive to adults who don't know you. But I encourage you to push through those concerns and hesitations and try to write in your own voice. That's what matters.

What are some basic dos and don'ts about college essay writing?

If you are a person who is humorous, please use it in your writing. If you are serious, reflect that in your writing, too. Don't feel you need to try out new material on the admission office. Don't try something new in your essay. Be yourself. You do not need a "hook" to be memorable. The most memorable essays I have read have not always been the best. Don't feel you need to shock to be memorable, and, while being memorable is not a bad thing, don't create an essay for that purpose; it can backfire. Also, as you think about what you want to write, don't forget that other parts of the application allow you to express yourself and address other aspects of who you are. Short answers are just as important in your application! Don't throw those away. Give them attention, too. The length of your work does not necessarily equate to importance. Short answers are very keenly read.

What suggestions do you have on the shorter writing pieces (activity paragraph, academic paragraph, why this school? etc.) and the role and importance they play in the application process?

As I mentioned before, all pieces of writing are equally important; my colleagues may not all agree with me on this. Colleges don't ask for short answers to keep you working harder or test your writing ability. Yes, your work should be grammatically correct, but the truth is I am using this information to hear more from you. If you have something compelling to say, I can accept a nontraditional approach and writing style. I like to think of it the way we read different authors. Each of us has different favorite authors, and the world's best authors are not necessarily mechanically the most sound. College essay writing poses a challenge since, as students, you are taught writing in a particular way and format, so this is sometimes an exercise you approach to try to follow the "right" method. Think of college application writing as allowing more freeform writing, and worry less about format and syntax and more about content. Not all of my colleagues will agree, but I can assess an ability to write and command of language and don't need an essay to do that for me.

What are your thoughts on letters of recommendation and interviews?

This may sound obvious, but make sure the person writing your letter has some good things to say about you. Don't overthink this: "I am applying as a bio major, and I need a letter from my science teacher. But my best letter-writer could be my art teacher. But maybe it would be a bit more impactful if my science teacher writes it." But maybe your science teacher doesn't know you as well as the art teacher does. The purpose of this letter is a third party speaking on your behalf and in support of you. So it ought to be from someone who will be able to write about you in a most impactful way. Choose your author carefully by who knows you best. Give advance warning to your teachers. In fact, recommendation letters should be the first thing you ask for as soon as you have your college list in order. The unfortunate truth is that if you don't give your teachers an early "head's up," you may get a rushed and poorly written letter.

Interview advice varies from school to school. Don't overthink the person who is giving the interview. While alumni interviewers are helpful and may know a lot, they might not be able to answer all of the same questions as an admission officer. Just as with essays, understand the purpose of them. At USC, we are not trying to trip you up or catch you in a trap. The interview is optional and just offers additional info to help our college be more fair and get a better perspective on all of our applicants. Don't fear the interview or be nervous. Embrace it. USC has over 47,000 applications per year, and we don't use alumni to interview students, so not everyone will be interviewed. Interviews are available on a first-come, first-served basis. Is this a disadvantage? Think about it: If an interview is optional, then don't stress out too much. Trust the college's process.

Do you have any other advice—words of wisdom—that you have cultivated through the years?

Choosing a college is about choosing a lifestyle; you need to keep options open and consider all of the elements of the experience. It is easy to become narrowly focused on one school or one element of the college experience, but I challenge you to look at a school from all points of view.

Are there any additional comments you would like to share about your university and the kinds of applicants you seek in terms of finding the right fit or match?

USC is a school that is keen on finding students who will fit best, not just benefit the university but who will themselves benefit from being here. The process of matching is a two-way street. Best fit is not just who we want but who also will themselves take most advantage of USC and get the greatest benefit from being a part of our community. Admission work here is done the old-fashioned way; we don't have any Early Decision schemes, and we don't cut corners or tweak the pool in any way. We also do not use a waiting list. We simply try to give it our best shot from the very start and have a transparent process. We make ourselves available to prospective students.

Douglas L. Christiansen, Ph.D., Vice Provost for Enrollment and Dean of Admissions
Vanderbilt University
Nashville, Tennessee

What are your suggestions on how to tackle the college application process in general—when to start and how to best approach it?

When you have narrowed down your college choices during the spring and summer before senior year, you should begin the application process. It is never too early to pull together your personal résumé, begin considering essay topics, or begin having test scores sent to the schools you will apply to (if not taking additional tests in the fall). Break down the components by school. If, for example, one section of an application is done per day, there will be no overwhelming, last-minute panic. Organization is the key! Create files on each school: keep copies of what is submitted, school contacts, teacher recommendation choices and completion of requests, and a checklist in each file so it is clear what has and has not been completed. By breaking down the tasks, one school at a time, there will be no confusion the day before the deadline. If you procrastinate, this will become such a nerve-wracking process, rather than the exciting, self-evolving process that it can be. Get organized, get tasks done early, and enjoy the ride!

What is your advice for essay writers: How do you know when you are done? How much time should you spend on the essay? When is enough, enough?

Essays provide the one opportunity for a college or university to hear your voice, and it is a critical component in the holistic admissions process practiced by many public and private colleges and universities. The essay should be written so that the admission officer reviewing the application gains insight into your character, life experiences, and critical-thinking abilities. While you may have had powerful experiences that have shaped your life—some tragic, some happy—what is important is to speak to how the experience changed your life, and what you have done to make your corner of the world better as a result of the experience. Invest enough time and energy into the thought process and writing of the essay so that it is clear and concise, and it has an impact. Once you have completed your writing, doing rewrites over and over will not be helpful. Be confident in the original premise, and let it rest a day or two. Reread the essay one last time with fresh eyes, and hit "submit."

What are some basic dos and don'ts about college essay writing?

- *DO FOLLOW DIRECTIONS! Stick to the word count given—no admissions officer has time to read essays that go on and on, and following directions is a critical skill that is noticed. So do what is asked. DO answer the question or give the description asked for in the essay question. While abstract thinking is great, giving an answer that in no way answers the question does not reflect well on you. DO spellcheck. Sounds simple, but sometimes this detail is forgotten, with disastrous results. DO proofread the final edits one last time to make sure the essay says what is intended.*
- *DO NOT wait until the last minute—essays require thought and personal investment, which require time and energy. DO NOT have anyone else write the essay—admissions counselors will know immediately! DO NOT write what parents, friends, or cousins say to write. Write from the unique, personal perspective that can only come from your heart.*

Would you share a memory or highlight of some stand-out (or poor) essays you've read through the years, if you are comfortable sharing some of those thoughts?

The best essays I have read were written by deep thinkers who overcame great difficulties and then used those experiences to change the world around them. The poorest essays are the ones that are obviously written by someone other than the applicant or at a level that is obviously different than what the student's grades and test scores would validate.

What suggestions do you have on the shorter writing pieces (activity paragraph, academic paragraph, why this school? etc.) and the role and importance they play in the application process?

It is very important to know why you are choosing this school over others. The best advice I can give is to give a REAL reason, not something like, "the city is nice," "I like the weather," or "my entire family went here." While all that information is nice, it gives no true insight into your FEELINGS about the school. It is better to speak to the true influences—a tour guide, a student met along the way, service work, or majors—that are unique to the school; give the reader something to hold on to that will be remembered long after reading the application. If there are 30,000 or more applications and they all say they want to come because the city is great, how can the admission counselor discern something critical about you, the writer?

What are your thoughts on letters of recommendation and interviews?

When choosing which teachers to ask to write letters of recommendation, think about those who have had great influence, not just in the classroom but at a deeper level. The teacher needs to speak to your intangible qualities, so choose carefully. Choose a teacher who you trust to speak highly of you, and one who will spend time on writing the letter. Very important: ask the teacher EARLY in the process—they all get lots of requests, so being one of the first to ask helps ensure getting the teacher who is most important to you to write a meaningful letter.

Do you have any other advice—words of wisdom—that you have cultivated through the years?

Throughout the application process, you should be true to yourself. Apply to the schools that interest you, not your parents, siblings, or friends. Be diligent about getting the application components submitted early. Follow through on all teacher requests, test-score submissions, and special forms required by the schools (Early Decision Agreements, for example), making sure all have been received by the schools. Once everything is submitted, RELAX, knowing all has been done that you have control over, and then trust that the process will work in your best interest.

Do you have any other advice—words of wisdom—that you have cultivated through the years?

You should get your applications in early so you can enjoy all that comes your way senior year! There is a great school for everyone! While you may not be admitted to your first-choice school, investing yourself wherever you are accepted creates a tie to that school. That "no" from the first choice may be a blessing in disguise! If you don't love the school after a year, transfer. But you should transfer knowing you worked hard to be a part of the culture and life of the school, and it was just not a good fit.

Are there any additional comments you would like to share about your university and the kinds of applicants you seek in terms of finding the right fit or match?

Vanderbilt University uses a holistic admissions process in which all parts of a student's application are considered—we do not employ cutoffs for standardized testing or grade point averages. Rather we look for students who have demonstrated strong academic skills and intellectual curiosity and who have engaged in activities outside the classroom that have nurtured their growth as leaders. Most successful applicants have taken a very rigorous course load and have challenged themselves at the highest levels of the available curriculum.

Nancy Hargrave Meislahn, Dean of Admission and Financial Aid
Wesleyan University
Middletown, Connecticut

What are your suggestions on how to tackle the college application process in general—when to start and how to best approach it?

Early in the process, as you begin researching colleges and visiting campuses, start taking notes and create whatever version of a file, journal, or folder works for you. Keep track of your reactions to what you've seen and heard. Make a copy of that essay you wrote for your English class that your teacher said was terrific. Jot a note to yourself when an idea for an application essay starts to percolate. When you actually start filling out applications, go back to those notes.

What is your advice for essay writers: How do you know when you are done? How much time should you spend on the essay? When is enough, enough?

Tough question! Many essays could benefit from additional work and editing, and others are "overcooked." A good editing trick applies here: Read your essay out loud, and really listen to what you are saying and how it flows. Is there a beginning, an end, and a substantial, engaging middle?

What are some basic dos and don'ts about college essay writing?

DO be Personal. Yes, it is a sample of your best writing. Yes, this is your opportunity to put flesh on the bones of your application. DO think about what you want the reader, the admission committee, to know about YOU.

Would you share a memory or highlight of some stand-out (or poor) essays you've read through the years, if you are comfortable sharing some of those thoughts?

Students often obsess over the topic of the essay rather than focusing on the story they want to tell or the qualities they want to amplify or demonstrate. Many of the best essays I've read over the years are about simple things, mundane topics. One of my favorite essays was about mowing the lawn—how it became a time to reflect rather than a chore. Another favorite essay was about sheet music that reminded the writer of piano lessons and how playing the piano became a passion.

What suggestions do you have on the shorter writing pieces (activity paragraph, academic paragraph, why this school? etc.) and the role and importance they play in the application process?

Many students waste the opportunities in the short answers. You should spend time thinking about how the pieces of the entire application come together as a mosaic, painting the full picture of who you are. The EC (extracurricular) grid, the personal statement, and short answer essays—along with what appears in your letters of recommendation—tell us about the whole person and what you might bring to the classroom and the campus.

Do you have any other advice—words of wisdom—that you have cultivated through the years?

John Paul Getty wrote, "The harder I work, the luckier I get." In the admission process—similar to day-to-day work in the classroom—hard work pays off. Make sure to plan the time necessary to do the research, write applications, and reflect on what you do well and want in the future.

Are there any additional comments you would like to share about your university and the kinds of applicants you seek in terms of finding the right fit or match?

Our president is fond of saying that Wesleyan isn't for everyone, and spots are too precious to waste. We seek curious, adventuresome students who love ideas and want to be in an environment with others who want to work hard and find their passions but those who are willing to collaborate and not just compete.

Concluding Remarks

My goal for *Writing Successful College Applications* was to offer enough professional advice and actual writing samples to make the college application writing process a bit less daunting and more manageable for you. Applying to college is just another of life's hoops to jump through, a rite of passage that you will conquer and survive. Use the opportunity to toot your own horn (within reason), and be the best advocate for yourself that you can be while retaining your authentic voice. Good luck on your academic journey, and savor and relish your college experience as much as you can. The real world awaits just beyond the classroom and will always be there. College, in my opinion, can be the best four years of your life, so try to pinch yourself every once in a while and appreciate your experience there.

—Cynthia Clumeck Muchnick

Student Contributors

Jacob Altman 42
George Andrews 128, 165, 182, 198
Ashley Appell 60
Cambria Arvizo 32
Adam Block 54, 94, 188, 240
Paige Bowie 148
Rachel Busic 71, 171, 177, 207b, 212a, 219b, 247
Kim Condino 44, 175, 234–239
Conner Cooper 85
Shelby Curran 130
Sadie Drucker 67, 164
Karli Dugan 57, 222
Lauren Edwards 36
Justin Etzine 102
Kay Fecker 167a, 180a, 205
Katie Flattum 97, 108, 159a, 210
Adam Fletcher 62
Sharon Ghelman 119, 126, 207a
Bryant Gilligan 134
Ben Glasser 51, 69
Zev Gollis 31, 66
Allison Holley 78, 201b, 220c, 221
Jeff Kahn 104, 111, 125, 159b, 168
Sarah Kahn 121, 153, 218
Michael Karamardian 123
Ben Karp 131
Christina King 169, 204

Virginia Rose La Puma 40, 56, 232
Amy Magill 39, 176b, 197
Mark Milner 140, 189, 208b, 216
Zachary Miot 113, 144, 163a
Coleman Moore 95, 142
Samantha Moore 99, 146, 162
Kylie Mugg 92
Andrew Noto 50
Madeena Rafiq 91, 115
Aaron Regunberg 109, 136, 167b
Brooke Rice 79, 106, 196, 212b
Lauren Rosen 83
Jordan Sandfer 64, 176a, 178, 203, 211
Abby Schwartz 89
Hope Secor 37, 86, 152, 163b, 166, 181, 201a
Sammy Shea 73
Allen Sifuentes 117
Cindy Stanwyk 27
Stephanie Tarle 81, 170a, 219a, 220b
Haley Thayer 29, 202, 208a
Riley Walker 101
Dylan West 74
Valerie Westhart 150
Cait Williamson 24, 170b, 180b
Jack Williamson 59
Andrew Yun 161, 200

Application Websites

The following URLs for the Common Application or for individual school websites, from which application questions were noted in this book, were accurate at the time of this book's publication. Please be aware that many colleges change their application questions each year, so it is best to check your school's website for the most up-to-date information.

Common Application 2014–15 Essay Prompts (pages 3–4):
https://collegeadmissions.uchicago.edu/apply/essay-questions

Common Application text-to-PDF conversion process (page 17):
https://appsupport.commonapp.org/ics/support/KBAnswer.asp?questionID=1649&subscribe=1

Brandeis University (page 214):
http://www.brandeis.edu/admissions/apply/checklist.html

Bucknell University (page 214):
http://www.bucknell.edu/Apply

Lafayette College (page 156):
http://admissions.lafayette.edu/apply/

St. Olaf College (page 221):
http://wp.stolaf.edu/admissions/files/2012/12/2013-14-Common-App-Supplement.pdf

Stanford University (pages 146 and 215–216):
https://www.commonapp.org/Login
http://admission.stanford.edu/application/transfer/essays.html

Tufts University (page 215):
http://admissions.tufts.edu/apply/essay-questions/

University of Chicago (pages 4–5):
https://collegeadmissions.uchicago.edu/apply/essay-questions

University of North Carolina Chapel Hill (page 6):
http://admissions.unc.edu/admissions-blog/2013/06/21/2014-application-essay-prompts/

University of Virginia (page 215):
http://uvaapplication.blogspot.com/2013/06/2013-2014-application-essay-questions.html

Wake Forest University (page 215):
http://static.wfu.edu/files/pdf/admissions/application.pdf